English Grammar
Easier Way

Published by :
Lotus Press Publishers & Distributors

English Grammar Easier Way

Shabnam Gupta

4735/22, Prakash Deep Building
Ansari Road, Darya Ganj,
New Delhi - 110002

Lotus Press : Publishers & Distributors
Unit No. 220, 2nd Floor, 4735/22, Prakash Deep Building,
Ansari Road, Darya Ganj, New Delhi- 110002
Ph.: 41325510, 98118-38000
• E-mail : lotuspress1984@gmail.com
www.lotuspress.co.in

English Grammar Easier Way

ISBN: 81-8382-079-4

Printed & Published by : **Lotus Press Publisher & Distributors,** New Delhi-02

Preface

Grammar is a very essential part of the usage of any language. Grammar can best be understood as a set rules which have been formulated for the correct and standardized usage of the language.

As such, an understanding of these rules is important for spoken as well as written English. These rules lend a uniformity to the language and make it an accepted standard world wide.

However, all rules have certain exceptions since it is as important to know these exceptions as it is to know the rules, it is only with regular practise and usage that one can gain mastery and command over any language.

This book attempts to present this set of rules in a simple way, such that learning grammar becomes easy and interesting.

— **Author**

Contents

1

Parts of Speech

Elementary Information

The words of a *speech/sentence* are divided into the following eight *parts of speech* according to their form, usage and structure. (i) Noun, (ii) Pronoun, (iii) Adjective, (iv) Verb, (v) Adverb, (vi) Preposition, (vii) Conjunction, (viii) Interjection.

Noun

Definition: A *Noun* is a word used as the name of a person, place, thing, quality, state/condition/position/attitude/action, etc.

Or

A *Noun* is the name of a person, place, or thing. Thing is a comprehensive word. It includes all objects which we can perceive and the objects that we can think of but cannot perceive *e.g.*

Person: Lalit, Monika, Aishna.

Place: Library, Dispensary.

Thing: Pencil, Doll.

Quality: Bravery, Depth.

State: Condition/Position/Attitude: Health, illness, sleep, poverty, life.

Action: Worship, game.

Look at the following sentences:

Lalit is a *boy*. *Life* is a *game*.

The *sun* shines in the *sky*. *Work* is *worship*.

Jupiter is a *planet*.

In the above sentences, the words printed in italics are *nouns*.

Pronoun

Definition: A *Pronoun* is a word used in place of a Noun or Noun Phrase *e.g.*

Anil is absent as *he* (Anil) is ill.

The scooter is there where Sonu left *it* (the scooter).

Sushma and Radha are taking *their* (Sushma's and Radha's) breakfast.

Remember that 'I, we' are *First Person Pronouns,* 'you, thou' are *Second Person Pronouns* and 'he, she, it, they, are *Third Person Pronouns.*

Adjective

Definition: An *Adjective* is a word that expresses some quality of a *Noun* or *Pronoun* or adds something to their meaning. *e.g.*

Sunita is a *bold* girl.

Ashoka was a *great* king.

Sonu's mother is a *kind* lady.

The words *bold, great* and *kind* are Adjectives here. They express the qualities of the Nouns *girl, king* and *lady* respectively.

She (Sarla) is *wise.* They are *silly.*

He (Madhu) is *dull.* I am *fat.*

You are *honest.*

The words *wise, silly, dull, fat,* and *honest* are Adjectives here. They express the qualities of the Pronouns *she* (Sarla), *they, he* (Madhu), *I* and *you* respectively.

Verb

Definition: A *Verb* is a word that expresses an action or a fact, as:

I *do* my work. Rani *sings* a song.

We *eat* rice. The children *are going*.

You *play* hockey. Mohan will *help* you.

The italicised words (*do, sings, eat, are going, play* and *help* are action words (*verbs*) here.

Adverb

Definition: An *Adverb* is a word that adds something to the meaning of a Verb, an Adjective or another Adverb, such as: *Never* mind. (The adverb *never* adds to the meaning of the verb *mind* here).

You are *really* sincere. (The Adverb *really* adds to the meanings of the Adjective *sincere* here).

She answered the call *much* hastily. (The Adverb *much* adds to the meaning of another Adverb *hastily* here).

Preposition

Definition: A *Preposition* is a word which is put before a noun or pronoun in order to show some relation between them, as:

The lamp is *on* the table. [The Preposition *on* shows the relation of the Noun (*the lamp*) with another Noun (*the table*) here].

She fell *into* the well. [The Preposition *into* shows the relation of the Pronoun (*she*) with the noun (*well*) here].

Mohan gives respect *to* me. [The Preposition *to* shows the relation of the noun (*Mohan*) with the Pronoun (*me*) here].

She is not *under* me. [The Preposition *under* shows the relation of the pronoun (*she*) with another pronoun (*me*) here].

Conjunction

Definition: A *Conjunction* is a word that joins words, sentences, phrases or clauses as:

One and one makes two. [The Conjunction *and* joins the word (*one*) with another word (*one*) here].

Meeru wept *as* she saw me. [The Conjunction *as* joins the sentence (Meeru wept) with another sentence (she saw me) here].

A wealthy man and a healthy man were friends. [The Conjunction *and* joins the Adjective Phrase (a wealthy man) with another Adjective Phrase (a healthy man) here]. We all admire a man of courage *but* we hate a coward.

The conjunction *but* joins the two co-ordinate clauses here.

Interjection

Definition: An *Interjection* is a word or phrase used to express some sudden feelings of wonder, joy, sorrow, annoyance, etc, as:

Alas! Her husband is dead. (The Interjection *Alas* expresses the feeling of sorrow here).

Hurrah! We have won the match. (The Interjection *Hurrah* expresses the feeling of joy here).

Ah! Has Rekha stood first? (The Interjection *Ah* expresses the feelings of joy and wonder here). Always put the mark of exclamation (!) after the interjection.

Some modern Grammarians include *Determiners* among the parts of speech. In this book, Determiners [Articles a, *an, the* and adjectives this, *that, these, those, each, some, every, any, my, his, one, two,* etc.].

2

Noun

Different Type of Nouns

Kinds of Noun: (i) Proper Noun (ii) Common Noun (iii) Collective Noun (iv) Abstract Noun (v) Material Noun.

Proper Noun

Definition: A *Proper Noun* is the (individual) name of a particular person, place or thing as Ganga, Bible, Red Fort. Look at the following sentences:

Roopangi is ten years old.

The *Taj* is in *Agra.*

Delhi is the capital of *India.*

March is the third month of the year.

In the above sentences, the words printed in italics are Proper Nouns. 'Roopangi' is the name of a particular girl. 'Taj' is the name of a building. 'Agra' and 'Delhi' are the names of places (cities). *India* is the name of a country. *March* is the name of a month.

Remember that the first letter of the Proper Noun is invariably written in capital letter irrespective of its (Proper Noun's) location in the sentence.

Sometimes, Proper Nouns are used as Common Nouns as:

Pt. Deep Chand was the *Lukman* (the wisest man) of his village. Here, *Lukman* is a Common Noun.

Kalidas was the *Shakespeare* (the greatest dramatist) of India. Here *Shakespeare* is used as a Common Noun.

Common Noun

Definition: A *Common Noun* is the name shared commonly by every person, place or thing of the same class or kind as book, toy, cow, lake, utensil, etc.

India is a *country*. Ayush is a *boy*.
Jaipur is a *city*. Priya is a *girl*.
Yamuna is a *river*. April is a *month*.
Cow is an *animal*. I write with a *pen*.

In the above sentences the words (country, boy, city, girl, river, month, animal and pen) are Common Nouns. These names are commonly shared by every person, place or thing of their kind or class. Collective Nouns and Abstract Nouns are also included in Common Nouns.

Collective Noun

Definition: A *Collective Noun* is the name given to a group (collection) of persons, places or things, etc. as: herd, flock, crowd, army, bunch.

There are four *sections* in our *class*.

Bahadur has joined the *army*.

Our *team* has eleven players.

My *family* lives in Delhi.

I am a member of your *club*.

The *police* scattered the crowd.

In the above sentences the italicised words give indication about the group (*collection*) of Nouns.

Remember that a collective noun is always taken as neuter gender. It is always singular in number. Collective nouns become Common nouns whenever they are used in the plural.

Also remember that a Collective Noun takes a Singular Verb when it is taken as a collection. However, it takes a plural verb whenever it stands for members of the collection; as — The committee is probing into his past life (committee as a collection).

The Committee are probing into his past life. (Members of the committee.)

Abstract Noun

Definition: An *Abstract Noun* is the name of a feeling, emotion, sentiment, action, quality, state or art, etc. as:

Honesty is the best policy.

Childhood is the period of *beauty*.

Her heart is full of *hatred*.

I like your *wisdom*.

Hatred is a bad quality.

Love begets *love*.

Everybody likes *goodness*.

In the above sentences, the italicised words are Abstract Nouns. They show some abstract quality.

Remember that an abstract noun is used in singular number. No article (A/An/The) is used before abstract nouns. The names of Arts and Sciences are also termed as abstract nouns.

For Recapitulation:

(a)	Happiness, love, hatred	show feelings
(b)	Deed, race, theft	show actions
(c)	Music, Hindi, Drawing	show arts
(d)	Beauty, truth, honesty	show qualities
(e)	Poverty, childhood, helplessness	show states

Material Noun

Definition: A *Material Noun* is the name given to a material substance of which various things (items) are made; as mud, glass, paper, gold, silver, copper, oil, plastics.

Sweets are made of *sugar, ghee, milk, maida,* and *water.*

Ornaments are made of *gold, silver, brass* and *copper.*

Tools are made of *iron.*

The table is made of *wood.*

Cloth is made of *cotton.*

Sweaters are made of *wool.*

In the above sentences, the italicised words are Material Nouns. These are raw materials with which other items can be prepared.

Remember that material nouns have no number. They cannot be counted. Material nouns have quantity. They can be measured or weighed. No article (A/An/The) is used before material nouns. Material nouns are always singular number.

Additional Information about Nouns

Countable Nouns (Countables): These nouns include the names of objects, people, etc. that we can count, *e.g.* pencils, girls, bananas, brothers, teachers, cows, etc. Common Nouns and Collective Nouns come under Countable Nouns, e.g. class, crowd, team, herd, flock, etc. Countable Nouns also have plural forms. We normally use *a* or *an* before Countable Nouns of Singular Number. Compound Nouns, composed of two or more words also come under Countable Nouns.

Uncountable Nouns (Uncountables): These nouns include the names of objects, people, etc. that we cannot count. Material Nouns and Abstract Nouns come under Uncountable Nouns. They show the quantity, mass or idea/feeling of an object, *e.g.* boyhood, beauty, cold, cotton, happiness, hatred, heat, milk, oil, rice, sugar, truth, water.

Numerals are not used with *Uncountable Nouns*. The meaning of the Uncountable Noun will change if we use it as a Countable Noun e.g.

I like your *work*. Here the Uncountable Noun *work* means 'job'.

I like Milton's works. Here the Countable Noun *works* means the books written by Milton.

Uncountable Nouns are normally plural in form. A/An are not used before Uncountable Nouns. However, *'some'* can be used before Uncountable Nouns.

Important Information about Classification of Nouns

According to Traditional Grammarians	According to Modern Grammarians
(i) Proper Noun	(i) Proper Noun
(ii) Common Noun	(ii) Countable Noun
(iii) Collective Noun	(iii) Uncountable Noun
(iv) Abstract Noun	
(v) Material Noun	

Miscellaneous Exercise (For Recapitulation)

Kinds of Nouns

Model Sentences

Who built the Red Fort in Delhi?

Can the oil float on water?

Ask Sarla to see me at once.

Love begets love and hatred begets hatred.

The Tapti falls into the Arabian Sea.

Is the Taj Mahal not made of marble?

The Ganges rises from the Himalayas.

Is the camel not the ship of the desert?

Lions live in the forest.

Honesty is the best policy.

The whole class is present today.

Is not beauty a gift of God?

Copper is not the most useful metal.

The youth must serve the nation.

The police dispersed the crowd.

Our table is made of wood.

The children are basking in the sun.

The sparrows make their nests.

The committee is enquiring into the matter.

Dhruvika is playing with a toy.

Number (of Nouns)

Nouns in English have two numbers.

Singular Number: A Noun that denotes one person or thing is said to be in the *Singular Number*; as book, boy, brother, child, city, class, chair, hand, king, sister, table, etc. The word *Singular* is the adjective form of *single* which means one (person or thing). *Number* means — quantity of units. Therefore, singular number means 'a single unit in counting'.

Plural Number: A Noun that denotes more than one person or thing is said to be in the *Plural Number*, as books, boys, brothers, children, cities, classes, chairs, hands, kings, sisters, tables, etc.

Remember that some languages have three numbers e.g.

(i) Singular Number (Single/one unit)

(ii) Dual Number (Two units)

(iii) Plural Number (More than two units)

English Language does not have 'a dual number'. The number showing two units is also considered as Plural Number.

Formation of Plurals from Singulars

Rule - 1. By adding 's' at the tail of the Noun

Singular	*Plural*	*Singular*	*Plural*
Actor	Actors	Beggar	Beggars
Article	Articles	Book	Books
Arm	Arms	Bride	Brides
Aunt	Aunts	Net	Nets
Base	Bases	Neighbour	Neighbours
Boat	Boats	Oak	Oaks
Boy	Boys	Oath	Oaths
Camel	Camels	Owl	Owls
Cook	Cooks	Oar	Oars
Cock	Cocks	Peacock	Peacocks
Cow	Cows	Pigeon	Pigeons
Dagger	Daggers	Pen	Pens
Doll	Dolls	Parrot	Parrots
Dog	Dogs	Quail	Quails
Day	Days	Queen	Queens
Egg	Eggs	Ram	Rams
Emperor	Emperors	Rabbit	Rabbits
Elephant	Elephants	Root	Roots
Examiner	Examiners	Rat	Rats
Feat	Feats	Roof	Roofs
Flag	Flags	Rider	Riders
Fig	Figs	Sea	Seas
Farmer	Farmers	Sister	Sisters
Girl	Girls	Servant	Servants
Goat	Goats	Sail	Sails
Hat	Hats	Tale	Tales
Hindu	Hindus	Tree	Trees

Contd...

Singular	*Plural*	*Singular*	*Plural*
Inkpot	Inkpots	Tail	Tails
Indian	Indians	Tailor	Tailors
Jewel	Jewels	Unit	Units
Joke	Jokes	Umbrella	Umbrellas
Job	Jobs	Urn	Urns
Jerk	Jerks	Van	Vans
Joint	Joints	Vote	Votes
Kite	Kites	Visitor	Visitors
Kid	Kids	Vulture	Vultures
Kettle	Kettles	Vocation	Vocations
Lad	Lads	Waiter	Waiters
Leg	Legs	Walnut	Walnuts
Lizard	Lizards	Waist	Waists
Lid	Lids	Wall	Walls
Lip	Lips	Year	Years
Monk	Monks	Yacht	Yachts
Mug	Mugs	Yak	Yaks
Master	Masters	Yoke	Yokes
Mat	Mats	Zebra	Zebras
Niece	Nieces	Zoo	Zoos
Nephew	Nephews	Zone	Zones

Rule- 2. By adding 'es' at the tail of the Noun ending in ch, s, sh, ss, x, or z as:

Nouns ending in 'ch'

Singular	*Plural*	*Singular*	*Plural*
Bench	Benches	Latch	Latches
Bunch	Bunches	Match	Matches

Contd...

Singular	*Plural*	*Singular*	*Plural*
Branch	Branches	Notch	Notches
Coach	Coaches	Patch	Patches
Crutch	Crutches	Speech	Speeches
Church	Churches	Switch	Switches
Ditch	Ditches	Watch	Watches
Finch	Finches		

Exceptions

Monarch	Monarchs	Stomach	Stomachs

Nouns ending in 's'

Bus	Buses	Circus	Circuses
Gas	Gases		

Nouns ending in 'sh'

Brush	Brushes	Bush	Bushes
Dash	Dashes	Dish	Dishes
Fish	Fishes	Gash	Gashes

Nouns ending in 'ss'

Glass	Glasses	Kiss	Kisses
Lass	Lasses	Princess	Princesses

Nouns ending in 'x'

Box	Boxes	Fox	Foxes
Hoax	Hoaxes	Tax	Taxes

Exception

Ox	Oxen

Nouns ending in 'z'

Buzz	Buzzes	Quiz	Quizes

Rule - 3. By changing 'y' into 'ies' if the noun ends in 'y' and is preceded by a consonant

Singular	*Plural*	*Singular*	*Plural*
Army	Armies	Gallery	Galleries
Baby	Babies	Gutty	Gutties
City	Cities	Gully	Gullies
Copy	Copies	Gunnery	Gunneries
Country	Countries	Library	Libraries
Cry	Cries	Lorry	Lorries
Duty	Duties	Lady	Ladies
Fairy	Fairies	Lily	Lilies
Family	Families	Pony	Ponies
Fury	Furies	Story	Stories
Fly	Flies		

Rule-4. By changing 'f or fe' into 'ves' of the nouns ending in f or fe:

Singular	*Plural*	*Singular*	*Plural*
Calf	Calves	Loaf	Loaves
Elf	Elves	Sheaf	Sheaves
Half	Halves	Thief	Thieves
Knife	Knives	Wolf	Wolves
Life	Lives	Wife	Wives
Leaf	Leaves		
Exceptions			
Belief	Beliefs	Chief	Chiefs
Dwarf	Dwarfs	Grief	Griefs
Handkerchief	Handkerchieves	Hoof	Hooves
Mischief	Mischiefs	Proof	Proofs
Roof	Roofs	Safe	Safes
Wharf	Wharfs		

Rule-5. By adding* 'en' *to certain nouns, as:

Singular	*Plural*	*Singular*	*Plural*
Ox	Oxen	Child	Children

Rule-6. By changing the inside vowel of certain nouns.

Singular	*Plural*	*Singular*	*Plural*
Foot	Feet	Man	Men
Goose	Geese	Woman	Women
Louse	Lice	Tooth	Teeth
Mouse	Mice		

Rule-7. By adding 's' to the nouns ending in double vowel.

Singular	*Plural*	*Singular*	*Plural*
Bamboo	Bamboos	Studio	Studios
Bee	Bees	Tree	Trees
Cuckoo	Cuckoos	Woe	Woes
Foe	Foes	Zoo	Zoos
Radio	Radios		

Rule-8. By changing 'man' into 'men' if a noun ends in man. No change is caused in the word preceding 'man', as:

Singular	*Plural*	*Singular*	*Plural*
Chairman	Chairmen	Milkman	Milkmen
Fisherman	Fishermen	Postman	Postmen
Gentleman	Gentlemen	Watchman	Watchmen
Layman	Laymen		

Rule-9. By adding s to the noun ending in 'y' if 'y' is preceded by a vowel (a, e, i, o, u), as:

Singular	*Plural*	*Singular*	*Plural*
Bay	Bays	Key	Keys
Boy	Boys	Lay	Lays

Contd...

Singular	*Plural*	*Singular*	*Plural*
Chimney	Chimneys	Monkey	Monkeys
Day	Days	Play	Plays
Donkey	Donkeys	Ray	Rays
Essay	Essays	Storey	Storeys
Fay	Fays	Toy	Toys
Guy	Guys	Valley	Valleys
Joy	Joys	Way	Ways

Rule-10. By adding 'es' to the noun ending in 'o' if 'o' is preceded by consonant, as:

Singular	*Plural*	*Singular*	*Plural*
Buffalo	Buffaloes	Mosquito	Mosquitoes
Echo	Echoes	Negro	Negroes
Hero	Heroes	Tomato	Tomatoes
Mango	Mangoes	Volcano	Volcanoes
Motto	Mottoes		
Exceptions			
Canto	Cantos	Dynamo	Dynamos
Photo	Photos	Piano	Pianos
Zero	Zeros		

Rule-11. By adding 's' to the principal word of Compound Nouns as:

Singular	*Plural*
Brother-in-law	Brothers-in law
Bed-room	Bed-rooms
Commander-in-Chief	Commanders-in-Chief
Daughter-in-law	Daughters-in-law
Father-in-law	Fathers-in-law

Contd...

Singular	*Plural*
Kite-maker	Kite-makers
Looker-on	Lookers-on
Mother-in-law	Mothers-in-law
Maid-servant	Maid-servants
Passer-by	Passers-by
Peacock	Peacocks
Peahen	Peahens
Sister-in-law	Sisters-in-law
Son-in-law	Sons-in-law
Step-mother	Step-mothers
Step-brother	Step-brothers
Step-son	Step-sons
Step-father	Step-fathers
Step-sister	Step-sisters
Exceptions	
Lord-Justice	Lords-Justices
Man-servant	Men-servants
Woman-servant	Women-servants

Rule - 12. By changing the noun 'ex, is, on, um, us, a' into; ices, es, a, a, i, ae respectively as:

ex-ices

Singular	*Plural*	*Singular*	*Plural*
ex-ices			
Index	Indices	Vertex	Vertices
is-es			
Axis	Axes	Basis	Bases
Crisis	Crises	Oasis	Oases

Contd...

Singular	*Plural*	*Singular*	*Plural*
on-a			
Criterion	Criteria	Phenomenon	Phenomena
Sanatorium	Sanatoria		
um-a			
Corrigendum	Corrigenda	Curriculum	Curricula
Medium	Media	Memorandum	Memoranda
us-i			
Focus	Foci	Locus	Loci
Radius	Radii	Syllabus	Syllabi
a-ae			
Formula	Formulae		

Rule-13. By adding 's' at the end of Figures and Letters, as:

Singular	*Plural*	*Singular*	*Plural*
B.A.	B.A.'s	M.P.	M.P's
B.Ed.	B.Ed.'s	M	M's
B.T.	B.T.'s	P	P's
C.A.	C.A.'s	Q	Q's
M.A.	M.A.'s	T	T's
M.L.A.	M.L.A's	d	d's
r	r's	4	4's
7	7's		

Rule - 14. Some Nouns do not follow any rules while they are changed from singular to plural. They are termed 'Special Plurals' as:

Singular	*Plural*	*Singular*	*Plural*
Child	Children	Madam	Madams
Mr. (Mister)	Messrs	Mrs. (Mistress)	"
Mr. Mathur	Messrs Mathur		
Miss Mathur	Misses Mathur		

Further Information about change of Nouns into Plural:

(i) Some Nouns like 'cannon, deer, series, species, dozen, fish, hair, pice, trout, cod, score, salmon, sheep, aircraft, swine, etc.' are alike in both Singular and Plural.

(ii) Some Nouns are used exclusively in singular, as:
Economics, fruit, furniture, hair, information, innings, machinery, mathematics, news, physics, politics, scenery, etc. Pair, dozen, core, gross, hundred, thousand, etc. are used in singular when used after numerals, as: She bought four dozen bananas.

(iii) Some nouns are used exclusively in plural, as cattle, gentry, people, riches, scissors, spectacles, bellows, thanks, pincers, tongs, trousers, vegetables, wages, etc.

Miscellaneous Exercise for Recapitulation

Noun: Number

Model Sentences

The dogs are barking in the street.

Many bushes are growing in our field.

We have bought ten benches today.

All the classes will assemble in the play-ground.

Why are the buses not plying today?

Ladies are dancing on the stage.

The armies are marching forward.

The dogs are chasing the cats.

The mosquitoes are humming around me.

The heroes are losing their importance nowadays.

Are the cuckoos not warbling in the trees?

Wolves are fighting in the zoo.

Have the roofs of these houses fallen?

Some men and some women are very selfish.

Are the mice holding a meeting?

The English (men) are very hard-working and punctual.

Why are you throwing stones on the passers-by?

Treat all men as your brothers (brethren).

The lookers-on (spectators) were clapping.

Do we not find many oases in a big desert?

The Gender

Gender denotes Sex: All living beings are either male or female. Lifeless things have no sex. Some Nouns are common for both the sexes.

Kinds of Gender:

Masculine Gender: The Nouns showing male sex are called *Masculine Gender,* as—boy, man, king, bull, nephew, actor, cock, etc.

Remember that all nouns associated with violence, vigour and strength are of Masculine gender, as—death, summer, winter, sun, thunder, time, wind, etc. e.g. Death has his own mood and schedule.

Feminine Gender: The Nouns showing female sex are called *Feminine Gender;* as—cow, daughter, hen, lioness, madam, poetess, queen, war, etc.

Remember that all nouns associated with beauty, grace, gentleness and fertility are of Feminine gender, as—earth, mercy, noon, peace, ship, autumn, spring, nature, liberty, etc., e.g. Peace hath her victory no less renowned than war. The moon does not show her face on a cloudy night.

Common Gender: The Nouns which show both the male and the female sex are called *Common Genders,* as — Painter, child, pupil, cousin, friend, foe, rival, neighbour, parent, servant, student, thief, enemy, person, orphan, baby, singer, infant, monarch, teacher, minister, etc.

Several languages have three genders. There is no common gender in Sanskrit Language. (All the names of persons or animals that do not indicate their sex are of common gender).

Neuter Gender: The Nouns showing non-living (lifeless, inanimate) things are called *Neuter Gender;* as—book, knife, pen, paper, room, table, tree, etc.

More Information about Neuter Gender:

(i) Lower animals and young children are also of Neuter Gender, as—ant, baby, etc.

(ii) Collective Nouns are invariably of Neuter Gender, as—Army, class, bunch, fleet, flock, herd, etc.

Rules for/of Forming Feminines from Masculines

Rule-1. By changing the words:

Masculine	*Feminine*	*Masculine*	*Feminine*
Bachelor	Maid	Husband	Wife
Beau	Belle	King	Queen
Boar	Sow	Lad	Lass
Boy	Girl	Lord	Lady
Bridegroom	Bride	Male	Female
Brother	Sister	Man	Woman
Buck	Doe	Master	Mistress
Bull	Cow	Monk	Nun
Cock	Hen	Mr.	Mrs.
Colt	Filly	Nephew	Niece
Czar	Czarina	Ox	Cow
Dog	Bitch	Papa	Momma
Drake	Duck	Prince	Princess

Contd...

Masculine	*Feminine*	*Masculine*	*Feminine*
Don	Donna	Ram	Ewe
Drone	Bee	Sir	Madam
Earl	Countess	Sire	Dame
Father	Mother	Son	Daughter
Fox	Vixen	Stag	Hind
Gander	Goose	Sultan	Sultana
Gentleman	Lady	Swain	Nymph
Hart	Roe	Uncle	Aunt
He	She	Viceroy	Vicereine
Hero	Heroine	Widower	Widow
Horse	Mare	Wizard	Witch

Rule-2. By forming the Feminine of the first-word of the Masculine Compound nouns:

Masculine	*Feminine*	*Masculine*	*Feminine*
Brother-in-law	Sister-in-law	Jack-ass	Jenny-ass
Bull-calf	Cow-calf	Male-doctor	Lady-doctor
Cock-sparrow	Hen-sparrow	Man-servant	Maid-servant
Father-in-law	Mother-in-law	Son-in-law	Daughter-in-law
He-buffalo	She-buffalo	Tom-goat	Filly-goat.

Rule-3. By forming the Feminine of the second-word of the Masculine Compound nouns:

Masculine	*Feminine*	*Masculine*	*Feminine*
Fisher-man	Fisher-woman	Mer-man	Mer-maid
Grand-father	Grand-mother	Milk-man	Milk-maid
Grand-son	Grand-daughter	Pea-cock	Pea-hen
Grand-uncle	Grand-aunt	Step-brother	Step-sister
Great-uncle	Great-aunt	Step-son	Step-daughter
Head-master	Head-mistress	Tom-cat	She-cat
Land-lord	Land-lady		

Rule-4. By adding 'ess' at the end of Masculine words, as:

Masculine	***Feminine***	***Masculine***	***Feminine***
Author	Authoress	Poet	Poetess
Baron	Baroness	Peer	Peeress
Count	Countess	Patron	Patroness
Giant	Giantess	Priest	Priestess
Heir	Heiress	Prophet	Prophetess
Host	Hostess	Shepherd	Shepherdess
Jew	Jewess	Tailor	Tailoress
Lion	Lioness	Tutor	Tutoress
Manager	Manageress	Viscount	Viscountess
Mayor	Mayoress		

Exceptions

God Goddess

Rule-5 (i). By adding 'ess' after dropping the last vowel along with the last consonant, as:

Masculine	***Feminine***	***Masculine***	***Feminine***
Abbot	Abbess	Sorcerer	Sorceress
Governor	Governess	Emperor	Empress
Murderer	Murderess		

(ii) By adding 'ess' in an irregular way; as:

Masculine	***Feminine***	***Masculine***	***Feminine***
Duke	Duchess	Master	Mistress
God	Goddess	Marquis/Marquess	Marchioness

Rule-6. By adding 'ess' after dropping the last vowel of the word:

Masculine	***Feminine***	***Masculine***	***Feminine***
Actor	Actress	Monitor	Monitress
Benefactor	Benefactress	Negro	Negress

Contd...

Masculine	*Feminine*	*Masculine*	*Feminine*
Conductor	Conductress	Prince	Princess
Editor	Editress	Tiger	Tigress
Hunter	Huntress	Traitor	Traitress
Inspector	Inspectress	Waiter	Waitress
Instructor	Instructress		

Hints to Remember about Genders:

1. We can address any male by calling him *Mr.*
2. Mrs. is a mode of address for a married female. Likewise, Miss is used as a mode of address for an unmarried female.
3. The words 'Dog', 'Horse' and 'Fox' are frequently used for both the masculine and feminine genders nowadays only in general sense.

Exceptions: The dog has given birth to two puppies. (wrong. Because 'Dog' is masculine here. The males do not give birth to children). The bitch has given birth to two puppies (correct because 'Bitch' is feminine. Only the females give birth to children).

Miscellaneous Exercise For Recapitulation

Noun: Gender

Model Sentences

All the lads and lasses are present today.

A bull and a cow are eating fodder.

A dog and a bitch are barking.

The king is talking to the queen.

The landlord and landlady of this house are gentle.

Is he riding a horse or a mare?

The husband and the wife have cooked the food together.

How many cocks and hens have you?

He had tamed many colts and fillies.

His uncles and aunts love him much.

Have both the hero and heroine reached the stage?

Both the lion and the lioness are dangerous.

Are the emperor and the empress not old?

Have the viceroy and the vicereine gone abroad?

Both the poet and the poetess are famous.

The mistress and the master of the house have boarded the train.

Her mother-in-law and father-in-law have died.

The prince and the princess have divided their property.

Who is tormenting the priest and the priestess?

Have you ever seen a stag and a hind?

Case: A case is a change in the form of a Noun, showing its relationship to another word.

Functions of Nouns: Use of Noun as the subject of a Verb. Look at the following sentences.

1. Bimla is making tea.
2. Kamla is doing the sums.
3. Sharda is weeping.
4. Chanchal helps Saroj.

In the above sentences, Bimla, Kamla, Sharda and Chanchal are the subjects of the verbs—making, doing, weeping and helps, because they pinpoint the doer of the action.

Remember that the subject of the verb is always in the Nominative Case.

Clue: We get the subject of the verb in answer to the questions:

1. Who is making tea? *Ans.* Bimla
2. Who is doing the sums? *Ans.* Kamla
3. Who is weeping? *Ans.* Sharda.
4. Who helps Saroj? *Ans.* Chanchal.

Remember that the Nominative Case normally precedes the verb but the Helping Verb precedes the Nominative Case in Interrogative Sentences.

Definition: The Noun (Pronoun) used as the Subject of a Verb is said to be in the Nominative Case.

Use of Noun as the object of a Verb. Look at the following sentences:

1. Hamid bought a book. 2. Niaz solved the sums.

In the above sentences, the words, *book* and *sums* are the objects of the verbs, *buy* and *solve* because they are directly affected by the action.

Clue: We get the object of the verb in answer to the questions.

1. What did Hamid buy? *Ans.* a book.
2. What did Niaz solve? *Ans.* the sums.

Remember that the Objective Case (Object of the verb), normally comes after the Verb.

Definition: The Noun (Pronoun) used as the object of a verb is said to be in the Accusative (Objective) Case.

Sometimes, we get two objects in a sentence, as:

1. He gave Mohini a pen.
2. She told us a secret.

Both of the sentences given above have two objects each. In sentence 1, the two objects are—Mohini (indirect object) and pen (direct object).

In sentence 2, the two objects are—us (Indirect object) and secret (Direct object).

Identification of Direct Object: We get the *'Direct Object'* in answer to the question. *'What'* as:

1. What did he give? *Ans.* a pen
2. What did she tell? *Ans.* a secret

Hence, a *pen* in sentence 1 and *a secret* in sentence 2 are *Direct Objects.* The ordinary *objects* are called the *'Direct Objects'.*

The Direct *Object* is always in the *Objective Case.*

Identification of Indirect Object: We get the *'Indirect Object'* in answer to the question 'Whom' as:

1. Whom did he give a pen? *Ans.* (For) Mohini.
2. Whom did she tell a secret? *Ans.* (For) us.

Hence, *Mohini* in sentence 1 and *us* in sentence 2 are *Indirect Objects.* The *persons* are called the *'Indirect Objects'* (to *whom/ for whom,* something is given).

The *Indirect Object* is always used in/for the *Dative Case e.g.*

1. He gave Mohini a pen.

   For whom did he give a pen? *Ans*- For Mohini (Dative case)
2. She told us a secret.

   To whom did she tell a secret? *Ans*-To us (Dative case)

As an object, the Noun can be used in the following two manners.

Object to a Transitive Verb:

1. She threw a ball.
2. I bought an orange.

In sentence 1, *throw* is the Transitive Verb of the Noun (a ball). In sentence 2, the Noun (an orange) has been used as the object of the Transitive Verb (*buy*).

Governed by a Preposition:

1. The ladder stands *against* the wall.
2. The sun shines *above* the trees.

In sentence 1, the noun (wall) has been used in the objective case and it (*wall*) is governed by the preposition (against).

In sentence 2, the noun (trees) has been used in the objective case and it (*trees*) is governed by the preposition (above).

The use of a Noun in the Form of Possession.

1. *Rohit's* doll is nice.
2. *Gita's* frock is silken.
3. *Babli's* game was fine.
4. *Mohan's* house is grand.

In sentence 1, the possessor (owner) of the doll is *Rohit.*

In sentence 2, the possessor (owner) of the frock is *Gita.*

In sentence 3, the game is related with *Babli.*

In sentence 4, the owner of the house is *Mohan.*

On reading the sentences, we can conclude that:

(i) Rohit, Gita, Babli, and Mohan are Possessive Nouns.

(ii) The Possessive Nouns are used in Possessive or Genitive case.

(iii) *'s'* is added with Possessive Nouns.

Note: The comma used before 's' of the Possessive Case is called the Apostrophe.

Formation of Possessive/Genitive Case:

Rule 1: Add *'s* at the end of Singular Nouns, as:

The boy's coat; a sister's affection; the land-lord's daughter.

Rule 2: Add *'s* at the end of the plural nouns which do not have *s* at the end; as:

The Children's Club; Women's sarees; Oxen's horns.

Rule 3: Add apostrophe (') at the end of such plural nouns as have *s* at the end; as—Cows' tails; tables' tops; watches' straps.

Remember that some modern Grammarians put apostrophe ('s) even though the plural nouns have *s* at the end, as:

Cows's tails; tables's tops; watches's straps, etc. But the use of cows' tails; tables' tops, watches' straps, etc. is equally correct.

Rule 4:

(i) Use *'s* after the latter noun in case, two nouns are closely related, as:

Many trees were planted during Indira and Rajiv's prime ministership.

(ii) Add *'s* after the latter noun, if the two nouns are used in apposition, as.

Rajeshwari stays with her neighbour, Radha's brother.

(iii) Add *'s* after the last noun if the title of a noun contains several nouns, as.

1. The Chief Justice of India's verdict.
2. The Pradhan of Village Panchayat's proclamation.

Remember that *'s* is not added while forming the Possessive Case of lifeless objects. Instead, we use the Possessive indeclinable (of) before the noun (s); as:

The table's leg is broken.

The house's roofs have fallen.

The tree's trunk is thin.

The coat's buttons have gone off.

(All of the above sentences are wrong).

Other Examples:

The leg of the table is broken.

The roofs of the house have fallen.

The trunk of the tree is thin.

The buttons of the coat have gone off.

(All of the sentences given above are correct).

Recapitulation of Important Tips: Possessive Case is generally used with Nouns denoting:

(a) Living Things—as bull's horns, Ramoo's book, cows' teats.

(b) Personified Things—as sorrow's tears, death's sting.

(c) Dignified things—as the mind's eye, heaven's sake.

(d) Weight, Value, Time, Space—as a stone's throw, five rupees' worth, a week's time, an arm's length.

(e) In certain phrases—as at one's fingers' tips, for heavens' sake, etc.

Avoid Double Possessives:

1. My friend's sister's daughter is a nurse. (wrong)
   The daughter of my friend's sister is a nurse. (correct)
2. One of these girls' performance is praiseworthy. (wrong)
   The performance of one of these girls is praiseworthy. (correct)
3. Also avoid using apostrophe (') or ('s) with possessive pronouns.
   Our's, your's, her's, their's (wrong)
   Ours, yours, hers, theirs (correct)

Important Information: Noun is also used in the following manners besides in the cases elaborated above.

4. The use of Noun as Complement of the Verb.

Look at the following sentences:

1. Ashoka was *a king.*
2. Mumtaz Mahal was *a queen.*
3. Pt. Deep Chand was *a headmaster.*
4. Birbal was *a wise minister.*

If the words a *king; a queen;* a *headmaster;* and *a wise minister* are removed from the above sentences, the remaining parts of the sentences will convey incomplete meanings. Because, the words a *king, a queen, a headmaster* and *a wise minister* complete the meanings of the above sentences. Hence, words which complete the meanings of the sentences are called *complements.*

More Information about complements:

Definition: The noun which is used to complete the meaning of the verb is termed as the complement of the verb.

Identification:

(i) Complement is normally used after the verbs given below.

is, are, am, was, were, appear, become, look, make, seem.

(ii) Complement is also used with certain transitive verbs, as we elected him, secretary. (In this sentence, the word *secretary* is the complement).

Use of Noun as Nomination of Address:

Definition: Those nouns, which are used in calling others are termed as 'Nomination of Address'. They are used in the Vocative Case, as:

1. Boys, keep quiet.
2. Class, stand up.
3. Workers, go to work.
4. Make a cup of tea, Rani.

The words *boys, class, workers,* and *Rani* have been used in the above sentences to attract/or invite their attention.

Hence, they have been used in Vocative Case or Nominative of Address.

Case in Apposition:

Definition: If two nouns are used together (simultaneously) and give indication of the same person, the latter noun will be termed as Case in Apposition of the former (previous) noun, as:

1. Sujata, your neighbour is a clever girl.
2. Roshan, your uncle is an athlete.
3. Neeru, your classmate is a flirt.

In the above sentence 1 *your neighbour* and *Sujata* give indication of the same person. Therefore, *your neighbour* has been used as Sujata's Case in Apposition.

In sentence 2 *your uncle* and *Roshan* refer to the same person. Therefore, *your uncle* has been used as Roshan's Case in Apposition.

In sentence 3 *your classmate* and *Neeru* give indication of the same person. Therefore, *your classmate* has been used as Neeru's Case in Apposition.

More Information about Case:

Cases in Hindi and Sanskrit

Name of the Case	*Clue/Identification*
1. Nominative Case	—
2. Accusative Case	To
3. Instrumental Case	With
4. Dative Case	For
5. Ablative Case	From
6. Genitive Case	of
7. Locative Case	in, at, into, on,
8. Vocative Case	Oh, Hey

Parsing

According to the revised syllabus, the candidates are required to write the part of speech, a particular word belongs to. Besides, he is also required to use the specified word in a sentence of his own. Look at the following sentences carefully.

1. *Ram* went there.	*Ram* Noun, Use: Ram came here.
2. I beat a *girl.*	*Girl* Noun, Use: You love a girl.
3. He was in the *room.*	*Room,* Noun, Use: My books are in the room.

4. *Hari's* clothes are dirty. *Hari's,* Noun, Use: Hari's sister was going to Mathura.

5. Come into the park, *Romesh.* *Romesh,* Noun, Use: Go there, Romesh.

6. Ashoka was a King. *King.* Noun, Use: Akbar was a famous king.

7. Niraj, our *captain,* made five runs. *Captain.* Noun, Use: Mukul, our captain, played well.

Common Errors in the Use of Nouns

	Incorrect	*Correct*
1.	She has many works to do.	She has much work to do.
2.	The cattles are grazing.	The cattle are grazing.
3.	She likes fruits and vegetable.	She likes fruit and vegetables.
4.	I have lost a five rupees note.	I have lost a five rupee note.
5.	I need two dozens bananas.	I need two dozen bananas.
6.	The bridge is close for repair.	The bridge is closed for repair.
7.	One of his uncle is a doctor.	One of his uncles is a doctor.
8.	The chair's leg is broken.	The leg of the chair is broken.
9.	There is no place on the desk.	There is no room on the desk.
10.	All his family's members are sick.	All the members of his family are sick.
11.	Mridula's hairs are curly.	Mridula's hair are curly.
12.	She gave me many advices.	She gave me much advice.
13.	Our teacher has sold all his furniture.	Our teacher has sold all his furnitures.
14.	Your scissor is blunt.	Your scissors are blunt.
15.	Politics are a dirty game.	Politics is a dirty game.
16.	Mohit got just passing marks.	Mohit got just pass marks.
17.	The girl showered many abuses on her neighbour.	The girl showered much abuse on her neighbour.
18.	My diary is full of informations.	My diary is full of information.
19.	Your spectacle is costly.	Your spectacles are costly.

Contd...

	Incorrect	*Correct*
20.	I want a paper.	I want a piece of paper.
21.	Give me a chalk.	Give me a piece of chalk.
22.	These news are true.	This news is true.
23.	He is true to his words.	He is true to his word.
24.	I bought two pairs of shoes.	I bought two pair of shoes.
25:	I have finished four-fifth of my book.	I have finished four-fifths of my book.
26.	We should love the poors.	We should love the poor.
27.	The judge passed order for his imprisonment.	The judge passed orders for his imprisonment.
28.	I shall spend my summer vacations in Kashmir.	I shall spend my summer vacation in Kashmir.
29.	The sceneries of Simla are charming.	The scenery of Simla is charming.
30.	Milk is sold by litre.	Milk is sold by the litre.
31.	Red Fort is made of stones.	Red Fort is made of stone.
32.	I gave the beggar five pices.	I gave the beggar five pice.
33.	He has taken his meals.	He has taken his meal.
34.	Madhu has no issues.	Madhu has no issue.
35.	Alas! Bhoj has no off-springs.	Alas! Bhoj has no off-spring.
36.	Are you fond of fruits?	Are you fond of fruit?
37.	Physics or Mathematics are an interesting subject.	Physics or Mathematics is an interesting subject.
38.	The first innings are over.	The first innings is over.
39.	Have you gone through contents of the question paper?	Have you gone through the content of the question paper?
40.	I cannot continue my study.	I cannot continue my studies.
41.	I shall spare no pain.	I shall spare no pains.
42.	Riches has wings.	Riches have wings.
43.	A summon was issued against the Ex-Prime Minister.	Summons were issued against the Ex-Prime Minister.

Contd...

	Incorrect	*Correct*
44.	The alm was given to the beggar.	The alms were given to the beggar.
45.	This tongs needs repair.	These tongs need repairs.
46.	Your trousers is torn.	Your trousers are torn.
47.	Many peoples were laughing at me.	Many people were laughing at me.
48.	The gentry of Delhi is unsocial.	The gentry of Delhi are unsocial.
49.	I saw many deers in the park.	I saw many deer in the park.
50.	He objected to his sister going there.	He objected to his sister's going there.
51.	Learn these poetries today.	Learn these poems today.
52.	The clock has struck seven hours.	The clock has struck seven.
53.	Ramoo has ten heads of cattle.	Ramoo has ten head of cattle.
54.	Twenty rupees are much for this ball-pen.	Twenty rupees is much for this ball-pen.
55.	Kukreja lives in the boarding.	Kukreja lives in the boarding-house.
56.	Where is your copy?	Where is your copy-book?
57.	The jury was divided in their opinions.	The jury were divided in their opinions.
58.	Pay my regard to your parents.	Pay my regards to your parents.
59.	There are two M.Ed-s in our school.	There are two M.Ed-'s in our school.
60.	I shall leave by 7.30 o'clock train.	I shall leave by 7.30 train.
61.	I can run a four miles race.	I can run a four-mile race.
62.	The Committee were unanimous in their decisions.	The Committee was unanimous in its decisions.
63.	The mice is playing.	The mice are playing.
64.	His tooth are aching.	His tooth is aching.

Common Errors in the Use of Cases

	Incorrect	*Correct*
1.	Your's faithfully.	Yours faithfully.
2.	He deals in childrens' items.	He deals in children's items.
3.	What is your doll's price?	What is the price of your doll?
4.	My house's location is ideal.	The location of my house is ideal.
5.	The chair's arms are broken.	The arms of the chair are broken.
6.	It is my friend's father's friend's car.	It is the car of the friend of my friend's father.
7.	This is Murli's my nephew's house.	This is the house of Murli, my nephew. *Or* This is my nephew, Murli's house.
8.	One of the girl's frocks was torn.	One of the frocks of the girl was torn.
9.	There was perfect law and order in William's and Mary's reign.	There was perfect law and order in Willam and Mary's reign.
10.	My classmate's Mohini's brother insulted me.	My classmate, Mohini's brother insulted me.

3

Pronoun

Kinds of Pronoun

There are the following eight divisions of pronouns:

(i) Personal Pronouns	(v) Distributive Pronouns
(ii) Relative Pronouns	(vi) Indefinite Pronouns
(iii) Interrogative Pronouns	(vii) Reflexive Pronouns
(iv) Demonstrative Pronouns	(viii) Reciprocal Pronouns

(i) Personal Pronouns are used for persons; as —I, we, you, he, she, they. We use ' I or we' for the speakers.

We use 'you' for the hearer.

We use 'he, she or they' for the persons about whom they both (I/we, you) talk.

Personal Pronouns are as under:

First Person Pronouns: The pronoun(s) which the speaker (s) uses (use) for himself (themselves) is (are) known as First *Person Personal Pronoun* (s), as:

I am speaking.	*We* are walking.
I do *my* work.	*We* go to *our* school.
Mohan helps me.	Sarla gives us toffees.
This book is *mine.*	That house is *ours.*

Second Person Pronouns: The pronoun(s) which the speaker(s) uses (use) for the hearer(s) is (are) known as *Second Person Personal Pronoun* (s), as:

You are a boy. Oh, God, *Thou* art great.

You should obey *your* parents. Is this house *yours?*

Oh, God, shower *Thy* blessings on this poor lady.

Is this book *thine* (yours)? I am offering *Thee* my prayers.

Please remember that 'you' is used both for a single hearer, as well as a number of hearers.

Third Person Pronouns: The pronoun(s) which the speaker(s) and the hearer(s) use for the person(s) about whom they both talk is (are) known as *Third Person Personal Pronoun*(s), as:

He is coming. *He* irons *his* shirt.

She is sleeping. *She* is cleaning *her* room.

They are reading. *They* are reading *their* books.

Are those bags *theirs?* Give *him* four rupees.

Is this book *hers?* Give *them* a warning.

Various Forms and Functions of the Personal Pronouns

Person	*Forms* *Number*	*Gender*	*Subject* *(Nominative)*	*Function* *Possessive*	*Object* *(Accusative)*
First	Singular	Common	I	my, mine	me
	Plural	Common	We	our, ours	us
Second	Singular	Common	You	your, yours	you
	Singular	Common	Thou	Thy, Thine	Thee
	Plural	Common	You	yours, yours	you
Third	Singular	Masculine	He	his	him
	Singular	Feminine	She	her, hers	her
	Singular	Neuter	It	its	it
	Plural	Common	They	their	them

Clarification about the Table given Overleaf

Important Information: *'I'* is 'Singular Number' and 'Common Gender'. It is used in Nominative Case. 'Me' is used in the objective case and *'My/ Mine'* is used in Possessive case.

'We' is 'Plural Number' and 'Common Gender'. It is used in Nominative Case. 'Us' is used in the Objective Case. *'Our/ Ours'* is used in Possessive Case.

'You' is used both in Singular and Plural numbers. It has Common Gender. It is used in Nominative Case as well as Objective Case. *'Your/Yours'* is used in Possessive Case.

'He' is 'Singular Number' and 'Masculine Gender'. It is used in Nominative Case. *'Him'* is used in the Objective Case. *'His'* is used in Possessive Case.

'She' is 'Singular Number' and 'Feminine Gender'. It is used in Nominative Case. *'Her'* is used in the Objective Case. *'Her/Hers'* is used in the Possessive Case.

'It' is 'Singular Number' and 'Neuter Gender'. It is used in Nominative Case and Objective Case. *'Its'* is used in the Possessive Case.

'They' is 'Plural Number' (of *he, she,* and *it*). It has both (Masculine and Feminine) genders. *'They'* is used in Nominative Case. *'Them'* is used in Objective Case. *'Their/ Theirs'* is used in Possessive Case.

Relative Pronouns: Join two sentences and show their relation with their antecedents; as.

1. I know the boy. He (the boy) is a swimmer. By joining these two sentences, we can re-write them as

   I know the boy *who* is a swimmer.

'Who' in the above sentences is a relative pronoun which joins the two sentences, 'who' shows its relation with 'the boy' (its antecedent).

2. This is the girl. I like her. By joining these two sentences, we can rewrite them, as

   This is the *girl whom* I like.

'Whom' in the above sentences is a Relative Pronoun which joins the two sentences, 'whom' shows its relation with 'the girl' (its antecedent).

Kinds of Relative Pronouns:

Continuative: The Continuative Relative Pronoun does not show the quality (speciality) of its antecedent Noun, as:

1. I met Sheela *who* (and she) gave me a pen.
2. Mr. Purcell released the pigeon *which* (and it) flew away.
3. He hit the glass *which* (and it) fell into pieces.

'*Who* and *Which*' in the above sentences add something to the statement existing before them. However, they do not qualify their antecedent Nouns (Sheela, Pigeon and Glass). Therefore, they do not introduce *Adjective Clauses.* They begin co-ordinate Clauses. Such types of co-ordinate clauses can often be separated from the remaining part of the sentences by inserting a comma.

Remember that no other pronoun except '*who* and *which*' can be used in continuative form.

Restrictive/Relative Pronouns: It qualifies its Antecedent Noun; as:

1. I know the girl *who* had stolen your purse.
2. Tell me the name of the boy *whom* you want to see.
3. Where is the frock *which* I presented you?
4. Bring me the book *that* is lying on the floor.

   In sentence 1. '*Who*' refers to a certain girl.

   In sentence 2. '*Whom*' refers to a certain boy.

   In sentence 3. '*Which*' refers to a certain frock.

   In sentence 4. '*That*' refers to a certain book.

Therefore, all of these relative pronouns (*who, whom, which,* and *that*) begin the subordinate Adjective Clauses.

Remember that the is invariably put before the antecedent Noun of a relative pronoun in restrictive sense, as:

the girl, *the* boy, *the* frock, *the* book

Necessary Information regarding the use of Relative Pronouns:

(i) The number and person of the Relative Pronouns will be the same as of its Antecedent Noun.

(ii) Relative Pronoun should be used, nearest to its Antecedent Noun.

(iii) '*Who, Whose* and *Whom*' will be used only for persons.

(iv) '*Which*' will be used only for lifeless objects and commonplace animals.

The use of "That" as Relative Pronoun:

(i) After Numeral Adjectives

Pt. Deep Chand was the *first headmaster* that received the Municipal Award.

(ii) After Uncertain Gender

The child that was lost has been traced.

(iii) After Interrogative Pronouns

Who are you that dare challenge me?

(iv) In Adverbial sense

This is the moment that (at which) you should report for duty.

(v) While/In talking about *persons, animals* and *things*

This is the scooter that I purchased yesterday.

I shall tell you about the people and animals that I saw in the village.

(vi) After Superlative Degree of Adjective

Munshi Prem Chand is the best writer that I know.

(vii) In the form of Defining word

The window pane that the boy broke has been fixed.

(viii) After all, any, it, none, nothing, only, same, etc. as:

All that glitters is not gold.

Anyone that heard of Rajiv's death shed tears.

It was Ram Kumar that ruined Hari's life.

There was *none* that did not curse the murderer.

It is not for *nothing* that I have come here.

It is *only* silly people that do not admire art.

It is the *same* cap that I bought yesterday.

Remember that *'that'* used after *'such'* is not called a 'Relative Pronoun'. It is rather called a *conjunction;* as:

He is not such a boy that he should miss the class.

The use of other words, used in the form of Relative Pronouns.

(i) *As,* used after *such* and *same* (*such as/same as*) is considered as a Relative Pronoun; as:

This is the same saree as my husband gave me.

Only such persons as are invited should enter the hall.

(ii) If *'But'* gives the sense of *who not; that not* or *which not,* it (but) will be considered as a Relative Pronoun; as:

There was none but (who not) wept.

There is no rose but (which not) has a thorn.

There is no book but (that not) has information.

(iii) *'What'* is sometimes used in lieu of *'that* which' as a Relative Pronoun. It is used exclusively for objects. Its Antecedent Noun is inferred; as:

(i) She buys *what* she likes. (Here, the antecedent Noun *'anything'* can be inferred)

(ii) I mean *what* I say. (Here the antecedent Noun of what *'something* can be inferred.)

Interrogative Pronoun

These Pronouns are used in asking questions; as:

1. When did you come here?
2. What is wrong with you?
3. Whom did you call?
4. How goes the world with you?
5. Which is your toy?
6. Where is your coat?
7. When did you come here?
8. Who teaches you English?
9. Whose pen is this?

Remember that:

'Who, Whose, Whom' are used for persons.

'What' is used for things.

'Which' is used both for persons and things.

It always denotes the selection

Demonstrative Pronouns: These Pronouns are used to pinpoint some Noun; as:

1. *This* is my umbrella.
2. *That* is your house.
3. *These* are your dolls.
4. *Those* are cows.

Remember that:

(i) Demonstrative Pronoun is immediately preceded by a *Verb.*

(ii) *'This* and *these'* show *'nearness'*

(iii) *'That* and *those'* show *'remoteness* or *distance'*

(iv) *'This* and *that'* are singular number.

(v) *'These* and *those'* are plural number.

(vi) *'That'* preceded by a verb will be termed as *Demonstrative Pronoun.* In the same way, *'that'* pinpointing (referring to) its antecedent Noun will be termed as *Relative Pronoun*; as:

1. It was he *that* led me to trouble.

   Here *'that'* is a Demonstrative Pronoun which refers to 'he' (a certain person).

2. That is the house where I live.

   Here *'that'* is a Demonstrative Pronoun which is followed by the verb (is) and it refers to the noun (house)

Distributive Pronouns: These Pronouns are used for each of the persons, things, etc. used in the sentences; as:

1. Choose *either* of these two frocks.
2. *Neither* of the two sisters is intelligent.
3. *Each* of you can attend the meeting.
4. *None* of them could catch the thief.
5. Why did you not buy *any* book?

Please Remember that:

Each, either and *neither* are followed by the noun, and verb of singular number.

'Either and neither' are used in speaking of two persons or things. *'Either'* means 'the one or the other of two'. Sometimes *'either'* means 'both' as there are trees on either bank of the river. *'Neither'* means 'not the one, nor the other of two'. It is the negative of *'either'*.

'Any' is used in the case of more than two persons or things.

Indefinite Pronouns: These Pronouns do not refer to some definite person or thing; as:

1. *All* of us were in danger.
2. *Many* of the passengers were killed.
3. *Everybody* does this work.
4. *None* but you could solve the sum.
5. *Nobody* came for my help.

6. *Some* are genius by birth.
7. *One* should do one's duty.
8. *Somebody* molested her.

Remember that: *All, any, anybody, everyone, everybody, few, many, no one, none, one, some, same, one, somebody,* etc. are Indefinite Pronouns.

More Information about Indefinite Pronouns:

(i) The possessive case of *one* is *one's;* as *one* should mind *one's* own work.

(ii) Use *he/she* after *everyone, everybody, anybody* according to the contextual requirement; as *everyone* likes *his* own circle of friends.

(Here, *'his'* has been used after *everyone* because the sex (Male/ Female) has not been mentioned here.

Reflexive Pronouns: These pronouns show that the subject alone is affected by the action (verb) and no one else; as

1. I iron my clothes *myself.*
2. We do the cooking *ourselves.*
3. You solved the sum *yourself.*
4. You can go home *yourselves.*
5. He can drive the scooter *himself.*
6. She can wash her clothes *herself.*
7. They can help *themselves.*
8. It cracked *itself.*
9. One should depend on *oneself.*

Remember that:

(i) 'Self' is used with *'my, him, her, it and one'.*

(ii) 'Selves' is used with *'our, your* (plural) and *them'.*

(iii) 'Self' is also used with *'your* (singular)'.

Examples:

1. Mohan! you prepare your food yourself. (Here, *'you'* stands for Mohan (Singular). Therefore, the use of *yourself* (your + self) is correct here).
2. Mohan and Shyam! You ate all the bananas yourselves. (Here *'you'* stands for both Mohan and Shyam (Plural). Therefore, the use of *yourselves* (your + selves) is correct here.

Reciprocal Pronouns: These pronouns are formed by joining two pronouns and show mutual/reciprocal relationship: as:

1. Mohan and Shyam love *each other.*
2. Sarla, Sharda and Monorama help *one another.*

Remember that:

(i) *'Each other'* is used in case of two persons or things.

(ii) *'One another'* is used in case of more than two persons or things.

Important Rules for the Use of Pronouns:

(i) If different pronouns are to be used in a single sentence, put them in the order of *'second person, third person and first person,* as:

You, he and I are close friends.

(ii) If different pronouns are to be used in a single sentence, and one's own fault is confessed, put them in the order of *first person, third person* and *second person,* as:

I, he and you are pick-pockets.

He and you have robbed me.

You and I have stolen this scooter.

(iii) If certain pronouns refer to different persons, use *first person plural* (*we*) instead of *second person* and *second person plural* instead *of third person,* as:

1. You and she have robbed your relatives.

2. We and you have spoiled our careers.

3. You and they should improve your handwriting.

(iv) Always use *Singular Number Pronouns,* in case a *Collective Noun* refers to the whole group; as:

The class respects its monitor.

(v) Always use *Plural Number Pronouns,* in case a *Collective Noun* refers to various persons of the group separately; as:

The committee left *their* seats in despair.

(vi) Use the *Plural Number Pronoun* if two or more than two Singular Number Nouns are joined by *and,* as:

Reeta *and* Renuka help each other.

(vii) Use the *Singular Number Pronoun* if two or more than two Singular Number Nouns, joined by *and* refer to a single person or thing (object), as:

1. Slow and steady wins the race.

2. The book and stationery stall is quite near.

(viii) Use the Singular Pronoun with Singular Nouns joined by *or, either ...... or, neither ..... nor,* as:

Neither Ragini nor Nagini has secured first division.

(ix) Use *'mine, ours, yours, hers* and *theirs'* in lieu of *'my, our, your, her* and *their'* if the Possessive Case Pronoun is separated from a Noun by means of a verb, as:

1. This scooter is *mine.*

2. That classroom is *ours.*

3. These toys are *theirs.*

(x) Use the *Nominative Case Pronoun* if a sentence begins with *'it'*, as:

1. It is I. 2. It is we.

3. It is she. 4. It is they.

(xi) Use the Objective case after *'let, like, between, but* and *prepositions'*, as:

1. Let me have my turn.
2. This is between her and us.
3. You should not rely on them.
4. Everyone was there but him.
5. You like me are also a loser.

(xii) Put the *Emphatic Pronoun* close to the *Subject* and the *Reflexive Pronoun* away from the Subject, as:

She herself caught the thief. (Emphatic)

She ruined herself in her youth. (Reflexive)

Miscellaneous Exercise For Recapitulation

Kinds of Pronouns

Model Sentences

We stitch our clothes ourselves.

He polishes his shoes himself.

They returned to their houses themselves.

Whom do you want to see?

What is she laughing at?

Is there someone in the room?

There is something wrong at the bottom.

Some of these novels are really praiseworthy.

That was a nice time when we were children.

Is this not my book?

This is the man who had kidnapped Rohit.

This is the boy whom she loves.

None of these stories is interesting.

Is either of the two sisters pretty?

Neither of these two boys is to blame.

These two parrots love each other.

Common Errors in the Use of Pronouns

Order of Pronouns

	Incorrect	*Correct*
1.	He, you and I are neighbours.	You, he and I are neighbours.
2.	I, he and you are relatives.	You, he and I are relatives.
3.	You, he and I are criminals.	I, he and you are criminals.

Wrong Use of the Cases

4.	You are stronger than me.	You are stronger than I.
5.	I am your's faithfully.	I am yours faithfully.
6.	It is him.	It is he.
7.	Only you and him can solve this sum.	Only you and he can solve this sum.
8.	If I were him, I should help her.	If I were he, I should help her.
9.	This is mine house.	This is my house, *or* This house is mine.
10.	There is no secret between you and I.	There is no secret between you and me.
11.	Good girls like you and she should not mix with bad boys.	Good girls like you and her should not mix with bad boys.
12.	You and I have done my homework.	You and I have done our homework.
13.	This doll is superior to your.	This doll is superior to yours.

Wrong use of Gender

14.	One should serve his country.	One should serve one's country.
15.	Everyone should try one's best.	Everyone should try his best.
16.	I supported everyone of those women in their election.	I supported everyone of those women in her election.
17.	Every teacher and every student should be regular in their work.	Every teacher and every student should be regular in his/her work.

Where Pronouns are not Needed

18.	The thief hid himself in a shed.	The thief hid in a shed.
19.	I have qualified myself as a doctor.	I have qualified as a doctor.
20.	Your explanation is to my hand.	Your explanation is to hand.

Contd...

Incorrect	*Correct*
Omission of Pronouns	
21. Never overeat.	Never overeat yourself.
22. The climate of Delhi is hotter than Dehradun.	The climate of Delhi is hotter than that of Dehradun.
23. I availed of the chance.	I availed myself of the chance.
24. They enjoyed heartily.	They enjoyed themselves heartily.
Miscellaneous	
25. She will not object to me seeing her dance.	She will not object to my seeing her dance.
26. Who is cleverer, Sarla or Saroj?	Which is cleverer, Sarla or Saroj?
27. All the students should honour each other.	All the students should honour one another.
28. The two brothers quarrelled with one another.	The two brothers quarrelled with each other.

4

Adjective

Kinds of Adjective

There are the following seven divisions of Adjectives:

(i) Adjective of Quality.

(ii) Adjective of Quantity.

(iii) Adjective of Number.

(iv) Demonstrative Adjective.

(v) Interrogative Adjective.

(vi) Distributive Adjective.

(vii) Possessive Adjectives.

Adjective of Quality: These adjectives show the qualities, disqualities or shape/colour, etc.; as:

1. Manoj is a *brave* boy.
2. Preet Kaur is a *black* woman.
3. Ashoka was a *great* King.
4. Hari is a *mean* fellow.
5. You are an *honest* girl.
6. The Ganges is a *holy* river.

Adjective of Quantity: These adjectives show the quantity of a thing; as:

1. I have *some* money to spend.

2. The lion ate up the *whole* goat.
3. I could not get *any* taxi.

Adjective of Number: These adjectives show the number of persons or objects; as:

1. I have a *dozen* pets.
2. The girl sitting in the *fourth* row is very naughty.
3. A student has *few* cares.
4. *Several* passengers died in the accident.

Types of Adjective of Number:

(i) Definite Adjective of Number denotes the exact number; as *a dozen* in sentence 1 and *the fourth* in sentence 2 above.

(ii) Indefinite Adjective of Number denotes the uncertainty of the number; as *few* in Sentence 3 and *Several* in Sentence 4 above.

Demonstrative Adjectives pinpoint the nouns, used immediately after them; as:

1. *This* boy is careless.
2. *That* girl is very smart.
3. *These* apples are rotten.
4. *Those* bananas are ripe.

Remember that:

'This' is Singular and *'These'* is plural. They (*This* and *These*) are used to pinpoint the persons or things present nearby.

'That' is Singular and *'Those'* is plural. They (*That* and *those*) are used to pinpoint the persons and things present at some distance.

Distinction between Demonstrative Adjective and Demonstrative Pronoun:

Demonstrative Adjective is succeeded by a Noun but a Demonstrative Pronoun is not succeeded (followed) by any Noun; as:

That is a picture. (Demonstrative Pronoun)

Those girls are intelligent. (Demonstrative Adjective)

Interrogative Adjective: These adjectives are used for making enquiries or asking questions; as:

1. *Whose* pen is this?
2. *Which* saree do you like?
3. *What* time is it?

Distinction between Interrogative Adjective and Interrogative Pronouns:

Interrogative Adjective is followed (succeeded) by a Noun but an Interrogative pronoun is not succeeded by any Noun; as:

Which book is hers? (Interrogative Adjective)

Which is her book? (Interrogative Pronoun)

Distributive Adjective: These adjectives are used to show each and every individual person or thing of a class/group; as:

1. *Each* boy took the breakfast.
2. *Every* teacher is honest.
3. *Either* drink (coffee or tea) will do.
4. *Neither* girl is lazy.

Distinction between Distributive Adjective and Distributive Pronoun:

Distributive Adjective is succeeded by a Noun but a Distributive Pronoun is not succeeded by any Noun; as:

Either of them should join the club. (Distributive Pronoun)

Either fruit will please her. (Distributive Adjective)

Remember that: *Each, every, neither, either are* used as Distributive Adjective.

Possessive Adjective: These adjectives show relation with certain persons or things; as:

1. *My* cousin is an officer.

2. *Your* books are useful.
3. *Her* saree is colourful.
4. *Their* house is large.

Miscellaneous Exercise For Recapitulation

Kinds of Adjectives

Model Sentences

Your brother is fat but you are skinny.
There is a little milk in this jug.
This is not a romantic novel.
Put a little ice in this water.
Some people are very greedy and selfish.
More workers are needed here.
The seventh boy in this row is naughty?
Do many plants not make their own food?
Is this toy not mine?
Whose is that umbrella?
This is the same turban as my father gave me.
A jeweller lived in a certain town.
The Mauryan empire was very large.
The Hindu religion is very simple.
At what time does your school close?
Whose watch have you stolen?
Where does your auntie live?
Their house is splendid.
Do the clothes not add to our appearance?
Here is a bird. Its feathers are not soft.

Types of 'Uses of Adjectives':

Attributively: When used attributively, the Adjective precedes a Noun; as:

The intelligent girl stood first.

Predicatively: Here, the adjective is used with the verb and becomes the part of the predicate; as:

The girl is intelligent.

Comparison of Adjectives

Look at the following sentences:

1. Dhruvika is a *smart* girl.
2. Dhruvika is *smarter* than Nupur.
3. Dhruvika is the *smartest* girl in our house.

In sentence 1, the word (adjective) — *smart* shows the quality of Dhruvika in the normal and usual way. In sentence 2, the word (adjective) — *smarter* compares the quality of Dhruvika with that of Nupur.

In sentence 3, the word (adjective) — *smartest* compares Dhruvika's quality with the qualities of other girls in her class.

The words—*smart, smarter* and *smartest* show comparison— As such, they are termed as Degrees of Comparison.

Kinds of Degree of Comparison:

Positive Degree: It shows the normal and general quality or disquality of a person or things; as:

Usha is a tall girl.

Comparative Degree: It shows the comparison between the qualities or disqualities or two persons or things; as:

Usha is taller than Kamla.

Superlative Degree: It shows the comparison of the quality or disquality of a person or thing with the qualities or disqualities of more than two persons or things of the same class; as:

Usha is the tallest girl in the class.

Remember that only Adjectives of Quality and Adjectives of Quantity have Degrees of Comparison.

Formation of Degrees of Comparison

Rule 1. 'er' and 'est' are added to the positive degree Adjectives to form their Comparative and Superlative respectively; as:

Positive	*Comparative*	*Superlative*
Black	blacker	blackest
Bold	bolder	boldest
Bitter	bitterer	bitterest
Bright	brighter	brightest
Brief	briefer	briefest
Calm	calmer	calmest
Clean	cleaner	cleanest
Clever	cleverer	cleverest
Cold	colder	coldest
Dear	dearer	dearest
Deep	deeper	deepest
Gay	gayer	gayest
Great	greater	greatest
Grey	greyer	greyest
Hard	harder	hardest
High	higher	highest
Keen	keener	keenest
Kind	kinder	kindest
Light	lighter	lightest
Mild	milder	mildest
Near	nearer	nearest
Poor	poorer	poorest
Proud	prouder	proudest
Rich	richer	richest

Contd...

Positive	***Comparative***	***Superlative***
Short	shorter	shortest
Small	smaller	smallest
Strong	stronger	strongest
Sweet	sweeter	sweetest
Tall	taller	tallest
Weak	weaker	weakest
Wild	wilder	wildest
Young	younger	youngest

Rule 2. 'r' and 'st' are added to the positive degrees of the Adjectives which have 'e' as their last letter to form their Comparative and Superlative degrees respectively; as:

Able	abler	ablest
Brave	braver	bravest
Fine	finer	finest
Large	larger	largest
Noble	nobler	noblest
Pure	purer	purest
True	truer	truest
Wise	wiser	wisest

Rule 3. 'ier' and 'iest' are added to the positive degrees of the Adjectives which have y as their last letters preceded by a consonant to form their Comparative and Superlative degrees respectively; as:

Dry	drier	driest
Early	earlier	earliest
Easy	easier	easiest
Happy	happier	happiest

Contd...

Positive	*Comparative*	*Superlative*
Healthy	healthier	healthiest
Heavy	heavier	heaviest
Jolly	jollier	jolliest
Lazy	lazier	laziest
Merry	merrier	merriest
Pretty	prettier	prettiest
Wealthy	wealthier	wealthiest

Rule 4. 'er' and 'est' are added to the positive degrees of the Adjectives which have consonants as their last letters preceded by a vowel on doubling the last consonant to form their Comparative and Superlative degrees respectively; as:

Big	bigger	biggest
Fat	fatter	fattest
Fit	fitter	fittest
Hot	hotter	hottest
Red	redder	reddest
Sad	sadder	saddest
Thin	thinner	thinnest
Wet	wetter	wettest

Rule 5. 'more and most' are added before certain adjectives to form their Comparative and Superlative degrees; as:

Active	more active	most active
Beautiful	more beautiful	most beautiful
Careful	more careful	most careful
Cheerful	more cheerful	most cheerful
Courageous	more courageous	most courageous
Difficult	more difficult	most difficult

Contd...

Positive	*Comparative*	*Superlative*
Diligent	more diligent	most diligent
Foolish	more foolish	most foolish
Harmful	more harmful	most harmful
Honest	more honest	most honest
Industrious	more industrious	most industrious
Important	more important	most important
Intelligent	more intelligent	most intelligent
Interesting	more interesting	most interesting
Obedient	more obedient	most obedient
Popular	more popular	most popular
Powerful	more powerful	most powerful
Urgent	more urgent	most urgent
Useful	more useful	most useful

Comparisons that defy all rules

Bad, ill, evil	worse	worst
Good, well	better	best
Far	farther/further	farthest
Fore	former	foremost, first
Hind	hinder	hindmost
Late	later/latter	last/latest
Little	less/lesser	least
Near	nearer	nearest/next
Nigh	nigher	nighest/next
Old	older/elder	oldest/eldest

Note that: *older* and *oldest* are used for all the persons who are senior in age to the speaker.

Elder and *eldest* are used for those persons who are one's blood relations and are senior in age to the speaker; as

I am Roshan's elder brother. Daya Nand is older than I.

Miscellaneous Exercise for Recapitulation

Degrees of Comparison

Model Sentences

The journey from Delhi to Madras is long.

My grandfather is an old but bold fellow.

This rope is shorter than that rope.

Ashoka was the noblest king in India.

A contented person is the happiest person.

Hard work is the easiest path to success.

Kamla is lazier than her mother.

The oak tree is taller than the mango tree.

Hari is the worst fellow on earth.

Rajni has obtained the least marks.

Which is the way to the nearest post office?

Who is the oldest man in your village?

You are the thinnest (slimmest) girl in your class.

He took a cup of hot tea.

Rohit is the richest boy in our class.

Sushma is abler than Manorama.

Your burden is heavier than my burden.

25th December was the saddest day of my life.

Tun-Tun is the fattest of all the heroines.

Lokesh was the gayest lad in the mob.

Important Information about Degrees of Comparison

(i) (a) Positive degree of the adjective is used to show the normal and general quality of a person or thing; as Misri Devi was a gentle lady.

(b) Positive degree of the adjective is used to show similarity or parity between two persons or things; as

He is as tall as his father. (positive)

The umbrella is not as costly as the watch. (negative)

(c) *Excellent, exterior, interior, major, minor* and *perfect* are invariably used in the positive degree; as

My house is located in the interior of the town.

(ii) '*Than* is normally used after the Comparative Degree but 'to' is invariably used after *junior, senior, inferior, prefer* and *preferable;* as:

I prefer milk to tea. She is junior to me in service. Cotton is inferior to silk.

(iii) 'The' is always put before a Superlative Degree; as

Sarita is the prettiest girl in our school.

Correct Use of Some Adjectives

All, whole

'*All*' shows both the quantity and the number but '*whole*' shows only the quantity; as:

All the apples are rotten.

She dropped *all* the milk.

She sold the *whole* milk.

Please remember that '*the*' is added before *whole* (*the whole*) and after *all* (*all the*)

Each, Every

'*Each*' is used for every person out of two or more persons and it provides understanding about a definite number; as:

Each of the four girls is absent.

The Principal has expelled *each* of the five late-comers.

'*Every*' is used to give indication of a group as a whole. It provides information about an indefinite number; as:

You have borrowed money from *every* teacher.

Some, any

'Some' is used in affirmative sentences in the sense of *'a little'*. *'Some'* is also used in interrogative sentences when the answer of the question is expected to be in the affirmative; as:

Shall I lend you *some* money?

Will you distribute *some* posters?

'Any' is used both in Negative and Interrogative sentences in the sense of 'a *little'; as:*

Have you *any* spare pen?

The bride did not speak *any* word.

Each other, One another

'Each other' shows the mutual relationship between two persons or things; as:

Sushma and Madhu quarrelled with *each other.*

'One another' shows the mutual relationship among three persons/objects (things) or more; as:

Sushma, Madhu and Anuradha quarrelled with *one another.*

Either, Neither, Any, Any other

'Either' means 'one or both of the two'

'Neither' means 'No one out of the two'

'Any' means 'one or more' but of many. (more than two)

There are trees on *either* side of the road. (Both)

I shall support *either* Mukul or Nikunj. (One)

Kavita belongs to *neither* group.

You may choose *any* saree you like.

Usha is taller than *any other* girl of (in) her class. (The word *'other'* must be used in this sentence. Otherwise, the meaning of the sentence will not become clear.)

Many, Many a, Much

Many' means 'consisting of a large number' it is used before Common Nouns to show their number. Plural Noun is used after it (*Many*); as:

There are *many* flower plants in the park.

'Many a' (also) means 'consisting of a large number'. It is (also) used before Common Nouns to show their number. A singular noun is used after it (*Many a*); as:

Many a flower fades unseen.

'Much' means 'great number'. It shows 'quantity or degree'; as:

There is *much* pollution in Delhi.

Little, A Little, The Little

'Little' means 'quite small; of smallest size; not much in size'; as:

There is *little* water in the bucket.

'A little' means 'nearly sufficient to fulfil requirement but not much'. It is used in the positive; as:

The calf is made to drink a *little* milk.

'The little' means 'the whole quantity of negligible size'. It points towards the aforementioned objects; as:

I have lost *the little* money I had earned.

Few, A few, The few

'Few' means 'a fair number; not many but more than one; a negligible and insignificant number'. It shows the negative side. It gives an indication of number; as:

I have *few* friends.

Few boys got first division.

'A few' means 'some or several but not many in number'.

It is used in the Positive to pinpoint a small number of persons or things; as:

A few girls can prepare dainty dishes.

Rajeshwari stayed with me for *a few* days.

'*The few*' means 'the whole number though small, negligible and insignificant' as:

The few friends he had, deserted him.

Later, Latest; Latter, Last

'*Later* and *Latest*' are an indication of time; as:

I shall tell you this secret *later*.

What is the *latest* news?

'*Latter* and *Last*' are an indication of position or order; as:

Out of the two students who came late, the former is a boy and the *latter* is a girl.

I handed over my answer book *last* of all.

Farther, Further; First, Foremost; Nearest, Next; Outer, Utter,
'Farther' means 'at a still more distance'; as:

The nearer the church, *the farther* from Christ.

'*Further*' means 'at more distance and additional' as:

You need *further* coaching.

'*First*' is an indication of order or position; as:

I was the *first* to oppose the proposal.

'*Foremost*' means 'most significant'; as:

To serve our aged parents is our *foremost* duty.

'*Nearest*' means 'located at a nearby place'; as:

I got admission in the *nearest* school.

'*Next*' means 'closely succeeding time, person or thing'; as:

I missed one bus but caught the *next*. Send the *next* man.

'Outer' shows *location, stage/state* or *phase;* as:

The thieves jumped over the *outer* wall and entered the house.

'Utter' shows the ultimate or extreme position; as:

Hari took up begging in *utter* poverty.

Miscellaneous Exercise for Recapitulation

Uses of Some Common Adjectives

Model Sentences

There is some milk in the jug.

Is there any milk in the jug?

Every man is mortal.

She did the sums without any difficulty.

I have little money.

Sharda has a little money.

She spent the little money she had.

There were many girls in the class.

There isn't much water in the tank.

My elder brother loves me much.

My eldest brother is the head of our family.

Is your girl friend not older than you (in age)?

Rewari is farther from Delhi than Gurgaon.

Have you anything further to say?

Which is the nearest market from your colony?

Kanta is going to Meerut by the next train.

She will be the last woman to bear this insult.

I have just few eggs, so I cannot lend you a dozen eggs.

I have never written any poems.

I have two scooters. Each scooter is of grey colour.

Common Errors in the Use of Adjectives

	Incorrect	*Correct*
1.	Those sort of mangoes *are* not to my taste.	Those sort of mangoes *is* not to my taste.
2.	The lily is lovelier than *any* flower.	The lily is lovelier than *any other* flower.
3.	You are more *wiser* than strong.	You are more *wise* than strong.
4.	I do not like *these* kind of people.	I do not like *this* kind of people.
5.	Old rice is superior *than* new one.	Old rice is superior *to* new one.
6.	Your composition is inferior *than* mine.	Your composition is inferior *to* mine.
7.	What is the *last* news?	What is the *latest* news?
8.	I could not hear the *later* part of the lecture.	I could not hear the *latter* part of the lecture.
9.	Ours is the *latest* house in the street.	Ours is the *last* house in the street.
10.	I am leaving by the *nearest* train.	I am leaving by the *next* train.
11.	The hind wheel of this car needs pumping.	The *hinder* wheel of this car needs pumping.
12.	The *interior* meaning of this sentence is not clear.	The *inner* meaning of this sentence is not clear.
13.	Our *previous* principal was a nice man.	Our *former* principal was a nice man.
14.	Will you please lend me *any* money?	Will you please lend me *some* money?
15.	*Some* policeman will direct you to her house.	*Any* policeman will direct you to her house.
16.	It rained *each* day during my absence.	It rained *every* day during my absence.
17.	Tea is taken *each* four hours.	Tea is taken *every* four hours.
18.	You come here *each* other day.	You come here *every* other day.
19.	I gave to the beggar *little* money I had.	I gave to the beggar *the little* money I had.
20.	There is a *little* hope of the survival of the patient of cancer.	There is *little* hope of the survival of the patient of cancer.
21.	Go and bring *little* milk.	Go and bring a *little* milk.
22.	The secretary was asked to say *few* words.	The secretary was asked to say a *few* words.
23.	A *few* men attain the age of a hundred years.	*Few* men attain the age of a hundred years.

Contd...

	Incorrect	Correct
24.	*Many a flowers bloom* in the spring season.	*Many a flower blooms* in the spring season. *Or* *Many flowers bloom* in the spring season.
25.	Does your cow give a *lot* of milk?	Does your cow give *much* milk?
26.	I haven't read much poems.	I haven't read *many* poems.
27.	This scooter is meant for *only you.*	This scooter is meant for *you only.*
28.	*Whole* the boys were present yesterday.	*All* the boys were present yesterday.
29.	*Whole the* country mourned Rajiv Gandhi's death.	*The whole* country mourned Rajiv Gandhi's death.
30.	I took *whole* jug of milk.	I took a *whole* jug of milk.
31.	Has the Inspector visited *more* schools?	Has the Inspector visited *the other* schools?
32.	You may take *anyone of the two sides.*	You may take *either of the two sides. Or* You may take *either* side.
33.	The river overflowed on *both of the sides.*	The river overflowed on *either side.*
34.	Let me see any *more* picture.	Let me see any *other* picture.
35.	Show me *other* pen; this one is not good.	Show me *another* pen; this one is not good.
36.	What is the *fresh* news?	What is the *latest* news?
37.	Manorama is our *mutual* friend.	Manorama is our *common* friend.
38.	Why did you wear *my this saree?*	Why did you wear *this saree of mine?*
39.	*His both* brothers are doctors.	*Both of his* brothers are doctors.
40.	*My all* friends are present.	*All my* friends are present.
41.	Delhi is a *worth-seeing place.*	Delhi is a *place worth-seeing.*
42.	Death is preferable *than* dishonour.	Death is preferable *to* dishonour.
43.	Who is *tallest,* you or I?	Who is *taller,* you or I?
44.	I am *more stronger* than you.	I am *much stronger* than you.
45.	*Little* money is better than none.	*A little* money is better than none.
46.	Chameli is my *older* sister.	Chameli is my *elder* sister.
47.	I have not *some* sugar.	I have not *any* sugar.
48.	She is a girl of a *few* words.	She is a girl *of few* words.
49.	It is *much* fine today.	It is *very* fine today.

Contd...

	Incorrect	*Correct*
50.	Kalidas is greater than *all the* dramatists.	Kalidas is greater than *all the other* dramatists.
51.	Sushma lost *her five-years* old son.	Sushma lost her *five-year* old son.
52.	Your wife is very *long*.	Your wife is very *tall*.
53.	Your father is a *miser*.	Your father is *miserly*.
54.	Never look down upon the *poors*.	Never look down upon the *poor*.
55.	Our examination begins on *next Friday*.	Our examination begins on *Friday next*.

Parsing

Parsing of Adjectives should be done in the following manner as per requirement of the revised syllabus.

1. Ramoo is a *good* boy.
   Good. Adjective. Use: Sita is a good girl.
2. She is *older* than Mohan.
   Older. Adjective. Use: Shyam is older than Hari.
3. Sushma is *junior* to Kamal.
   Junior. Adjective. Use: She is junior to me.
4. The rope is *long*.
   Long. Adjective. Use: The queue is long.
5. I ate *some* rice.
   Some. Adjective. Use: He bought some milk.
6. Look at this pen.
   This. Adjective. Use: I like this frock.
7. *Every* boy can do it.
   Every. Adjective. Use: Every man dies sooner or later.
8. I have done *much* work.
   Much. Adjective. Use: You have taken much milk.
9. *Whose* pen is this?
   Whose. Adjective. Use: Whose pen is this?
10. *This* paper is white.
    This. Adjective. Use: This girl is smart.

5

Verb

Kinds of Verb

Verbs can be divided into the following classes:

(i) Auxiliary Verbs

(ii) Ordinary Verbs

(iii) Verbs of Incomplete Predication

Auxiliary Verbs: They are the verbs that help their principal verbs to form their tenses, voices, moods or negative sentences; as:

1. I *do* not sing a song.
2. She *is* writing a letter.
3. You *have* eaten a banana.
4. *Did* we go to school yesterday?
5. *Was* he solving the sums?
6. They *had* returned our books.
7. You *will* read the book.
8. O! that you *might* write neatly.
9. A rat *is* killed by a boy.

The verbs printed in italics in sentence 1, 2, 3, 4, 5, and 6 help the main verbs and form tenses. Sentence number 1 is a negative sentence.

The verbs printed in *italics* in sentences 4 and 5 help the main verbs and form tenses. Being used in the beginning of the sentences they form Interrogative sentences.

Sentence 8 shows the mood (desire).

Sentence 9 is a Passive Voice Sentence.

Kinds/Types of Auxiliary Verbs:

Chief/Primary Auxiliary Verbs:

To be (is, am, are, was, were)

To do (do, does, did)

To have (has, have, had)

Chief/Primary Auxiliary Verbs can be used as Main/Finite Verbs; as:

I *do* my work.

She *does* her work.

You *did* your sums.

Delhi *is* the capital of India.

You *are* a clever girl.

I *am* fifteen years old.

My mother *was* tall.

I *have* a scooter.

He *has* no pen.

Nikunj *had* a toy.

They *were* at home.

Modal Auxiliaries: Will, shall, can, could, may, might, would, should, must, dare, need, used to, ought to, etc. are called Modal Auxiliaries.

Modal Auxiliaries can be used invariably as Helping Verbs; as:

We *should* do our duty.

You *can* speak English.

It *may* rain today.

She *might* not come.

You *must* try your luck.

We *ought* to serve our parents.

You *need* not worry.

Dare he go against you?

She *used* to take exercise daily.

Remember that Modal Auxiliaries are never used alone. They are always used with the chief (Main/Principal) Verbs.

Hints: 1. can, 2. may, 3. might, 4. will, 5. would; should, 6. must, 7. need, 8. dare, 9. ought, 10 used to.

Ordinary Verbs

Ordinary Verbs are of the following two kinds: (a) Finite Verbs, (b) Non-Finites

Finite Verbs: These verbs change their forms according to the persons, number and tense of the subjects; as:

I/we/you/they play.

He/she plays. It rains.

Types of Finite Verbs:

(i) Transitive Verbs
(ii) Intransitive Verbs
(iii) Auxiliary Verbs

Transitive Verbs: Transitive Verbs are followed by an object; as:

1. Rashmi *bought* a ball.
2. Sharad *recited* a poem.
3. Children *like* toffees.
4. She *gave* me a book.

Find out the answer to 'What or Whom' to locate the object

In sentence 1 — What did Rashmi buy? *Ans.* a ball.

In sentence 2 — What did Sharad recite? *Ans.* a poem.

In sentence 3 — What do the children like? *Ans.* toffees.

In sentence 4 — What did she give me? *Ans.* a book.

and

Whom did she give the book? *Ans.* me.

Remember that the verbs (bought, recited, like and gave) used before the objects (a ball, a poem, toffees, me and a book) in the above sentences are Transitive Verbs.

Remember that a Transitive Verb is sometimes followed by two objects, like me and a book in sentence 4 above.

In sentences with two objects, the object which is the answer to *'what'* is called the Direct Object.

What did she give me? *Ans.* a book.

Therefore, a *book* is the Direct Object.

Similarly, in sentences with two objects, the object which is the answer to *'whom'* is called the Indirect Object.

Whom did she give a book? *Ans.* me.

Therefore, *me* is the Indirect Object.

Indirect Object Generally Precedes the Direct Object:

The following Verbs, normally have two objects each:

ask, give, grant, offer, promise, teach, tell, show, etc.

Intransitive Verbs: No objects are needed after these (Intransitive) Verbs; as:

1. The scooter *runs* fast.
2. The slate *breaks*.
3. Wood *floats* on water.
4. The fire *burns*.

These sentences do not respond to the answer of 'What and Whom'.

Therefore, the Verbs (runs, breaks, floats, burns, etc.) used here are — Intransitive Verbs.

Some Verbs can be used both transitively and intransitively; as:

Verbs used Intransitively	*Verbs used Transitively*
Kites fly.	The children fly kites.
She runs.	She runs a race.
The glass broke.	She broke the glass.

Remember that some Intransitive Verbs are followed by Nouns which have similar meanings to the meanings of the Verbs. Those nouns are termed as Cognate objects; as

She saw a dreadful *sight*. (*See* Verb—*Sight* Noun)

I slept a disturbed *sleep*. (*Sleep* Verb—*Sleep* Noun)

You fought a brave *fight*. (*Fight* Verb—*Fight* Noun)

The nouns—*sight, sleep* and *fight* in the above sentences are cognate objects.

Some Intransitive Verbs can be turned into Transitive Verbs by adding a preposition after each of them; as

Don't laugh at the widow.

The Director looked into the matter.

Prepositions (like at/into) are added immediately after the verbs (laugh/looked) in the above sentences. Therefore, they are termed as *Prepositional Verbs.* The Intransitive Verb becomes a Transitive Verb, if it is used in the causative sense; as:

Intransitive	*Transitive*
I sang.	She made me sing a song. (caused to sing)
The tree fell.	The woodcutter felled the tree. (caused to fall)

Rules for Intransitive use of Transitive Verbs:

(i) When a Verb is used in its normal situation without going through to the object; as:
Mohini cried all of a sudden.
The tonga stopped suddenly.

(ii) If the Reflexive Pronoun (self/selves) is dropped; as:
Move (yourself) a bit.
Keep (yourself) away from fire.

(iii) *Auxiliary Verb:* It has been discussed at length in this chapter.

Non-Finites: These Verbs do no change according to the number, person or tense of the subjects.

Kinds of Non-finites

Infinitive: These verbs do not have application in any sentence. They are simply mentioned; as:

1. They wish *to go.*
2. *To err* is human.

3. My ambition is *to become* a teacher.
4. We eat to *live.*
5. She began *to weep.*
6. Have you a pen to *spare?*
7. I expect her *to solve* this problem.
8. She knows how *to iron* the clothes.

On reading the above sentences it can be observed (gathered) that an *Infinitive* is formed by adding *'to'* to the first form of the Verb (to + V^1)

Remember that an Infinitive can sometimes be used without to; as:

Please let her *speak.*

We saw the actress *dance.*

You need not *come* here.

I made him *sing.*

'To' has not been used with the verbs (*speak, dance, come* and *sing*) in the above sentences.

Please note that *'to'* is not normally used with the verbs.

Bid, behold, dare, feel, hear, help, know, let, like, make, need, observe, please, watch, etc.

However, *'to'* is not used with/after *'but'* meaning *'except'*; as:

She did nothing but (except) cry.

You would do nothing but (except) gossip.

'To' is not used with/after *'had better'*, *'had rather'*, *'had sooner'*, *'rather than'* *'sooner* than' and *'would rather'*, as:

You had better wash your face.

You had rather done your home work.

I would rather quit the job than apologise.

I would sooner die than drink.

Some other uses of Infinitives:

After 'Too+Adjective' as:

1. She is too weak to walk.
2. He is too bulky to run.

After 'Enough'; as:

She is strong enough to defend herself.

She is wise enough to solve this problem.

By using 'to' on removing the Relative Clause; as:

1. My mother gave me a toffee which I could eat.

Or

My mother gave me a toffee to eat.

2. No one is here who can (will) help you.

Or

No one is here to help you.

To show disappointment/despair; as:

She opend the box and found it empty.

Or

She opened the box to find it empty.

Remember that 'Infinitives, are normally used as objects of the verbs given below:

Agree, arrange, attempt, consent, care, cease, choose, claim, decide, determine, expect, endeavour, forget, fail, hope, hesitate, learn, long, manage, neglect, offer, propose, promise, prepare, pretend, remember, regret, refuse, swear, seem, try, threaten, undertake, want, wish.

Example: I wish to *tell* you a secret.

Miscellaneous Exercise for Recapitulation

Non-Finites (Infinitive-'to')

Model Examples

I want to drink a little water.

To err is human and to forgive is divine.

To gamble will prove ruinous for your family.

He was made to run a mile.

She stood from the chair to welcome me.

I am delighted to see you here.

She has much (enough) money to spare.

She does not know how to drive a car.

You are wise enough to understand my objective.

It is kind of her to help you.

I shall go to school to see the class-teacher.

The police set out to search the thief.

It is harmful for your health to drink.

To speak the truth is a virtue.

She is the best actress to act in this play.

He survived the air-crash only to drown in the river.

It was brave of the woman to catch the thief.

What do you want to say in this matter?

Give me a book to read.

To drink in public places is prohibited.

Gerund: The *Gerund* is used to show an action. The Nouns, working as *non-finite verbs* are termed 'Gerunds'; as:

1. *Smoking* is a bad habit.
2. Her favourite hobby is *dancing.*
3. He likes *drinking.*
4. I am sick of *waiting.*
5. It is no use *crying* over spilt milk.

A Gerund may be used at the beginning, in the middle (interior) or at the end of a sentence.

On reading the above sentences, we can safely say that Gerunds can be used in the following manners.

(i) As *subject* of the sentence.

(ii) As *subject complement* of the verb.

(iii) As *object* to the *verb.*

(iv) As *object* to the *preposition.*

(v) As *case in Apposition* of 'It' pronoun.

Other Information about the use of Gerunds:

(i) As Full Gerunds; as:

Reading the religious books being his habit, we like him.

(ii) The use of Gerund as Perfect form (Having + 3rd form of Verb); as:

He will never admit having broken the glass.

(ii) A 'Gerund' is used in place of an 'Infinitive' after the prepositions; as:

She is good at singing songs.

(iv) Possessive Pronouns can also be used with Gerunds; as

I know Rajus's visiting her frequently.

Remember that Infinitives and Gerunds are called Verbal Nouns. We can apply both Infinitives and Gerunds as objects of the following Verbs.

Advise, allow, attempt, begin, be afraid (of), continue, can't bear, go hate, intend, love, like, mean, needs, prefer, permit, propose, recommend, requires, remember, request, start, stop, try, used to, wants.

Example: He began to go to school. *Or* He began going to school.

We normally use Gerunds as Objects of the following Verbs:

Avoid, admit, anticipate, complete, consider, can't stand (endure), detest, deny, delay, defer, enjoy, excuse, fancy, finish, forgive, give up, involve, imagine, keep, miss, mind, prevent, postpone, pardon, put off, practise, risk, resent, recollect, resist, suggest, save.

Example: He cannot give up smoking.

Miscellaneous Exercise For Recapitulation

Non-Finites (Gerunds)

Model Examples

Drinking is a curse for good health.

When I returned home, I found my sister laughing.

Seeing Sheela alone, a man entered her house.

Driving a van needs a licence and carefulness.

Riding a horse is a useful exercise.

Walking in the hot sun at noon dazzles the eyes.

I hate stealing and hoarding the most.

She is fond of back-biting about others.

She intends coming here next week.

My reading room is neat and clean.

She is skilled at dancing and painting.

Urmila was fined for coming late to school.

She is thinking of settling in Delhi.

Sitting here is sheer wasting of time.

The reading of romantic stories is my favourite pastime.

Stop wasting money on viewing cheap films.

It is no use crying over spilt milk.

I shall manage reaching there in time.

Teaching is a noble profession and an art.

Avoid mixing with girls of loose morals.

Participle: These non-finite verbs can be used both as adjectives and as adverbs. Therefore, they are also called Verbal adjectives.

Kind of Participles

Present Participle: (V^1 + ing), (First form of the Verb + ing); as:

1. *Flowing* water is pure. (Here, the word *flowing,* shows the continuity of the action)

2. I hate a *complaining* child. (Here, the word *complaining* has been used as an adjective to qualify the noun *'Child'*)
3. The sight was *charming*. (Here, the word *charming*, being the complement of the verb 'was' is also the complement of the subject *'The sight'*)
4. I saw her *smoking*. (Here, the word *smoking* is the complement of the object *'her'*).
5. Meera came to me *crying*. [Here, two actions (*came* and *cry*) have taken place at the same time (simultaneously). Therefore, the more significant out of the two actions 'Cry has been shown by Present Participle.]
6. *Seeing* the Police, the thief hid behind the wall. [Here, the same subject *(thief)* performs two actions ('See and *hide*)]. The former action takes the Present Participle under such situations.
7. He took up his bag. He ran away. (Here, both the actions take place simultaneously.)

Or

Taking up his bag, he ran away. (Here, Present Participle has been used to connect two sentences. *'Taking up his bag'* is a 'Participle Phrase'.)

8. God *willing*, I shall get first division. [Here, *Present Participle* has been used in *'God willing'* because it (*which*) is an Absolute Phrase].

Past Participle: (V^3) Third form of the Verb. Examples:

1. This is a *spoilt* child. (Here, the use of the word *'spoilt'* shows the completion of the action *'spoil'*.)
2. The *tired* traveller fell asleep. (Here, the word, *'tired'* functions as the adjective of the Noun *'traveller'*).
3. She looks *worrried* and *dejected* (Here, the words *'worried* and *dejected'* are functioning as adjectives). Being, the complements of the verb *'looks'*, they are (also) the complements of the subjects *'she.*

4. He got his hair *cut*. (Here the word *cut* is the complement of the subject *'hair'*).
5. The decision *taken at the right time* is always rewarding. (Here, the word *'taken'* is a Past Participle. While qualifying the Noun 'decision' it also helps in the formation of an adjectival phrase.)

   Remember that such Adjectival Phrases are often used after the noun, they qualify.
6. The chairman left the meeting fully *satisfied*. (Here, the word *'satisfied'* is a Past Participle which is modifying the Verb *'left'*. Hence, it is functioning as an adverb).

Perfect Participle: (Having + V^3)

Examples:

1. Sheela has taken her breakfast. She is getting ready for school.

   Or

   Having taken her breakfast, Sheela is getting ready for school.

(Here, two such sentences which lack quickness in action have been combined by using a/the perfect participle)

Remember that the second action 'got ready' came into force on the completion of the first action ('taken her breakfast'). There can be a little or more duration of time between both the actions.

2. School over, the students came out. (Here, *School over school having been over* Perfect Participle 'having been' can be inferred).

   Or

   School having been over, the students came out.
3. The sun rose and we returned home (As soon as the sun rose, we returned home).

   Or

No sooner did the sun rise than we returned home.

The above sentence is a compound structure. The second action has been completed, immediately after the completion of the first action. The sentence can also be written as 'The sun having risen, we returned home' by using the Perfect Participle.

4. (i) The order has been placed. (ii) No change is possible now. Here, sentence 4 (i) is a Passive-Voice sentence and Sentence 4 (ii) is an Active-Voice sentence. We can also use Perfect Participle and write the two sentences as:

The order having been placed, no change is possible now.

Miscellaneous Exercise for Recapitulation

Non-Finites (Participles)

Model Examples

I do not like a weeping girl.

Your remark is insulting and pricking.

I caught my brother gambling.

Sudesh greeted me laughing.

It being stormy, we did not venture out.

I threw the broken pieces of glass into the dust-bin.

It being Diwali, all the shops are closed today.

Out of greed for gold, ladies get their ears pierced.

The chairman left the chair fully satisfied.

The candidates selected for this post have not turned up.

You look a bit dejected.

The broken glass cannot hold water.

Having picked up my bag, I boarded the school bus.

Having been wounded in the battle the commander gave in.

Having finished his home-work, Gita put her bag away.

Having seen a snake in the grass, she ran in fear.

Having seen the Principal, the girls rushed into the rooms.

Having put off the lamp I lay down on the bed to rest.

The failed candidates are eligible to reappear.

Verbs of Incomplete Predication –

These Verbs do not convey full sense. Therefore, some complement is needed to complete their sense; as

1. Kamla *was* present.
2. You *look* gay.
3. Quinine *tastes* bitter.
4. You *made* mischief.

The words *'was, look, tastes* and *made'* in the above sentences are *Verbs* of *incomplete predication* (linking verbs) because the words *'present, gay, bitter* and *mischief* have been used here to complete the incomplete sense. Such words are called complements.

Kinds of Complements

Subjective Complement: The complements which describe some subject are called *Subjective Complements,* as:

1. The ice is *cold.*
2. My father was *unhappy.*
3. Sarla is *active.*

In the above sentences, the words *'cold, unhappy* and *active'* are subjective complements because they describe the subjects (*ice, father* and *Sarla*) used in the sentences.

Objective Complement: The complements which describe some object are called *objective complements;* as:

1. The Congress chose Rajiv their *leader.*
2. You made me *prefect.*
3. We appointed Ranjika our *secretary.*

In the above sentences, the words leader, prefect and secretary are objective complements because they impart some information about the objects (*Rajiv, me* and *Ranjika*) used in the sentences.

Moods of Verbs

There can be no sentence without a Verb. The Verb is the soul of the sentence because it expresses actions or facts. However, actions and facts are expressed in the different moods shown below.

1. I get up early every morning.	Statement
2. Who teaches you English Grammar?	question
3. Be off.	order
4. Please grant me leave, sir.	request
5. Never mix with bad girls.	advice
6. May you succeed in your mission!	wish
7. Run fast so that you may catch the bus.	purpose.
8. If I go to Bombay, I shall bring a camera for you.	condition.

Please remember that the Verb is bound to take form according to the mood of the subject.

The mood of a Verb indicates the manner (mode) in which its action or fact is made expressive.

Classification of Moods

The Indicative Mood:

1. Ashoka was an ideal ruler.
2. If the sky falls, we shall catch larks.
3. The humiliated girl could not utter a word.
4. Wasn't Ashoka an ideal ruler?
5. Shall we catch larks if the sky falls?
6. Why couldn't the girls utter a word?

In the sentences 1 to 3, the Verbs simply assert or deny an action or fact. Similarly, in the sentences 4 to 6, the Verbs ask questions about an action or fact.

The mood in which a Verb simply indicates (expresses a statement or asks a question) is called 'The Indicative Mood'.

The Imperative Mood:

1. Show me your work, today.
2. Never step into my room in future.
3. Repay my loan or get ready for the consequences.
4. Do not waste away your precious time.
5. Always speak the truth.
6. Help the poor and the needy.
7. Grant me a son, O God.
8. Give me a lift upto the next crossing, please.
9. Excuse me this time, sir.
10. Let us go out for a picnic.
11. Let us enjoy ourselves.
12. Let us eat, drink and make merry.

Sentences	1 to 3	Show command
"	4 to 6	Show advice
"	7 to 9	Show request
"	10 to 12	Show proposal

This mood expresses actions which are urgent and obligatory. Therefore, it is called 'The Imperative Mood'.

The Subjunctive Mood:

1. The grandmother said, "May you get a son!"
2. The beggar said, "O, that I were rich!"
3. If wishes were horses, beggars would ride them.
4. She talks as if she were the princess.
5. I feel as if I were drunk.
6. See that you do not lag behind.
7. She burnt midnight oil so that she might get first division.
8. Bhagat Singh died that the nation might live.

Sentences	1 to 3	Show command
"	4-5	Show similarity
"	6-8	Show purpose

This mood is called subjunctive mood because in it the verb lies in a clause that has a subjunction with another clause.

The Infinitive Mood:

1. To smoke is a bad habit.
2. To worship (God) is always paying.
3. I love to befriend diligent students.
4. I promise to visit your house tonight.
5. This room is to let.
6. The sky is not going to fall.
7. Let me swim.(Let me to swim)
8. The guests are about to reach.
9. Hari had no option but to commit suicide.
10. To think that my neighbour should rob me!
11. To see that the healthy girl should die!
12. How to manage now?
13. Whom to contact under the situation?

Sentences 1-2 Infinitive function as Subject of a verb

""	""	3-4	""	""	""	Object of a verb
""	""	5-7	""	""	""	Complement of a verb
""	""	8-9	""	""	""	Object of a Preposition
""	""	10-11	""	""	""	Part of an Exclamation
""	""	12-13	""	""	""	Part of a question

In this mood, the Verb is infinitive in nature. It can be used with any subject and is in no way limited by the person or number of any particular subject. Therefore, it is called 'The Infinitive Mood'.

Causative Verbs

Definition: A sentence in which the subject does not act but gets the action done through some other agency is called a Causative sentence.

1. I *made* her laugh.
2. Her father *got* her married.
3. *Get/Have* it done.
4. She *helped* me solve the sums.
5. I *caused* him play football.
6. He *had* his hair cut.
7. *Make* her prepare breakfast.
8. *Cause* this letter to be sent.

In the above sentences, the italicised words have been used as Causative Verbs.

Points to Remember:

(a) In an active - voice sentence, the Causative Verbs, 'Make' and 'Help' should never be succeeded by an infinitive (to)

(b) In a passive - voice sentence, the Causative Verbs, 'Make' and 'Help' should invariably be succeeded by an infinitive (to)

Examples:

1. I made him to realize. (Active Voice - Incorrect)
   I made him realize. (Active Voice - Correct)
2. I helped him to carry the load. (Active Voice - Incorrect)
   I helped him carry the load (Active Voice - Correct)
3. He was made write a letter. (Passive Voice - Incorrect)
   He was made to write a letter. (Passive Voice - Correct)
4. He was helped solve the sums. (Passive Voice - Incorrect)
   He was helped to solve the sums. (Passive Voice - Correct)

(c) The word *'Cause'* is invariably succeeded by an infinitive (to) (both in Active and Passive voice) when it is used as a *Causative* Verb.

Examples:

1. I caused him run a race. (Active Voice - Incorrect)
   I caused him to run a race (Active Voice - Correct)
2. He was caused rob a traveller (Passive Voice - Incorrect)
   He was caused to rob a traveller. (Passive Voice - Correct)

Form of the Causative Sentence:

Subject + get/have + object (Noun/Pronoun) + V^3 /to infinitive

Forms of Verbs

Simple Form	*Causative Form*
To bind	To get bound.
To cut	To get/have cut.
To drink	To drench/To make drink.
To do	To get done.
To eat	To feed/To make eat.
To erase.	To get erased.
To full	To fill.
To know	To inform.
To laugh	To make laugh.
To lie	To lay.
To marry	To get married.
To run	To make run.
To rise	To raise/To rouse.
To remember	To remind.
To see	To show.
To sink	To make sink/To soak.
To stand	To make stand.
To send	To have/get sent.
To understand	To make understand.
To weep	To make weep.
To write	To make write.

We have to use different tenses while learning English. The knowledge of the different forms of Verbs is essential for the same.

The following are the Different Forms of the Verbs:

1. Present (Ist form)
2. Past (2nd Form)
3. Past Participle (3rd form)
4. Present Participle (V^1 + ing form)

The different forms of some important Verbs are given below. You should read them carefully and memorize them.

Conjugation of Strong Verbs

GROUP 1

Without adding 'n' in forming Past Participle forms

Present (Ist Form)	***Past (2nd form)***	***Past Participle (3rd Form)***	***Present Participle V^1 + ing Form***
Awake	awoke	awoke	awaking
Become	became	become	becoming
Begin	began	begun	beginning
Behold	beheld	beheld	beholding
Bid	bid	bid	bidding
Bend	bent	bent	bending
Bind	bound	bound	binding
Cling	clung	clung	clinging
Come	came	come	coming
Dig	dug	dug	digging
drink	drank	drunk	drinking
Feed	fed	fed	feeding
Fight	fought	fought	fighting
Find	found	found	finding
Get	got	got	getting

Contd...

Present (Ist Form)	*Past (2nd form)*	*Past Participle (3rd Form)*	*Present Participle V^1 + ing Form*
Grind	ground	ground	grinding
Hang	hung	hung	hanging
Hold	held	held	holding
Lie	lied	lied	lying
Ring	rang.	rung	ringing
Run	ran	run	running
Shine	shone	shone	shining
Shoot	shot	shot	shooting
Shrink	shrank	shrunk	shrinking
Sit	sat	sat	sitting
Spit	spat	spat	spitting
Stand	stood	stood	standing
Stick	stuck	stuck	sticking
Sting	stung	stung	stinging
Strike	struck	struck	striking
Swim	swam	swum	swimming
Swing	swung	swung	swingging
Win	won	won	winning
Wind	wound	wound	winding
Wring	wrung	wrung	wringing

GROUP 2

By adding 'n' in forming Past Participle form

Present (Ist Form)	*Past (2nd form)*	*Past Participle (3rd Form) V*	*Present Participle V^1 + ing Form*
Arise	arose	arisen	arising
Bear	bore	borne	bearing

Bear	bore	born	bearing
Bite	bit	bitten	biting
Blow	blew	blown	blowing
Bid	bade	bidden	bidding
Break	broke	broken	breaking
Choose	chose	chosen	choosing
Do	did	done	doing
Draw	drew	drawn	drawing
Drive	drove	driven	driving
Eat	ate	eaten	eating
Fall	Fell	fallen	falling
Fly	flew	flown	flying
Forbid	forbade	forbidden	forbidding
Forget	forgot	forgotten	forgetting
Freeze	froze	frozen	freezing
Give	gave	given	giving
Grow	grew	grown	growing
Hide	hid	hidden	hiding
Know	knew	known	knowing
Lie	lay	lain	lying
Ride	rode	ridden	riding
Rise	rose	risen	rising
See	saw	seen	seeing
Shake	shook	shaken	shaking
Slay	slew	slain	slaying
Speak	spoke	spoken	speaking
Steal	stole	stolen	stealing
Swear	swore	sworn	swearing
Take	took	taken	taking
Tear	tore	torn	tearing
Throw	threw	thrown	throwing

Contd...

Present (Ist Form)	*Past (2nd form)*	*Past Participle (3rd Form) V*	*Present Participle V^1 + ing Form*
Wear	wore	worn	wearing
Weave	wove	woven	weaving
Write	wrote	written	writing

GROUP 3

By adding -d, -ed with the Verb in forming their Past (2nd) and Past Participle (3rd) forms.

Present (Ist Form)	*Past (2nd form)*	*Past Participle (3rd Form) V*	*Present Participle V^1 + ing Form*
Abuse	abused	abused	abusing
Act	acted	acted	acting
Add	added	added	adding
Admire	admired	admired	admiring
Advice	advised	advised	advising
Allow	allowed	allowed	allowing
Answer	answered	answered	answering
Appear	appeared	appeared	appearing
Appoint	appointed	appointed	appointing
Arrest	arrested	arrested	arresting
Arrive	arrived	arrived	arriving
Ask	asked	asked	asking
Attack	attacked	attacked	attacking
Bake	baked	baked	baking
Bark	barked	barked	barking
Bathe	bathed	bathed	bathing
Beg	begged	begged	begging
Behave	behaved	behaved	behaving

Contd...

Present (Ist Form)	*Past (2nd form)*	*Past Participle (3rd Form) V*	*Present Participle V^1 + ing Form*
Believe	believed	believed	believing
Bleed	bled	bled	bleeding
Bless	blessed	blessed	blessing
Boil	boiled	boiled	boiling
Boast	boasted	boasted	boasting
Borrow	borrowed	borrowed	borrowing
Call	called	called	calling
Carry	carried	carried	carrying
Change	changed	changed	changing
Check	checked	checked	checking
Clap	Clapped	clapped	clapping
Clean	cleaned	cleaned	cleaning
Climb	climbed	climbed	climbing
Close	closed	closed	closing
Collect	collected	collected	collecting
Complain	complained	complained	complaining
Complete	completed	completed	completing
Confuse	confused	confused	confusing
Consult	consulted	consulted	consulting
Cook	cooked	cooked	cooking
Copy	copied	copied	copying
Count	counted	counted	counting
Cover	covered	covered	covering
Cross	crossed	crossed	crossing
Crow	crowed	crowed	crowing
Cry	cried	cried	crying
Dance	danced	danced	dancing

Contd...

Present (Ist Form)	*Past (2nd form)*	*Past Participle (3rd Form) V*	*Present Participle V^1 + ing Form*
Deceive	deceived	deceived	deceiving
Defeat	defeated	defeated	defeating
Decide	decided	decided	deciding
Desire	desired	desired	desiring
Die	died	died	dying
Dip	dipped	dipped	dipping
Divide	divided	divided	dividing
Drown	drowned	drowned	drowning
Dye	dyed	dyed	dyeing
Earn	earned	earned	earning
Employ	employed	employed	employing
Enter	entered	entered	entering
Examine	examined	examined	examining
Explain	explained	explained	explaining
Face	faced	faced	facing
Fear	feared	feared	fearing
Feed	fed	fed	feeding
Fell	felled	felled	felling
Fine	fined	fined	fining
Finish	finished	finished	finishing
Flee	fled	fled	fleeing
Float	floated	floated	floating
Gather	gathered	gathered	gathering
Graze	grazed	grazed	grazing
Hang	hanged	hanged	hanging
Hate	hated	hated	hating
Have	had	had	having

Contd...

Present (Ist Form)	*Past (2nd form)*	*Past Participle (3rd Form) V*	*Present Participle V^1 + ing Form*
Hear	heard	heard	hearing
Help	helped	helped	helping
Improve	improved	improved	improving
Invite	invited	invited	inviting
Join	joined	joined	joining
Jump	jumped	jumped	jumping
Kill	killed	killed	killing
Knit	knitted	knitted	knitting
Laugh	laughed	laughed	laughing
Lay	laid	laid	laying
Lead	led	led	leading
Lie	lied	lied	lying
Like	liked	liked	liking
Listen	listened	listened	listening
Live	lived	lived	living
Look	looked	looked	looking
Love	loved	loved	loving
make	made	made	making
Marry	married	married	marrying
Meet	met	met	meeting
Melt	melted	melted	melting
Mend	mended	mended	mending
Mix	mixed	mixed	mixing
Move	moved	moved	moving
Name	named	named	naming
Need	needed	needed	needing
Nip	nipped	nipped	nipping

Contd...

Present (Ist Form)	*Past (2nd form)*	*Past Participle (3rd Form) V*	*Present Participle V^1 + ing Form*
Obey	obyed	obeyed	obeying
Open	opened	opened	opening
Oppose	opposed	opposed	opposing
Order	ordered	ordered	ordering
Pay	paid	paid	paying
Peep	peeped	peeped	peeping
Play	played	played	playing
Plant	planted	planted	planting
Plough	ploughed	ploughed	ploughing
Pluck	plucked	plucked	plucking
Praise	praised	praised	praising
Preach	preached	preached	preaching
Pray	prayed	prayed	praying
Prepare	prepared	prepared	preparing
Prevent	prevented	prevented	preventing
Promise	promised	promised	promising
Prove	proved	proved	proving
Pull	pulled	pulled	pulling
Punish	punished	punished	punishing
Push	pushed	pushed	pushing
Quarrel	quarrelled	quarrelled	quarrelling
Rain	rained	rained	raining
Reach	reached	reached	reaching
Receive	received	received	receiving
Refuse	refused	refused	refusing
Remember	remembered	remembered	remembering
Repair	repaired	repaired	repairing

Contd...

Present (Ist Form)	***Past (2nd form)***	***Past Participle (3rd Form) V***	***Present Participle V[1] + ing Form***
Reply	replied	replied	replying
Resign	resigned	resigned	resigning
Rest	rested	rested	resting
Return	returned	returned	returning
Roar	roared	roared	roaring
Save	saved	saved	saving
Say	said	said	saying
Saw	sawed	sawed	sawing
Select	selected	selected	selecting
Sell	sold	sold	selling
Slip	slipped	slipped	slipping
Stand	stood	stood	standing
Stay	stayed	stayed	staying
Stop	stopped	stopped	stopping
Study	studied	studied	studying
Talk	talked	talked	talking
Tell	told	told	telling
Tie	tied	tied	tying
Touch	touched	touched	touching
Try	tried	tried	trying
Trust	trusted	trusted	trusting
Understand	understood	understood	understanding
Use	used	used	using
Wait	waited	waited	waiting
Walk	walked	walked	walking
Wander	wandered	wandered	wandering
Watch	watched	watched	watching

Contd...

Present (Ist Form)	*Past (2nd form)*	*Past Participle (3rd Form) V*	*Present Participle V^1 + ing Form*
Waste	wasted	wasted	wasting
Wash	washed	washed	washing
Wind	wound	wound	winding
Wish	wished	wished	wishing
Wonder	wondered	wondered	wondering
Work	worked	worked	working
Worship	worshipped	worshipped	worshipping
Wound	wounded	wounded	wounding
Wed	wedded	wedded	wedding
Wrap	wrapped	wrapped	wrapping
Yield	yielded	yielded	yielding

GROUP 4

By adding* - t *with the crude form (1st form) of the Verb, (V^1) in forming their Past (2nd) and Past Participle (3rd) forms

Bring	brought	brought	bringing
Build	built	built	building
Burn	burnt	burnt	burning
Buy	bought	bought	buying
Catch	caught	caught	catching
Creep	crept	crept	creeping
Dream	dreamt	dreamt	dreaming
Feel	felt	felt	feeling
Keep	kept	kept	keeping
Kneel	knelt	knelt	kneeling

Learn	learnt	learnt	learning
Leave	left	left	leaving
Lend	lent	lent	lending
Lose	lost	lost	losing
Mean	meant	meant	meaning
Seek	sought	sought	seeking
Send	sent	sent	sending
Sleep	slept	slept	sleeping
Spend	spent	spent	spending
Sweep	swept	swept	sweeping
Teach	taught	taught	teaching
Think	thought	thought	thinking
Weep	wept	wept	weeping

GROUP 5

The following Verbs have all the three (Present, Past and Past Participle) forms alike

Bet	bet	bet	betting
Bid	bid	bid	bidding
Burst	burst	burst	bursting
Cast	cast	cast	casting
Cut	cut	cut	cutting
Hurt	hurt	hurt	hurting
Let	let	let	letting
Put	put	put	putting
Quit	quit	quit	quitting
Read	read	read	reading
Set	set	set	setting
Shed	shed	shed	shedding
Spread	spread	spread	spreading
Thrust	thrust	thrust	thrusting

Common Errors in the Use of Verbs

	Incorrect	*Correct*
1.	You said that you *saw* her last year.	You said that you *had seen* her last year.
2.	I did not stop because he *had* already *went* out.	I did not stop because he *had* already gone out.
3.	You got angry before *I uttered* a word.	You got angry before I *had uttered* a word.
4.	This was going on *since* a long time.	This was going on *for* a long time.
5.	If I *did* this, I shall be wrong.	If I *do* this, I shall be wrong.
6.	When she *will come* to Delhi, she will visit our house.	When she *comes* to Delhi, she will visit our house.
7.	If he *would have* done this, he would have been wrong.	If he *had* done this, he would have been wrong.
8.	She knows *to drive.*	She knows *how to drive.*
9.	I *said to* him leave the room.	I *asked* him to leave the room.
10.	I *told* the master to excuse me.	I *asked* the master to excuse me.
11.	She has got a *hurt* on her leg.	She has *hurt* her leg.
12.	Sarla *gave* a wonderful speech.	Sarla *made* a wonderful speech.
13.	I have *given* my examination.	I have *taken* my examination.
14.	She does not *hear me.*	She does not *listen* to me.
15.	*Keep* this lamp on the table.	*Put* this lamp on the table.
16.	The hunter *shot* the tiger but missed.	The hunter *shot at* the tiger but missed.
17.	The ship was *drowned.*	The ship *sank.*
18.	Columbus *invented* America.	Columbus *discovered* America.
19.	I *lived* in a hotel for a day.	I *stayed* in a hotel for a day.
20.	Our team *made* four goals.	Our team *scored* four goals.
21.	I *hope* she must come.	I *am sure* she will come.
22.	Coal *finds* in many countries.	Coal *is found* in many countries.
23.	Let me know who *found* Delhi.	Let me know who *founded* Delhi.
24.	He *filled* milk in the jug.	He *filled* the jug with milk.
25.	I *won* him in the long race.	I *beat* him in the long race.
26.	You can *avail* of this golden golden opportunity.	You can *avail yourself* of this opportunity.
27.	The notorious terrorists were *hung.*	The notorious terrorists were *hanged.*
28.	She *said to* me to come in.	She *told/asked* me to come in.

Contd...

	Incorrect	Correct
29.	*See* this word in the dictionary.	*Look up* this word in the dictionary.
30.	He told me that I *shall* help you.	He told me that he *would* help me.
31.	I would do this if I *was* you.	I would do this if I *were* you.
32.	He denied that he *was not* a thief.	He denied that he *was* a thief.
33.	*Being* a very cold day, I *did* not go to office.	It being a very cold day, I *did* not go to office.
34.	Kamlesh *has left* for Bombay night.	Kamlesh *left* for Bombay last last night.
35.	I *will* call you tomorrow.	1 *shall* call on you tomorrow.
36.	I *will definitely* help you.	I *shall definitely* help you.
37.	Sushma *is* ill for two months.	Sushma *has been* ill for two months.
38.	The audience did nothing but *cheered.*	The audience did nothing but *cheer.*
39.	Which novel *you* like most?	Which novel do *you* like most?
40.	You do nothing but *to sing and dance.*	You do nothing but *sing and dance.*
41.	Come what may, nothing *shall* stop her coming.	Come what may, nothing *will* stop her from coming.
42.	Bread and butter *are* my favourite food.	Bread and butter *is* my favourite food.
43.	Every girl and every boy *were* present in the class.	Every girl and every boy *was* present in the class.
44.	Neither Shyam nor Ram *were* present in the class.	Neither Shyam nor Ram *was* present in the class.
45.	No nook or corner *were* left unexplored.	No nook or corner *was* left unexplored.
46.	Either Satya or Bimla *have* stolen my pen.	Either Satya or Bimla *has* stolen my pen.
47.	Kanta or her brothers *has* done this.	Kanta or her brothers *have* done this.
48.	Either, you or he *are* to blame.	Either, you or he *is* to blame.
49.	I met Rohit who *was* my tutor ten years ago.	I met Rohit who *had been* my tutor ten years ago.
50.	I who *is* his sister, shall help him.	I who *am* his sister, shall help him.
51.	Justice as well as mercy *allow* it.	Justice as well as mercy *allows* it.
52.	Either he or you *is* a fault.	Either he or you *are* at fault.

Contd...

	Incorrect	Correct
53.	The jury *was* divided on this point.	The jury *were* divided on this point.
54.	She *tells* that she is going to school.	She *says* that she is going to school.
55.	She *said to* me not to worry.	She *told* me not to worry.
56.	How did you *reach at the* station?	How did you *reach the* station?
57.	She *shirks from* hard work.	She *shirks* hard work.
58.	I joined the college *with* a view to *study*.	I joined the college *with a view to studying*.
59.	It is no use *to go* there.	It is no use *going* there.
60.	Law and order *have* to be maintained.	Law and order *has* to be maintained.
61.	None but the brave *deserve* the fair.	None but the brave *deserves* the fair.
62.	A hue and cry *were* raised.	A hue and cry *was* raised.
63.	I wish it *was* over.	I wish it *were* over.
64.	Neither she *reached* there nor I did.	Neither did she *reach* there nor did I.
65.	He went *for seeing* his aunt.	He went to *see* his aunt.
66.	He stopped her *to* shed tears.	He stopped her *from* shedding tears.
67.	How you *know* me?	How *do you know* me?
68.	She *laid* in bed for four months.	She *lay* in bed for four months.
69.	The woodcutter has *fallen* many a tree.	The woodcutter has *felled* many a tree.
70.	Our enemy has *flown* away.	Our enemy has *fled* away.
71.	Ten rupees *are* a short amount.	Ten rupees *is* a short amount.
72.	*I know* him for five years.	*I have known* him for five years.
73.	I forbade him *not to smoke.*	I forbade him *to smoke.*
74.	He missed to *say* that.	He missed *on saying* that.
75.	She made me to *repeat* the whole incident.	She made me *repeat* the whole incident.
76.	Tell me why did she *come* here.	Tell me why she *came* here.
77.	I wish I *was* a doctor.	I wish I *were* a doctor.
78.	Your hair *seem* to be grey.	Your hair *seems* to be grey.
79.	Each of them likes to *sing*.	Each of them likes *singing*.
80.	She avoided to *meet* her sister.	She avoided *meeting* her *sister*.

6

Adverb

Kinds of Adverb

(i) Simple Adverbs

(ii) Relative Adverbs

(iii) Interrogative Adverbs

Simple Adverbs: These adverbs only modify certain words. The following are their divisions.

Adverbs of Time

1. I have seen you *before.*
2. See me *after* an hour.
3. Return my book *soon.*

The italicised words in the above sentences are Adverbs of time.

Ago, early, formerly, afterwards, late, immediately, now, then, recently, today, tomorrow, shortly, etc. are also Adverbs of Time.

Adverbs of Place

1. We shall sit *here.*
2. You may go *out.*
3. You can play *anywhere.*

The italicised words in the above sentences are Adverbs of place.

Above, below, away, backward, down, far, up, inside, outside, near, everywhere, besides, within, without, etc. are also Adverbs of Place.

Adverbs of Manner

1. I received him *warmly.*
2. Monika speaks *clearly.*
3. You should write *neatly.*

The italicised words in the above sentences are Adverbs of manner.

Badly, certainly, gladly, ill, quickly, so, thus, well, etc. are also Adverbs of Manner.

The Adverbs which have 'ly' at their end and are formed from Adjectives are known as Adverbs of Manner.

Adverbs of Number or Frequency

1. I *have failed* once.
2. She *often* makes false promises.
3. She *never* sits idle.

The italicised words in the above sentences are Adverbs of Number/Frequency.

Always, again, frequently, twice, thrice, seldom, thirdly, etc. are also Adverbs of Number/Frequency.

Adverbs of Quantity or Degree

1. She sang *very* well.
2. His speech was *rather* dull.
3. You are *partly* honest.

The italicised words in the above sentences are Adverbs of Quantity or Degree.

Any, as, almost, enough, fully, little, more, much, pretty, quite, rather, too, very, wholly, etc. are also Adverbs of Quantity/Degree.

Adverbs of Affirmation or Negation

1. I do *not* know him.
2. He will *surely* help me.

In sentence 1, the italicised word *'not'* is an Adverb of Negation. In sentence 2, the italicised word *'surely'* is the Adverb of Affirmation.

Certainly, truly, yes, etc. are also Adverbs of Affirmation Nay, never, no, not, etc. are also Adverbs of Negation.

Adverbs of Reason or Result

1. She was, *therefore,* unable to dance.
2. The offices were closed *on account* of Diwali.

The italicised words in the above sentences are Adverbs of Reason or Result.

As, because, for, since, that, now, that, seeing that, etc. are also Adverbs of Reason. Similarly so, therefore, thus, so that, on account of such that, etc. are also Adverbs of Result.

Adverbs of Purpose

1. She works hard *so that* she may get-first division.
2. He came to my house *in order to borrow* some money.

The italicised words in the above sentences are Adverbs of Purpose.

In order to, with a view to, with the purpose of, with the intention to, for, etc. are also Adverbs of Purpose.

Adverbs of Concession or Contrast

1. *Though* he works hard, he has little hope of success.
2. *However* hard you may try you cannot win a prize.

The italicised words in the above sentences are Adverbs of Concession or Contrast. *Though/although, yet, all the same, even if, granting that, etc. are also Adverbs of Concession/ Contrast.*

Adverbs of Comparison

1. *Kalu is not* so black *as* Sundri (is).
2. She is *as* tall *as* her sister.

The italicised words in the above sentences are Adverbs of Comparison. *More than, less than, the most, the least, than, etc. are also Adverbs of Comparison.*

Adverbs of Condition

1. *Had* you worked hard, you would have passed.
2. *If* you go to the post office, bring some post-card for me.

The italicised words in the above sentences are Adverbs of Condition.

As long as, if, if not, on condition that, provided that, supposing that, unless, etc. are also Adverbs of Condition.

Adverbs of Extent

1. There was sand *as far as* I could see.
2. *The faster* you run, the sooner you would reach school.

The italicised words in the above sentences are Adverbs of Extent.

As far as, the-the, so far as, etc. are also Extent Showing Adverbs.

Relative Adverbs: The Adverbs, showing Time (when); Place (where) and Reason (why) are called Relative Adverbs. These adverbs combine two clauses. They point towards their antecedent Noun or Pronoun. They show *'Time'*, *'Place'* or *'Reason'*, as:

1. This is the place *where* I lived.
2. This is the reason *why* she left the house.
3. Please tell me *when* you reached home.

Two clauses have been combined in each of the above sentences. *'Where'* points to a *place: Why* points to *reason* and *when* points to *time.*

Interrogative Adverbs: These adverbs are used in/for asking questions — they show time, place, number, quantity, manner and reason; as:

Why are you angry? *How* are you feeling now?

Where does your uncle live? *When* do you get up?

The italicised words in the above sentences are Interrogative Adverbs. They are used in the very beginning of the sentences.

When, where, why, how far, how many, how much, how long, how often, whence, etc. are interrogative Adverbs.

Distinction between Relative Adverb and Interrogative Adverb

Relative Adverb	*Interrogative Adverb*
It is used in the interior of the sentence.	It is used in the very beginning of the sentence.
It is normally preceded by a Noun.	It is not preceded by a/any Noun.
It connects two sentences.	It asks questions.
It shows its relation with its preceding Noun/Pronoun.	

Formation of Adverbs

Adverbs are formed.

By Adding 'ly'

(a) To Nouns; as — daily, hourly, monthly, timely, weekly, yearly.

(b) To Adjectives; as — beautifully, carefully, cheerfully, diligently, foolishly, honestly, powerfully, urgently, usefully, lately, nearly, etc.

(c) To participles; as — charmingly, lovingly, surprisingly, markedly, hurriedly, blessedly, decidedly, desiredly.

By Adding Prepositions:

(a) To Nouns; as — Abed (on-bed), afoot (on foot), ahead, ashore, beside, today.

(b) To Adjectives; as — Across, aloud, anew, behind, below, between.

(c) To Adverbs; as — Hereby, herein, herewith, henceforth, thereby, therein, thenceforth.

(d) By combining a Noun and an Adjective; as — East-ward, mean-time, mid-day, side-ways, some-times, other-wise, etc.

(e) Adverbs of Number are formed in the following manner: One-once; Two-twice; Three-thrice; Four-fourfold.

Comparison of Adverbs

Like Adjectives some Adverbs too have Degrees of Comparison; as:

	Positive Degree	*Comparative Degree*	*Superlative Degree*
(a)	Early	earlier	earliest
	Fast	faster	fastest
	Hard	harder	hardest
	Long	longer	longest
	Near	nearer	nearest
	Soon	sooner	soonest
(b)	Beautifully	more beautifully	most beautifully
	Carefully	more carefully	most carefully
	Neatly	more neatly	most neatly
	Slowly	more slowly	most slowly
	Swiftly	more swiftly	most swiftly

Wisely	more wisely	most wisely

Contd...

	Positive Degree	*Comparative Degree*	*Superlative Degree*
(c)	Badly, ill, evil	worse	worst
	Far	farther	farthest
	Forth	further	furthest
	Late	later	latest, last
	Little	less	least
	Much	more	most
	Near, nigh	nearer	nearest
	Well	better	best

Hint/clue: Only the Adverbs showing *manner, degree* and *time* can be compared.

Important Information: The above table must have made it clear that the forms of some Adverbs are similar to those of their corresponding Adjectives. In other words, some words are sometimes used as Adjectives and as Adverbs at other times; as

Adjective	*Adverb*
1. This is a *hard* question.	1. It is raining *hard.*
2. Come by an *early* train.	2. Come *early.*
3. He has *long* ears.	3. May you live *long*!

Parsing

Parsing of Adverbs should be done in the following manner as per requirement of the revised syllabus.

1. She will come *now.*

   Now. Adverb. Use: Rani will not go now.

2. They work *hard.*

   Hard. Adverb. Use: Sheela works hard to get through.

3. *Where* do they live?

   Where. Adverb. Use: Where has Anjana gone?

4. This is the place *where* Neelam lives.

   Where. Adverb.

   Use: I shall go to school where he is reading now.

5. *When* did he go?

   When. Adverb. Use: When did you sleep yesterday?

6. This is a *very* sweet mango.

   Very. Adverb. Use: This is a very easy question.

7. He comes here *daily.*

   Daily. Adverb. Use: I go to my school daily.

8. He *often* makes mistakes.

   Often. Adverb. Use: He often sleeps late.

9. He is *as* his brother.

   As. Adverb. Use: Hari is as cunning as Ram.

10. You are *quite* wrong.

    Quite. Adverb. Use: His opinion is quite sound.

Position of Adverbs: Always keep the Adverb quite close to the word, it modifies. The change in the position of the Adverb brings about a great difference in its meanings; as:

Only I saw Sushma's frock.	(Only here means no one, other than me)
I saw Sushma's frock only.	(" " " , nothing else but the frock)
I saw Sushma's only frock.	(" " " , the one frock she had)
I saw only Sushma's frock.	(" " " , no one else's)
I only saw Sushma's frock.	(" " " ', simply saw, did not touch)

The above sentences must have made it clear that there has been a tremendous change in the meaning of the Adverb *'only'* with the change in its position. Therefore, the learners, of English are advised to use the Adverbs judiciously.

General Rules Regarding the Use of Adverbs:

(a) At the beginning of the sentence:

(i) The use of Interrogative Adverb:

Examples:

1. *Where are* you coming from?
2. *How* dare you oppose me?
3. *When* will she give a tea party?

(ii) If an Adverb modifies the whole sentence:

Surely she will stand first.

Probably you are in the wrong.

(iii) To lay emphasis on the sentence:

Here comes the actress. *There* stands the devil.

(b) In the Interior of the sentence:

(i) Some time — denoting Adverbs (Always, ever, never, often, seldom, sometimes, etc.) are used before the Verbs, they modify; as:

1. She *always* plays foul.
2. I *often* worry about my parents.

(ii) Insert the Adverb in between the Auxiliary Verb and the Finite Verb, if an Auxiliary Verb is present in a sentence: as:

1. She will *never* dupe you.
2. He is *highly* respected.
3. You have *wisely* acted.
4. They do *surely* recognise her.

(iii) Fix the Adverb, after the Verb if the Verb 'To be' is used as a Finite Verb; as:

1. I am *never* wrong.
2. She is *ever* green.

(c) At the end (tail) of the sentence:

(i) If an Adverb modifies an Intransitive Verb, put that Adverb after the Verb; as:

1. He writes *legibly*.
2. Sarla plays *honestly*.
3. Sarita sings *confidently*.
4. Gita loves *passionately*.

(ii) If an Adverb is to be used with the Transitive Verb, put that Adverb after the Verb; as:

1. She learns the poem *silently*.
2. She can solve this problem *quickly*.

Uses of Some Adverbs

'Very'

(a) Put the Adverb *'very'* before Adjectives and Adverbs in the Positive Degree; as:

Smoking is *very* harmful.

He gets up *very* early.

(b) Put the Adverb *'very'* before Adjectives in Superlative Degree; as:

I tired my *very best* to help my neighbour.

She did her *very* best to please her in-laws.

(c) Put the Adverb *'very'* before Present and Past Participle; as:

She told me a *very* encouraging tale.

He was *very* delighted to see me.

(d) The Adverb *'very'* is used to modify another Adverb 'much'; as:

Your saree is *very* much costlier than hers.

(e) The Adverb *'very'* is used as an Adjective, before a Noun; as:

This is the *very* pen I was searching for.

'Much'

(a) The Adverb *'much'* is used before the Comparative Degrees of Adjectives and Adverbs; as:

You look *much* happier today.

I am *much* more worried to hear about your failure.

(b) The Adverb *'much'* is used before the Superlative Degrees of Adjectives; as:

You are *much* the smartest player in the team.

(c) The Adverb *'much'* is used as an Adjective; as:

It gives her *much* pleasure to scold her servant.

(d) The Adverb *'much'* is used before Past Participle; as:

She was *much* confused to read my letter.

(e) The Adverb *'much'* is used to modify the Adverb *'too'*; as:

She talks too *much*.

This problem is *much* too easy for her.

Remember that the Adverb *'very'* never modifies any Verb *'the'* is used before *'very'* (The very) and after *'much'* (Much the). *'Very'* and *'much'* are both used with *delighted, experienced, pained, pleased, surprised* and *tired.*

'Too'

(a) *'Too'* is sometimes used to replace *'very'* and *'much'*; as:

She is too stupid. (Stupid beyond measure/limits)

(b) Whenever *'too'* is used in Negative Sense, it means *'so that.......* not', *'to'* is used after 'too' in that case; as:

She is *too* proud *to* accept her defeat.

Or

She is so proud that she will not accept her defeat.

(c) *'Too'* is sometimes used in the sense of *'also'*: as:

He too was fined. (This means 'He was also fined with/like others.)

(d) *'Much too'* is used before an Adjective but *too much* is used before a noun; as:

You are *much too* weak to lift this heavy load.

Too much wealth makes one proud.

'Enough'

(a) The Adverb *'enough'* is put immediately after the Adverb, it modifies; as:

Will you be kind *enough* to grant me four days' leave?

(b) As an Adjective *'enough'* is used before the Noun, it qualifies; as:

I have *enough* money for the journey.

'Quite'

Quite means *'fairly'*; *'to some extent'*, *'not very'*; as:

Is she *quite* hopeful? She is *quite* a (fairly a) tall girl.

The bull is *quite* dead.

'Since', Ago' and Before'

(a) As Adverbs *'since'* and *'ago'* can safely be used for each other; as:

I received your progress report a few days since/ago.

(b) As an Adverb, *'before'* means *'formerly'*; as:

I have seen the Taj before (formerly).

'Perhaps' and 'Probably'

(a) *'Perhaps'* is fraught with *'suspicion/doubt'*; as:

Perhaps she will help me.

(b) *'Probably'* contains *'likelihood/chance'*; as:

Probably Nikunj will win the scholarship.

'Yes' and 'no': *'Yes'* is used for the reply in Affirmative and *'No'* is used for the reply in Negative; as:

Question: Will you lend me one thousand rupees?

Answer: Yes, I shall — No, I shan't.

'But': As an Adverb 'But' = 'only'; as

You are *but* (*only*) a mean fellow.

Miscellaneous Exercises for Recapitulation

Uses of Adverbs

Model Sentences

Some persons speak too fast to be understood.
His salary is high enough for his work.
This book is much better than that.
He was much disgusted with his life.
An elephant walks majestically.
Why did you reach the school late?
How did she solve these sums?
This is how we can settle the dispute.
Do you play football daily? Yes, I do.
The shepherd shouted loudly for help.
I shall leave for school soon.
I have already finished my breakfast.
We could find him nowhere.

Or

We could not find him anywhere.
She often comes to see me.
My aunt seldom goes to the market.
Finally, they had to give in.
Ultimately, she had to discontinue her studies.
She failed because she did not appear in the examination.
Do not swallow the food hurriedly.
The old woman was weeping bitterly.

Errors in the Use of Adverbs

Incorrect	*Correct*
1. I'm too pleased to greet you.	I'm very pleased to greet you.
2. She comes here seldom.	She seldom comes here.
3. I'll come directly from Jaipur.	I'll come direct from Jaipur.

Contd..

Incorrect	*Correct*
4. The rose smells sweetly.	The rose smells sweet.
5. I'll be very much glad to see you.	I'll be very glad to see you.
6. This book is much entertaining.	This book is very entertaining.
7. He was enough kind to help me.	He was kind enough to help me.
8. Supposing if she comes, what will you say?	Supposing (If) she comes, what will you say?
9. He works hardly.	He works hard.
10. They left Delhi two years before.	They left Delhi two years ago.
11. Please kindly help me.	Please (Kindly) help me.
12. I do not know to drive a scooter.	I do not know how to drive a scooter.
13. It is nothing else than arrogance.	It is nothing else but arrogance.
14. She will be very obliged to me.	She will be much obliged to me.
15. The deer ran fastly.	The deer ran fast.
16. I am in need of a pen badly.	I am badly in need of a pen.
17. He seldom or ever learns his lesson.	He seldom or never learns his lesson.
18. She only rests when she is tired.	She rests only when she is tired.
19. I am very well here.	I am quite well here.
20. He's enough rich to help me.	He's rich enough to help me.
21. You speak very hasty.	You speak very hastily.
22. She has too high an opinion of herself.	She has a very high opinion of herself.

7

Preposition

Kinds of Preposition

(i) Simple Prepositions; as:

At, after, by, down, in, over, to, up, with, etc.

(ii) Compound Prepositions; as:

About, across, against, before, beside, into, until, within, etc.

(iii) Participial Prepositions; as:

Accepting, consider, during, etc.

(iv) Phrasal Prepositions; as:

Along with, by virtue of, by way of, in the event of, instead of, on account of, on behalf of, etc.

(v) Double Prepositions; as:

From among, from beneath, from under, out of, etc.

Uses of Certain Prepositions

The uses of 'At'

1. I get up *at* 6 A.M. (To show definite time).
2. My mother is *at* home. (To show definite location).
3. I live *at* village Dichaon Kalan. (Before the name of a village).

4. I was born *at* Rohtak. (Before the name of a city).
5. Urmilla lives *at* Mohan Garden. (Before the name of a colony).
6. On my way to Aligarh, I stayed *at* Ghaziabad. (Before the name of the city where one stays for some time).
7. I go to the temple *at* dawn, *at* noon and *at* night. (Before *dawn, noon* and *night*).
8. Ghee is selling *at* one hundred rupees a litre. (To show the rates).

The Uses of 'In'

1. The Principal is *in* his office. (To indicate a definite place).
2. I was born *in* Haryana. (Before the name of a province).
3. I study *in* Lucknow. (Before the name of a big city).
4. Allahabad University is *in* India. (Before the name of a country).
5. I shall finish my breakfast *in* ten minutes. (To show the duration of an action).
6. *In* my opinion, she is quite blank. (To show context).
7. Kamla was born *in* poverty. (To show financial condition).
8. Gandhi was born *in* October in 1869. (To show the month and year which prolong for some time).
9. I study *in* the morning and *in* the evening but rest *in* the afternoon. (Before *morning, evening* and *afternoon*).

The Uses of 'To'

1. I go *to* school daily. (Before destination).
2. It is ten minutes *to* two. (To tell/show time).
3. I want *to* buy a pencil. (Before an Infinitive Verb).
4. What is she *to* you? (To show relation).

The Uses of 'Into'

1. She fell *into* the well. (To show movement towards a place).
2. Translate this passage *into* Hindi. (To change the form).

The uses of 'On'

1. I have written a book *on* translation. (To clarify the position of something).
2. We sleep *on* the roof. (To show contact with a place).
3. I shall visit your house *on* Monday. (Before a day).
4. India became a Republic *on* 26th January, 1950. (Before a date).

The use(s) of 'Upon'

The cat pounced *upon* the rat. (To show movement towards a higher position).

The use (s) of 'After'

It was after 10 p.m., when we ran *after* the thief. (To show some *time* or *position* meaning *later than*).

The use of 'Behind'

Who is hiding *behind* the wall? (To show some place 'at the back of).

The uses of 'Within'

1. He will return *within* a week. (To show the position of time in between the specified limit).
2. Women live *within* the four walls of the house. (To show the boundary/ boundlines of a place).

The use of 'Before'

I shall finish my work *before* sunset. (prior to some time).

The uses of 'Above' and 'Over'

1. Keep your head *above* water. (To show upper position).
2. The sky is *over* our heads. (To show a much higher position).

The uses of 'Between'

1. My book is *between* Kareena and Varuna. (With two persons).

2. There is a distance of 50 km *between* Delhi and Gurgaon. (Showing the intervening places).
3. There is no secret *between* him and you. (Showing two pronouns).
4. There is no similarity *between* your book and my book. (Showing two things/items).

The uses of 'Among'

1. There is no difference of culture *among* Gurgaon, Rohtak and Sonepat. (In between more than two places).
2. Divide these bananas *among* these ten boys. (In between more than two persons).

The uses of 'By'

1. Tea has been taken *by* the guests. (Shows persons as doers).
2. What is the time *by* your watch? (according to).
3. You have to finish this work *by* 6 p.m. (To show last limit of time).
4. We go to school *by* train. (To show means of an action).
5. She caught you *by* the collar. (To show the way of an action).
6. Apples are sold *by* the kilogram. (To show measuring instruments).

The uses of 'With'

1. Why did you stab him *with* a knife? (Showing helpful instrument).
2. Who was playing *with* you? (To show a companion doing same action).

The use of 'Till'

1. I shall wait for you *till* sunset. (To show time limit).

The uses of 'Under' and 'Below'

1. A cat is sitting *under* the table. (To show a lower position in place).
2. Sarla is *below* Sharda in the office. (To show a lower rank in service).

The uses of 'Beside' and 'Besides'

1. The baby is sleeping *beside* its mother. (By the side of).
2. *Besides* being punished, he was expelled from school. (In addition to).

The use of 'of'

1. She is the daughter *of* a rich man. (To show relationship).

The uses of 'off'

1. Switch *off* the light. (To disconnect the function).
2. She fell *off* the tree. (To show separation from upwards to downwards).

The uses of 'From'

1. She has come direct *from* home. (To show the starting point).
2. I shall start my revision *from* tomorrow. (To show time).
3. This is a quotation *from* Kalidas. (To show the source).

The uses of 'Since'

1. I cannot take exercise *since* I am ill. (To show reason).
2. I have been reading *since* morning. (To show point of time).

The uses of 'For'

1. She has been reading *for* five hours. (To show an indefinite period of time).
2. Lend me your book *for* a day. (To show exact period of time).

The use of 'Towards'

1. She went *towards* the Post office. (To show direction).

Miscellaneous Exercise 1 (For Recapitulation)

Prepositions (On, In, At, Upon, Into, Within) Model Sentences

My father has full command *on* English.

I shall return *within* a week.

Have you no influence *on* your neighbour?

I shall return *in* a week.

A long discussion took place *on* this matter.

The prince sat upon the throne *on* his father's death.

He threw himself *into* his work heart and soul.

I shall write to you a letter *within* a week.

There is no harm *in* going there.

Who is standing *at* the gate?

We are living *at* peace with our neighbours.

He was born *at* Ghaziabad in U.P.

She takes great pride *in* never making a mistake.

After the partition we settled *at* Delhi in India.

She is putting all her money *into* her purse.

I leave the bed *at* 6 o'clock every morning.

The book is lying *on* the table.

The sun shines brightly *at* noon.

Pour a little more tea *into* the cup.

Water can be converted *into* ice by freezing.

The tiger sprang *upon* the deer.

Miscellaneous Exercise 2 (For Recapitulation)

Prepositions (after, before, over, under, below, above)

Model Sentences

He is *over* head and ears in debt.

They quarrelled *over* a trifle.

Is the sky not *over* our heads?

Tether the bullocks *under* a shady tree.

She is *below* many students in the class.

My house is *above* the road.

Keep your head *above* water.

To mix up with him is *below* my dignity.

See me *after* the period is over.

We ran *after* the thief in vain.

Where had you gone *before* sunrise today?

Why did you arrive *before* the scheduled time?

His elder sister was born four years *before* him.

Is the cat sitting *under* the table?

Is he not *under* the thumb of his wife?

He is *below* me in rank.

Her performance was much (far) *below* my expectations.

Never hit anybody *below* the belt.

She will settle in Delhi *after* a few years.

It is harmful to sleep *under* a tree at night.

Miscellaneous Exercise 3 (For Recapitulation)

Prepositions (by, with, for, of, to, towards, from)

Model Sentences

We have *to* do the whole of our work by ourselves.

We assess the people *by* their appearance.

I shall return *by* 8 o'clock.

I rise *with* the sun.

He was much disgusted *with* his wife.

Ram killed Ravana *with* an arrow.

I am waiting *for* my friend.

Vitamins are essential *for* maintenance of health.

All these presents are *for* you.

Gandhi was quite worthy *of* people's trust.

I shall relieve him *of* his duties.

The judge found him guilty *of* murder.

The cat is afraid *of* the dog.

We ought not to make fun *of* the poor.

I gave a rupee *to* a beggar.

At what time do you go *to* school?

I saw him going *towards* the post office.

The villagers are always friendly *towards* the tourists.

Now he is heading *towards* the age of retirement.

Leaves are falling *from* the trees.

Where are you coming *from*?

She has been debarred *from* appearing at the examination due to shortage of attendance.

He is abstaining *from* drink after the accident.

Miscellaneous Exercise 3 (For Recapitulation)

Prepositions (away, across, behind, beyond, against)

Model Sentences

Keep that devil far *away*.

Our school is two miles *away* form our house.

Have you cleared *away* your books from the table?

The hut was swept *away* by the flood.

Can you swim *across* this river?

The river is half a mile *across*.

The boatman rowed me *across* the river.

My house is just *across* the street.

Who is the girl standing *behind* you?

Why are you standing close *behind* me?

We left our companions a long way *behind*.

Don't look *behind* or you will fall.

There is a road *beyond* the village up into the hills.

It is *beyond* my power to help you.

This bicycle is *beyond* repairs.

She is living *beyond* her means.

You are rowing *against* the current.

She was married *against* her will.

The ladder is standing *against* the wall.

He was leaning *against* a tree.

Miscellaneous Exercise 4 (For Recapitulation)

Prepositions (off, about, beside, besides, between, among)

Model Sentences

Switch *off* the fan.

He put *off* his cigarette in the ash tray.

The plane took *off* exactly at 7 o'clock.

The strike was called *off* unconditionally.

Are you not anxious *about* the result of your examination?

The boys became very enthusiastic *about* their trip.

Don't ask me anything *about* her.

Do not beat *about* the bush.

My study (room) is *beside* the kitchen.

The baby is lying *beside* its mother.

Come and sit *beside* me.

He was *beside* himself with rage when I rebuked him.

Besides Rajni, we, a group of four girls will take tea at your house.

No one else writes (a letter) to me, *besides* you.

Pappu is my younger brother and I have three other brothers *besides* him.

Besides punishing him, the Principal rusticated him also.

The school is situated *between* the post office and the hospital.

Divide these mangoes *between* the two sisters.

Among Ram, Sham and Gopal, who got the maximum number of marks?

Distribute this milk *among* the five girls.

Miscellaneous Exercise 5 (For Recapitulation)

Prepositions (through, upto, without, beneath, around)

Model Sentences

We went *through* the field and reached the forest.

The thief got in the house *through* the window.

The water flowed *through* the pipe.

My aunt nursed me *through* my long illness.

It is upto you *whether* to help him or not.

If you go *upto* the post office, bring a few envelopes for me.

Your reply is not *upto* the mark.

I think he is *upto* some mischief.

You should not board a train *without* a ticket.

Beauty is a curse *without* intelligence.

Why did you go to his house *without* my permission?

There is no taste *without* teeth.

Shall we take rest in the shade *beneath* this tree?

The police found the dead body buried *beneath* a pile of leaves.

The boat sank *beneath* the high and large waves.

A graduate girl considers the job of a peon *beneath* her status.

There is a beautiful lawn *around* our house.

There is a fence *around* our field.

We went to Lucknow and walked *around* the city.

Some guests arrived in our house *around* twelve at night.

Common Errors in the Use of Prepositions

	Incorrect	*Correct*
1.	It has been raining *from* morning.	It has been raining *since* morning.
2.	Is there any remedy *of* this?	Is there any remedy *for* this?
3.	She invited me *for* tea.	She invited me *to* tea.
4.	Compare Ashoka *to* Shah Jahan.	Compare Ashoka *with* Shah Jahan.
5.	She died *from* cancer.	She died *of* cancer.
6.	I refrain *to tell a* lie.	I refrain *from telling a* lie.
7.	Write to me *on* this address.	Write to me *to* this address.
8.	Open your book *on* page four.	Open your book *at* page four.
9.	Why is the teacher angry *upon* you?	Why is the teacher angry *with* you?
10.	Let us sit *under* the shade of a tree.	Let us sit *in* the shade of a tree.
11.	Never quarrel *on* trifles.	Never quarrel *over* trifles.
12.	I am searching *after* my book.	I am searching *for* my book.
13.	Distribute these toffees *between* twenty girls.	Distribute these toffees *among* twenty girls.
14.	What is the time *in* your watch?	What is the time *by* your watch?
15.	Our examinations will begin *from* Monday.	Our examinations will begin *on* Monday.
16.	Savita has been very kind *on* me.	Savita has been very kind *to* me.
17.	I shall say this *on* her face.	I shall say this *to her* face.
18.	I have been waiting for you *from* two hours.	I have been waiting for you *for* two hours.
19.	You can see me *behind* the period is *off*.	You can see me *after* the period is *over*.
20.	Switch *away* the light.	Switch *off* the light.
21.	Look! the mouse is running *in* the hole.	Look! the mouse is running *into* the hole.

Contd...

	Incorrect	*Correct*
22.	The Punjab is to the North *from* India.	The Punjab is in the North *of* India.
23.	There is little water *into* the jug.	There is little water *in* the jug.
24.	I live *in* village Mundhela *at* New Delhi.	I live *at* village Mundhela *in* New Delhi.
25.	*In* my way to Agra, I met *some* from my relatives.	*On* my way to Agra, I met some *of* my relatives.
26.	Can you jumped *in* the river?	Can you jump *into* the river?
27.	The cat jump *on* the table.	The cat jumped *upon* the table.
28.	He killed snake *by* a stick.	He killed a snake *with* a stick.
29.	A button *from* my coat has come *out.*	A button *of* my coat has come *off.*
30.	He plays *since* morning to evening.	He plays *from* morning *till* evening.
31.	I have known them *from* 1990.	I have known them *since* 1990.
32.	You have been cheating me *from* five years.	You have been cheating me *for* five years.
33.	She returned home at *over* 9 p.m.	She returned home *after* 9 p.m.
34.	The train is running *after* time.	The train is running *behind* time.
35.	The sun shines *above* the earth.	The sun shines *over* the earth.

Words Followed by Appropriate Prepositions

A

1. Abide by: She failed to abide by her promise.
2. Absorb in: My mother is absorbed in household duties.
3. Abstain from: A wise man should abstain from drink.
4. Accede to: I cannot accede to your silly request.
5. Access to: We have an easy access to the librarian.
6. Accuse of: He was accused of murder.
7. Admitted to: I have been admitted to the 9th class.
8. Agree to: She did not agree to my proposal.
9. Agree with: Do you agree with me or not?
10. Aim at: The fowler aimed at the crow.
11. Alarmed at: I was alarmed at the sight of a snake.

12. Amuse with: I amused him with titbits.
13. Angry with: Why are you angry with me?
14. Afraid of: I am afraid of my teachers.
15. Appeal to: The red colour does not appeal to me.
16. Apologise to, for: I apologise to you for my folly.
17. Apply to, for: He applied to the Principal for leave.
18. Approve of: I never approve of her conduct.
19. Arrive at: The train arrived at the station in time.
20. Annoyed with, at: You were annoyed with me at my misbehaviour.
21. Associate with: You will ruin yourself if you associate with bad girls.
22. Assure of: The teacher assured us of help.
23. Astonished at: I was astonished at your failure.
24. Ask of, for: I asked of my neighbour for a loan of five hundred rupees.
25. Abound in: The pond abounds in fish.
26. Attend to: Attend to what your mother says.
27. Attend upon: You should attend upon your aged parents.

B

28. Believe in: I believe in Godly help.
29. Beg of: The beggar begged a rupee of me.
30. Beware of: Beware of your neighbour's dog.
31. Bark at: Dogs bark at the strangers.
32. Back out: Never back out of your promise.
33. Belong to: Nikunj belongs to the family of writers.
34. Bent on: Our neighbour is bent on harming us.
35. Bless with: Naresh has been blessed with a son.
36. Blind of: Sarup was blind of one eye.
37. Blind to: You are blind to the defects of your brother.
38. Boast of: Never boast of your riches.

39. Born in: Suchitra was born in Gautam's family.
40. Born of: I was not born of rich parents.
41. Born to: A daughter was born to Krishna.
42. Busy with: Always remain busy with your work.
43. Borrow from: You had borrowed a pen from me.

C

44. Call at: I shall call at your house tonight.
45. Call on: Will you call on me today?
46. Care for: Nobody cares for a poor man.
47. Charge with: Jaggu was charged with murder.
48. Cheat of: Hari Chand cheated me of ten rupees.
49. Complain of: She always complains of headache.
50. Complain to: I have complained to the Post Master against the postman.
51. Come by: How did you come by this suitcase?
52. Collide with: Two buses collided with each other.
53. Cling: The baby is clinging to its mother.
54. Comply with: I cannot comply with your request.
55. Compare to: Eyes are compared to a lily.
56. Compare with: Compare Lal Bahadur with Jawahar Lal.
57. Control over: The teacher has no control over his class.
58. Confident of: I am confident of my success.
59. Congratulate on: I congratulate you on your success.
60. Conscious of: You are not conscious of your weakness.
61. Consist of: This exercise book consists of one hundred pages.
62. Contented with: Nobody is contented with his lot.
63. Cured of: She could not be cured of cancer.

D

64. Deal in: I deal in tea leaves.
65. Depend upon: Never depend upon others.

66. Deprived of: Nobody can deprive me of my share.
67. Desire for: I have no desire for wealth.
68. Die of: He died of pneumonia.
69. Die from: He died from over-work.
70. Differ with: The two brothers differ with each other in their views.
71. Different from: Your younger brother is totally different from you.
72. Devoid of: You are devoid of common sense.
73. Disgusted with: I am disgusted with over-work.
74. Dispense with: The mill-owner has dispensed with his services.
75. Dispose of: I want to dispose of my scooter.
76. Distinguish between: I cannot distinguish between gold and brass.

E

77. Eligible for: I am not eligible for this post.
78. Envious of: Don't be envious of others' success.
79. Equal to: One kilogram is equal to one thousand grams.
80. Enquire after: I enquired after his well-being.
81. Enquire of: I enquired of him about his parents.
82. Escape from: The thief escaped from the police station.
83. Essential to: Good health is essential to success in life.
84. Expect of: She never expected this of him.
85. Exception to: There is an exception to every rule.
86. Exempt from: The headmaster has exempted Rajneesh from the payment of fine.

F

87. Familiar to: Her face is familiar to yours.
88. Familiar with: I am not familiar with Mohit.
89. Faith in: Have you no faith in me?

90. Famous for: Agra is famous for the Taj.
91. Feed on: The tiger feeds on flesh.
92. Feel for: The rich should feel for the poor.
93. Free from: Nobody is free from worries.
94. Free with: I am not free with my teachers.
95. Fight for: We should fight for our rights.
96. Filled with: His brain is filled with dirt.
97. Fond of: Children are fond of toys and toffees.
98. Furnished with: Your house is not furnished with modern items.

G

99. Gifted with: Rohit is gifted with a sweet voice.
100. Give up: Give up smoking.
101. Glad at: I am glad at your success.
102. Good at: I am not good at painting.
103. Grateful to: I am grateful to you for your help.
104. Grumble at: Never grumble at your lot.
105. Guard against: Guard yourself against silly companions.
106. Guilty of: You are guilty of misbehaviour.
107. Glance at: Don't glance at strangers.

H

108. Hard up: My father is hard up these days.
109. Hanker after: Do not hanker after wealth.
110. Heir to: The eldest son used to be the heir to his father's property.
111. Hinder from: Don't hinder me from doing graduation.
112. Hatred for: I have a great hatred for smugglers.
113. Honest in: Try to be honest in your dealings.
114. Hope for: Always do your very best and hope for the best.
115. Hopeful of: I am quite hopeful of my success.

I, J

116. Ignorant of: Man is ignorant of his success.
117. Ill with: Today, I am ill with fever.
118. Inform of: I shall inform you of my arrival.
119. Indifferent to: He is indifferent to his health.
120. Inferior to: Cotton is inferior to terene.
121. Injurious to: Drinking is injurious to health.
122. Interest in: I have no interest in painting.
123. Introduce to: I shall introduce you to my sister.
124. Insist on: She insisted on accompanying me.
125. Intimate with: I am not intimate with Reshma.
126. Invite to: I am inviting you to a tea party.
127. Jealous of: Why is he jealous of my success?
128. Junior to: I am junior to Rohit in service.

K, L

129. Kind to: Be kind to all the creatures.
130. Knock at: Who is knocking at the door?
131. Known by: We are known by the company we keep.
132. Known for: Birbal was known for his witty remarks.
133. Known to: She is not known to me.
134. Lame of: Bimla is lame of one leg.
135. Laugh at: Never laugh at the poor.
136. Lead to: This road will lead you to the hospital.
137. Lean against: Do not lean against the wall.
138. Listen to: Listen to what your teacher says.
139. Long for: Who does not long for a long life?
140. Look at: Look at this silly fellow.
141. Loyal to: Be loyal to your master.

M, N, O

142. Match for: Dimple is no match for John.
143. Meddle with: Don't meddle with others' affairs.

144. Mix with: Don't mix with bad children.
145. Need of: I am in need of a house-maid.
146. Notorious for: Rajeshwari is notorious for pick-pocketing.
147. Obedient to: Be obedient to your elders.
148. Object to: I object to your proposal.
149. Oblivious of: I am not oblivious of my surroundings.
150. Oblivious to: I was quite oblivious to the risk.

P, Q

151. Part from: The bride parted from her girl friends in tears.
152. Part with: I cannot part with this costly pen.
153. Pity on: Take pity on this poor lady.
154. Play upon: I cannot play upon the harmonium.
155. Pray to: I shall pray to God for success.
156. Preside over: Pt. Deep Chand presided over the function.
157. Prevent from: Don't prevent your sister from studying further.
158. Pride in: Your pride in your achievement is justified.
159. Pride of: The new car was the pride of the whole family.
160. Popular with: Our library incharge is popular with the students.
161. Profit by: You should profit by others' experiences.
162. Proud of: Damyanti was not proud of her beauty.
163. Qualified for: I am fully qualified for the post of a superintendent.
164. Quarrel with: Never quarrel with anybody on trifles.
165. Quarrel over: The two ladies quarrelled over their children.

R

166. Recover from: I have recovered from illness.
167. Refer to: Please refer to my application dated the 18th instant.

168. Refrain from: You should refrain from telling a lie.
169. Rejoice at: She rejoiced at her success.
170. Rely on: I cannot rely on that fair-weather friend.
171. Related to: I am not related to her.
172. Remember to: Remember me to your parents.
173. Remind of: Should I remind you of my application again?
174. Repent of: Rajnish repented of his meanness.
175. Reply to: Why did she not reply to your letter?
176. Respect for: I have no respect for cheats.
177. Rob of: A drunkard is robbed of his health and wealth.

S

178. Send for: Send for the doctor at once.
179. Search for: I am reaching for my lost diary.
180. Search of: He is in search of a suitable job.
181. Satisfied with: I am not satisfied with my present job.
182. Shiver with: Everyone shivers with cold in winter.
183. Shocked at: I was shocked at my uncle's death.
184. Sick of: The beggar is sick of his wretched life.
185. Sorry for: I am sorry for being late.
186. Stare at: Why are you staring at that gentle lady?
187. Stare in: Death ever stares us in the face.
188. Superior to: My watch is superior to yours.
189. Sure of: Everyone is sure of death.
190. Surprise at: Everybody was surprised at my success.
191. Suspect of: The police suspected Hemu of murder.
192. Sympathy for: I have no sympathy for mean fellows.
193. Sympathise with: I sympathised with the old woman and gave her some money.

T

194. Take for: I took Rupa for Kanta.

195. Talk about: Let us talk about modern politicians.
196. Taste for: I have no taste for painting.
197. Teem with: Our farm-house teems with rats.
198. Think over: I am thinking over my problems.
199. Tired of: I am tired of this miserable life.
200. Tremble with: He was trembling with fear.
201. True to: I am always true to my word.
202. Trust in: Trust in God and do the right.
203. Trust with: Do not trust the stranger with your suitcase.
204. Treat as: I treated his remark as joke.

U, V, W, X, Y, Z

205. Unfit for: A lame person is unfit for military jobs.
206. Useful to, for: A morning walk is useful to us for our health.
207. Vie with: The two rivals vied with each other.
208. Vote for: I always vote for a suitable candidate.
209. Wait for: I was waiting for your letter.
210. Wait upon/on: The waiter waits upon the customers.
211. Wait in: I waited in all days but you did not come.
212. Want in: Madhuri is wanting in common sense.
213. Warn of: I warned him of the results of drinking.
214. Weary of: I am weary of old age.
215. Wonder at: I wondered at the beauty of the Taj.
216. Worthy of: The one-eyed and ugly girl is not worthy of her husband.
217. Yield to: I shall not yield to any temptation.
218. Zeal for: She has a great zeal for outdoor life.

Points to Remember about Fixed Prepositions

1. The Preposition *'to'* is normally used after the words showing *'habit'*; as:

Accustomed to, habituated to, addicted to, given to, used to, etc.

2. *The preposition 'For'* is used after the words meaning 'reputation/fame', etc.; as:

   famous for, known for, popular for, notorious for, remarkable for, renowned for, etc.

3. (i) The preposition *'of'* is used after the words meaning 'dispossession'; as:

   Bereft of, deprived of, destitute of, devoid of, etc.

   (ii) The preposition *'of'* is also used after the words meaning 'pride, glory, desire, decision', etc.; as:

   Ambitious of, boast of, certain of, confident of, envious of, greedy of, proud of, sure of, vain of, etc.

4. The Preposition *'from'* is used after the words meaning *'taboos'*; as:

   Abstain from, check from, debar from, desist from, discourage from, hinder from, obstruct from, prevent from, prohibit from, refrain from, restrain from, etc.

5. The preposition *'at'* is generally used after the exclamatory words; as:

   Amazed at, astonished at, alarmed at, astounded at, perplexed at, started at, surprised at, etc.

There are certain words which can be used both as Adverbs and as Prepositions as:

1. Go and run about. (Adverb)
2. She often talks about you. (Preposition)
3. Could you not come before? (Adverb)
4. You came an hour before me. (Preposition)
5. Let them move on. (Adverb)
6. The lamp is on the table. (Preposition)

Explanation: Noun/Pronoun succeeds the preposition invariably. If a Noun/Pronoun does not succeed a word, the word may be termed as an adverb.

Recapitulation of the uses of Prepositions:

At: It is used with the names of villages, small colonies and towns.

It also shows point of time, value, degree, result and position.

In: It (In) is used with the names of big cities and countries. It also shows points of reference, state, place, time and rest/motion within.

It also shows the expiry of stated time.

After: It denotes the past time and also refers to order or position or object of search.

Behind: It refers to place (at the back of).

Between: It is used for two persons or things (in the middle of two).

Among: It is used for more than two. (in the midst of more than two).

Into: It shows motion or direction in words and change of direction.

Before: It refers to a point of time. It also means 'in front of' and 'earlier than'.

Within: It means 'before the end (expiry) of a period of time'.

On: It refers to things at rest.

Upon: It refers to things in motion.

For: It refers to a period of time. It shows the three main notions e.g. *Substitution, Casualty* and *Opposition.*

Since: It refers to a point of time.

Remember that *'for'* and *'since'* are used in some forms of Perfect Tense only.

From: It refers to a point of time. It also denotes the ideas of *starting point, cause, distinction* and *separation.* It can be used in every tense.

Beside: It means *'by the side of'* and *'overflowing with'.*

Besides: It means 'in *addition to'.*

By: It refers to the agent or the doer. It also shows nearness in relation to *time* (not later than) *space, agency, measure, amount, standard, manner,* etc. It also shows swearing in the name of. It also gives the sense of *near, alone, in respect of, according to.*

With: It shows the instrument. It also gives the sense of *'in spite of, 'in the company of'* and *having,* etc.

Till: It means *upto the point, as late as, to the time.*

Above: It (above) is the opposite of below. It shows rest in a higher position, a higher rank, overhead, etc.

Under: It (under) is the opposite of over and implies the relation of low in position or space. It also means *'lower than* or *in less than , in the/supervision/subordination of, at the foot of, inferior to, subject to,* etc.

Below: It (below) is the opposite of above. It shows rest in a lower position.

Over: It (over) is the opposite of under. It implies the relation of highest in position or space. It (over) also indicates *position beyond; Motion above* and *Position above.*

About: It (about) shows nearness of some kind. It also means *on every side of; concerning; here and there,* etc.

Across: It (across) means *intersection; from side to side of; forming a cross with;* to *or on the other side of.*

Against: It (against) refers to a time of necessity or danger. It also means *opposition, in contrast to, into collision with; in anticipation of,* etc.

Along: It (along) means *in the same line with; parallel to; from end to end of; through any part of the length of; side by side with; close to.*

Amidst: It (amidst) means *'in the middle of;* in *the course of.* (*amid* is the abbreviated form of *amidst*)

Around: It (around) means *'on every side; here and there; about; approximately'.*

Beneath: It (beneath) means *'below; under; underneath'.*

Beyond: It (beyond) means *to the other side of;* to *the further side of; out of reach/comprehension* or *range'.*

But: It (but) means *'except; apart from; without'.*

Of: It (of) means *'concerning;* out *of; relating to'.*

Off: It (off) means *'away, down, or up from; disengaged* or *distant from* (so as to be no longer on).

Through: It (through) means *'from end to end or side to side of, from beginning to end of; by reason of; upto and including; by means (agency) of.*

To: It (to) means 'in *the direction of; as far as; the end point of a journey, etc.'*

Towards: It (towards) means *'in the direction of; as regards; in relation to; near; as contribution to.*

Up: It (up) means 'to *a higher point of; on or along in ascending direction; at* or *in a higher part of.*

Without: It (without) means 'outside *of, lacking in; not having; free from; devoid of; not with; unless'.*

Parsing

Parsing of prepositions should be done in the following manner as per requirement of the revised syllabus.

1. The inkpot is *on* the desk.

   On. preposition. Use: The pen is on the table.

2. Let us go *for* a picnic.

   For. Preposition. Use: He did the work for me.

3. He was *among* the crowd.

   Among. Preposition. Use: Distribute these sweets among the students.

4. Hamid acted *according* to my advice.

   According to. Preposition. Use: The work was undertaken according to their plan.

5. *Owing to* hard work, he fell it.

   Owing to. Preposition. Use: Owing to his bad character, nobody liked him.

8

Conjunction

Kinds of Conjunction

(i) Co-ordinate Conjunctions.

(ii) Subordinate Conjunctions.

Co-ordinate Conjunctions

Read the following sentences:

1. She took her breakfast *and* boarded the bus.
2. I tried to catch him *but* I failed to do so.
3. She was angry yet she did not abuse me.

The above sentences can also be written as follows:

1. She took her breakfast. She boarded the bus.
2. I tried to catch him. I failed to catch him.
3. She was angry. She did not abuse me.

All the sentences given above are conveying their individual meanings. In them, the first sentence is the Principal clause and the second sentence is a Co-ordinate clause. The Conjunctions *'and'*, *'but'*, *'yet'* which have been used to combine them are called Co-ordinate conjunctions.

Coordinating Conjunctions

Cumulative Conjunctions

1. Help the needy *and* forget.

2. Kalidas was *both* a poet *and* a dramatist.
3. Mridula is pretty *as well as* kind.
4. Rani no *less than* Kanta is to blame.

The words printed in italics in the above sentences are Cumulative Conjunctions, because they are combining one sentence with the other statement.

Adversative Conjunctions

1. He ran fast *but* he could not catch the bus.
2. Mohini burnt mid-night oil *nevertheless* she missed first division.
3. Vijay is strong *still* he does not torment the weak.
4. The lion did not pounce upon the goat *only* he (the lion) started licking it (the goat).

The words printed in italics in the above sentences are Adversative Conjunctions, because they are combining such sentences as are contradictory to each other.

Alternative Conjunctions

1. He must leave the place *or* he will be insulted.
2. You must work hard, *otherwise* you are sure to lose one year.
3. *Either* she is pretty or she is cheerful.

The words printed in italics in the above sentences are Alternative Conjunctions, because they are combining such sentences as show the choice of one out of the alternatives.

Illative Conjunctions

1. You will win the race *for* you can run fast.
2. Madhu was arrogant, *therefore,* she was expelled from school.
3. She missed the bus, *so,* she reached the school late.
4. It is time to leave the bed, let us leave the bed *then.*

The words printed in italics in the above sentences are

Illative Conjunctions because they are combining such sentences as show one sentence as the result of the other sentence.

Please Remember that Co-ordinate Conjunctions are used when two simple sentences are combined into a compound sentence.

List/Categorisation of Coordinating Conjunctions:

(i) And; both................. and; also; too; not only................. but also; no less than; well; as well as; now.

(Showing addition)

(ii) But; however; nevertheless: only; still; whereas; while; yet; though................. yet.

(Showing Contrast/Opposition)

(iii) Else; neither................. nor; either................. or; or; otherwise; whether .... or . (Showing Choice)

(iv) For; hence; so; so then; then; therefore.

(Expressing Result/Inference)

Subordinate Conjunctions

1. *If* you work hard, you will pass.
2. Since I am old, I cannot eat much.
3. I ran fast *lest* I should be late.
4. Sher Khan had died *before* his wife came.

All of the above sentences comprise two clauses each out of them, the Principal Clause is conveying its meaning independently. The other (Subordinate) clause depends on the Principal Clause to convey its meaning clearly.

Principal clause	*Subordinate clause*
1. You will pass,	*if* you work hard.
2. I cannot eat much,	*since* I am old.
3. I ran fast,	*lest* I should be late.
4. Sher Khan had died,	*before* his wife came.

In the above sentences, *'if, since, lest,* and *before'* are subordinate conjunctions because they are joining the subordinate clause with the Principal clause.

According to their meanings, the subordinate conjunctions express the sense as follows.

Time

1. You were not at home, *when* I gave you a ring.
2. *As soon as* she saw a thief, she raised an alarm.
3. Do not go *until* I return.
4. I reached the school *after the bell had gone.*
5. She has been ill *since* she arrived in Bombay.

The words printed in italics in the above sentences are time-denoting subordinate conjunctions.

As; after; as soon as; as long; just as; since; till; until; when; whenever; while; etc. are subordinate conjunctions which show time'.

Place

1. I shall sit *where* I find the place.
2. *Wherever* Rajeshwari went, the hoodlums followed her.
3. He put the book *whence* (from where) he had taken it.

The words printed in italics in the above sentences are place-denoting subordinate conjunctions.

Whence (from where; where; wherever, whither, etc. are subordinate conjunctions which show 'place')

Purpose

1. We eat rich food *so that* we may keep fit.
2. He worked hard *lest* he should fail.
3. I took the scooter in *order that* I might reach my office in time.

The words printed in italics in the above sentences are Purpose-denoting subordinate conjunctions.

In order that; lest, so that, that, etc. are Subordinate Conjunctions which show 'purpose'.

Result

1. She is *such* a cheat *that* nobody trusts her.
2. Geeta *is* so charming *that* she wins everyone's heart.

The words printed in italics in the above sentences are result-denoting subordinate conjunctions.

So-that, Such-that, etc. are Subordinate Conjunctions which show 'Result'.

Cause

1. As it is already late, *so* let us go to bed.
2. I am glad *that* you have arrived.
3. Sarita took a taxi *because* it was raining.

The words printed in italics in the above sentences are Cause-denoting subordinate conjunctions.

As, because, for, that, since, etc. are Subordinate Conjunctions which show 'cause'.

Manner

1. She talks *as if* she were an officer.
2. *So far as* I know Seh Dev is insane.
3. *As* you sow, so shall you reap.

The words printed in italics in the above sentences are Manner-denoting subordinate conjunctions.

As; as if; as .... so, as though; so far, etc. are Subordinate Conjunctions-which show 'Manner'.

Condition

1. You cannot catch the thief *unless* you run fast.
2. *Supposing* your mother dies, what will you do.
3. I shall lend him the required money if he asks me.

The words printed in italics in the above sentences are Condition-denoting subordinate conjunctions. If, provided, in case, supposing, unless, etc. are Subordinate Conjunctions which show *'condition.*

Contrast

1. *Though* Kusum is very beautiful, *yet* she is humble.
2. *Although* she is unwell, she attends the school.
3. You cannot win her heart, *however* cunning you may be.

The words printed in italics in the above sentences are Contrast-denoting subordinate conjunctions.

Although; although .... yet; however, though; though................ yet, etc. are Subordinate Conjunctions which show 'contrast'.

Comparison

1. He is *as* shy *as* his sister.
2. The hills are not *so* pretty *as* they look.
3. Silk is not more useful *than* cotton.

The words printed in italics in the above sentences are Comparison-denoting subordinate conjunctions.

As; as............ as; so............ as, than, etc. are Subordinate Conjunctions which show *'comparison.*

> Remember that subordinate conjunctions are used when two Simple Sentences are combined into a Complex Sentence.

More Information about Conjunctions

1. Conjunctions join some words, phrases or sentences. They are also called *linkers.* The conjunctions which combine the sentences are also termed as Sentence-linkers (connectors).
2. Sentence connectors are helpful in connecting one sentence with the next sentence or one idea with the next idea.

3. The conjunctions which are used in pairs are called correlative conjunctions; as - both............ and; but............ also; as............ as; so............ as; if............ then; not only............ but also, either............ or; neither............ nor; whether............ or; so............ as; although............ yet; though yet; no............ sooner............ than.

Examples:

1. You are *either* mistaken *or* mad.
2. An umbrella is *neither* useful for a scooterist *nor* essential.
3. She *not only* studies in a college *but also* teaches in a private school.
4. I do not care *whether* he fails *or* passes.
5. *Though* I am poor *yet* I am not greedy.

Miscellaneous Exercise 1 (For Recapitulation)

Conjunctions (And, but, yet, both, as well as, no less than, nevertheless, still)

Model Sentences

He is a wealthy and generous person.

Two and two make four.

Trust in God and do the right.

She is a promising girl but her brother is a dunce.

Babar was cruel but his son was kind.

She is rich but she is very humble.

He is poor yet he is honest.

The girl worked hard yet she failed.

He did not study at all yet he stood first in the examination.

Mohan as well as his sisters is wise.

Ram as well as his wife Sita went to the forest.

Rajni no less than Sushma is guilty.

Savitri no less than Sita was chaste.

He is often rude to me, nevertheless, I like him.

She is very intelligent, nevertheless, she is polite.

She is poor, nevertheless, she will help you with money.

He worked very hard, still he could not get a scholarship.

A man gave me a lift on his scooter still I could not reach school in time.

Miscellaneous Exercise 2 (For Recapitulation)

Conjunctions (Either............ or, or, Neither............ nor, Otherwise, Else)

Model Sentences

Either you or your son has done it.

Has she written this letter herself or copied it from someone?

I shall take either tea or coffee. Do or die is our belief.

Either you or your brother has broken this glass.

Mend your ways, otherwise you will be a sufferer.

Either Rohit or Mohit has stolen my purse.

Repay her debt, otherwise she will drag you to the court.

Neither your sister nor you have taken tea.

Serve your father, otherwise he will curse you.

She has neither gone to hospital nor to school.

Work hard, otherwise you will fail.

She has neither prepared the breakfast nor has she taken a bath.

Walk fast, else we will miss the train.

Neither lend nor borrow.

Reach home in time, else your parents will be angry.

Is he at home or in the park?

Hold your tongue, else I shall give you a slap.

Is she wearing a blue saree or red?

Work hard, else you will repent life-long.

Miscellaneous Exercise 3 (For Recapitulation)

Conjunctions (Not only............. but also, as, since, while, because, just, therefore)

He is not only foolish but also ugly.

I don't like Karuna because she is rude and impertinent.

The robbers not only robbed him but also shot him dead.

He does not like to mix up with me because (just because) I am poor.

You have not only to give away the prizes but also to deliver a speech.

She is getting weaker since she does not get rich diet.

He behaved as a foolish fellow.

Ramoo slipped away while I was searching my book.

As a soldier, he had to go on the war-front.

Some one picked my pocket while I was boarding the bus.

As your elder brother, I advise you to leave bad company.

Some guests poured into my house while I was taking tea.

She did not talk to me as she was unknown to me.

While I was crossing a field, a snake hissed at me.

She has done no work since she has arrived here.

Do only as you are told.

Tripta has gained weight since she married.

As I had no money for bus fare I had to walk home (on foot).

Since you are ill, you should not overstrain yourself.

The child is crying because he is hungry.

Miscellaneous Exercise 4 (For Recapitulation)

Conjunctions (therefore, however, notwithstanding, nonetheless. nevertheless, rather than, no sooner than, hardly/scarcely -when)

Model Sentences

I have been suffering from fever for a week and therefore, I am unable to attend the school.

She is very intelligent, nevertheless (nonetheless) she is modest. He did not do his home work, therefore he was fined.

He is often rude to me, nevertheless, I like him.

She met with an accident, therefore, she could not come.

I would rather break than bend.

You cannot stand first, however hard you may study.

He would rather die than seek help from anybody.

He failed thrice, however he did not lose heart.

No sooner did she get the news of her husband's death than she started weeping bitterly.

You cannot move that heavy stone, however strong you are.

No sooner did we step out of the house, than it began to rain heavily.

She walks bare-footed however hot the sand may be.

No sooner did Lord Krishna see Sudama than he came to him running.

He settled down abroad, notwithstanding the language problems.

Hardly/Scarcely had she stepped out of the house when she was kidnapped.

She went to the forest notwithstanding her father's warning.

Hardly (scarcely) had the mother reached the kitchen when the telephone bell rang.

This pen is costly, nevertheless (nonetheless), I think we should buy it.

Parsing

Parsing of conjunctions should be done in the following manner as per requirement of the revised syllabus:

1. He worked hard but he failed.
   But. Conjunction. Use: Rani came but Sheela went.
2. Raju passed *because* he worked hard.
   Because. Conjunction. Use: He failed because he did not work.
3. We work *that* we may be happy.
   That. Conjunction. Use: She earns that she may be rich.
4. Rohit *as well as* Ram passed this year.
   As *well as.* Conjunction. Use: Rama as well as Sita went into the forest.
5. She looks *as if* she were tired.
   As if. Conjunction. Use: He talks as if he were a king.
6. I like you better *than* him.
   Than. Conjunction. Use: Chhoti is stronger than you.
7. He *neither* reads *nor* does he let others read.
   Neither.... Nor. Conjunction. Use: Neither he reads nor does he play.

Errors in the Use of Conjunctions

Incorrect	*Correct*
1. As she is bulky, so she walks slowly.	As she is bulky, she walks slowly.
2. Because she is smart, therefore everybody likes her.	Because she is smart, everybody likes her.
3. He called her *as* a fool.	He called her a fool.
4. Supposing if he fails, what will he do?	If he fails, what will he do?

Contd...

	Incorrect	*Correct*
5.	She was angry, therefore, I ran away.	She was angry, so I ran away.
6.	You must finish your work *when* you go home.	You must finish your work *before* you go home.
7.	She wants a ring twice costly as this.	She wants a ring twice as costly as this.
8.	She hates you much as I.	She hates you as much as I.
9.	Many people regard you *like* a silly.	Many people regard you *as* a silly girl.
10.	She wept bitterly *so* she told her woeful tale.	She wept bitterly *as* she told her woeful tale.
11.	She looked at you *if* you were mad.	She looked at you *as if* you were mad.
12.	I reached your house *as* you had left.	I reached your house *after* you had left.
13.	I have no money I cannot buy a car.	Since I have no money, I cannot buy a car.
14.	It is just a month *as* we arrived here.	It is just a month *since* we arrived here.
15.	He said *as* he would help me.	He said *that* he would help me.
16.	Bring it nearer *so* I may see it clearer.	Bring it *nearer so that* I may see it clearer.
17.	It was raining heavily *as* she stepped in.	It was raining heavily *when* she stepped in.
18.	As speaking English, she often makes mistakes.	*While* speaking English, she often makes mistakes.
19.	She asked *that why* I was late.	She asked why I was late.
20.	Wait here *until he does not* come.	Wait here *until he* comes.
21.	Walk carefully *lest you* fall down.	Walk carefully lest *you should* fall down.
22.	Run fast *lest you should not* miss the bus.	Run fast lest *you should* miss the bus.
23.	Although she is poor but she is honest.	Although she is poor yet she is honest.
24.	Unless you do not labour hard, you will never score a good division.	Unless you labour hard, you will never score a good division.

Contd...

	Incorrect	*Correct*
25.	I remembered her name *as* she had left.	I remembered her name *after* she had left.
26.	You can visit me *when* you desire.	You can visit me *whenever* you desire.
27.	She does not know *that when* her mother would return.	She does not know *when* her mother would return.
28.	He cannot do it; *or* can I.	He cannot do it; *nor* can I.
29.	She will not come unless she *is not* invited.	She will not come unless she *is* invited.
30.	Unless you have no objection, he will continue writing to you.	If you have no objection, he will continue writing to you.
31.	I doubt *that* she will pass.	I doubt *whether* she will pass.
32.	She is as smart *like* her mother.	She is as smart *as* her mother.

9

The Interjection

Feelings are expressed by the use of Interjection

Joy

1. *Hurrah* ! we have won the match.
2. *Ha* . *Ha !* sweets will be distributed in the school.
3. *Ah* ! my son has stood first in his class.

The words printed in italics in the above sentences are Joy-denoting Interjections.

Sorrow

1. *Ah me* ! my purse is missing.
2. *Ha* ! you had a nasty fall.
3. Ah ! your mother has died.
4. *Alas* ! I am undone.

The words printed in italics in the above sentences are Sorrow-denoting Interjections

Remember that *'Ah'* and *'Ah* me' are used, both as joy-denoting and sorrow-denoting Interjections.

Surprise

1. *Oh* ! you are here.
2. *Good Heavens* ! the scooter is missing.

3. *Good God* ! he has won the lottery twice.
4. *What* ! my brother has failed.

The words printed in italics in the above sentences are Surprise-denoting Interjections.

Remember that *Oh, Good Heavens, Good God* and *What* are used, both as joy-denoting and sorrow-denoting Interjections.

Attention

1. *Lo* ! finish your breakfast at once.
2. *Hush* ! the train has reached the platform.
3. *Behold* ! a crow has injured a sparrow.
4. *Listen* ! you have to deliver my message to Rohit.
5. *Look* ! never go outside in the dark.

The words printed in italics in the above sentences are Attention-denoting (diverting/detracting/interjections)

Calling/Address

1. *Ho* ! come here, Sonu.
2. *Holla* ! let us go out for a picnic.
3. *Halloo* ! start the race.

The words printed in italic in the above sentences are Calling/Address (Mode of address-denoting) Interjections.

Approval

1. *O.K.* ! I shall visit your house.
2. *Well done* ! I praise your performance.
3. *Bravo* ! you have made all the arrangements.

The words printed in italics in the above sentences are Approval-denoting Interjections.

Shame or Reproof/Contempt

1. *For shame* ! your sister has run away from home.
2. *Fie* ! *fie!* you have not repaid my loan.
3. *Fie* ! A soldier afraid of death.

The words printed in italics in the above sentences are Shame/Reproof/ Contempt-denoting Interjections.

Remember that

1. Words like *Alack ! Adieu ! O ! Lo ! Pooh!,* etc. can also be used as Interjections when they express the instant feelings of *sorrow, joy,* curiosity, etc. arising in the heart.
2. The phrases like *Cheer up ! Dear me ! Fool ! Good bye ! Good Gracious ! Good Heavens ! Well done!,* etc. can also be used as Interjections. When they convey some feeling arising instantly in the heart.

The following Parts of Speech are also occasionally used as Interjections:

1. In the form of a Noun Infinitive; as:
   To think that your mother would leave us too soon !
2. In the form of a Noun; as:
   A horse ! My kingdom for a horse !
3. In the form of a Pronoun; as:
   What a shameful act it is !
4. In the form of a Verb; as:
   1. Would that I were with you ! (wish)
   2. Hark ! Hark (applause)
5. In the form of an Adverb; as:
   1. How stupid you are ! (wonder)
   2. How charming the sight is ! (wonder)
6. In the form of a Conjunction; as:
   If I could only meet her once ! (wish)
   Remember that an Interjection has no grammatical relation with any other word in the sentence.

Parsing

Parsing of Interjection should be done in the following manner as per requirement of the revised syllabus.

1. *Hello* ! What are you searching here?
   Hello. Interjection
2. *Alas* ! I am doomed.
   Alas. Interjection.

Common Errors in the Use of Interjections

Incorrect	*Correct*
1. *Alas!* our team has won the match.	*Hurrah!* our team has won the match.
2. *Hurrah !* she has died so young.	*Alas !* she has died so young.
3. *Hark !* what's up over there?	*Behold !* what's up over there?
4. *Woe,* she too has come back.	Lo, she too has come back.
5. *Ah !* how horrible.	*Oh* ! how horrible.
6. *Oh !* so grandly is she dressed.	*Oho !* so grandly is she dressed.
7. *Fie !* a good deed indeed.	*Bravo !* a good deed indeed.
8. *Behold !* what is she saying?	*Hark!* what is she saying?
9. *Oh !* how are you?	*Hello !* how are you?
10. *Uf!* the rogue is coming.	*Hush !* the rogue is coming.
11 *Hi!* untidy ! throw it away.	*Fie !* untidy ! throw it away.
12. *Fie !* Banga is such a mean fellow.	*Pooh !* Banga is such a mean fellow.
13. *Fie!* remove this nauseating object from here.	*Pshaw!* remove this nauseating object from here.
14. *Bravo !* how hot it is !	*Ugh !* how hot it is !
15. *Why !* has he taken to begging?	*What!* has he taken to begging?
16. *Oho !* come over here, Sweety.	*Hi!* come over here, Sweety.
17. *Oh me !* what a nasty deed you have done !	*Ah me!* what a nasty deed you have done !
18. *Welcome !* Rejeshwari has committed suicide.	*For shame!* Rejeshwari has committed suicide.
19. *Farewell!* you've come in time.	*Hail !* you've come in time.
20. *Welcome !* see you !	*Adieu/Farewell!* see you !
21. *Hail* this useless fellow !	*Damn* this useless fellow !
22. *Wonderful* ! you have failed.	*Strange !* you have failed.
23. *Shocking!* my son, you have stood first.	*Well done!* my son, you have stood first.

10

Article

A, An and The are Called Article

Remember that the 'Articles' are virtually 'Demonstrative Adjectives'.

Kinds of Articles

(i) Indefinite Articles
(ii) Definite Article

Indefinite Articles

'A' and *'an'* are termed as 'Indefinite Articles' because they do not hint at any definite person, place or thing.

Uses of A

The Article A is used under the following conditions.

1. I read a book.
2. This is a hat.
3. She lives in a hut.
4. Do you study in a college?
5. A house is to live in.
6. A pen is to write with.
7. I saw a cat and a rat.
8. Seven days make a week.

You have read the above sentences. You must have understood that the Article *'A'* is used before that singular Noun which begins with a consonant and gives the sound of a consonant.

1. I saw a European lady.
2. You must make a united effort.
3. I have bought a uniform.
4. My sister is a university student.

You have read the above sentences. You must have understood that the Article *'A'* is used before that Singular Noun which begins with the vowels 'e' or 'u' but gives the sound of 'y' a consonant.

1. Saroj had a one-rupee note.
2. Sarup was a one-eyed man.
3. This is *a* one-sided game.

You have read the above sentences. You must have understood that the Article 'A' is used before that Singular Noun which begins with the vowel *'O'* but gives the sound of 'w' a consonant.

Important Information about Indefinite Article 'A'

To pinpoint an unknown Noun; as:

1. There was a king in Mathura.
2. A thief broke into our house.

To represent a class/group, etc.

1. A dog is a faithful animal.
2. A junior should obey his senior.

While using a Proper Noun, like an ordinary Adjective; as:

1. Prem Chand is a Kalidas (as able as Kalidas):
2. Dr. Satbir Singh is a Lokman. (as expert as Lokman)

To give understanding of something in Numeral sense; as:

1. Thirty days make a month.
2. He did not speak a word.

To give understanding of similar meaning; as

1. Men of a caste eat together.
2. Birds of a feather flock together.

Uses of 'An'

The Article *'An'* is used under the following conditions.

1. I eat *an* apple every day.
2. Do you take *an* egg at breakfast?
3. I have bought *an* ink-stand.
4. You have eaten *an* Orange.
5. I took *an* umbrella with me.

You have read the above sentences. You must have understood that the Article *'An'* is used before the/that Singular Noun which begins with a vowel (a, e, i, o, *u*) and gives the sound of a vowel.

1. I am *an* M.A.
2. Your brother is *an* M.L.A.
3. Your father is *an* S.H.O. in Haryana.
4. My uncle is *an* F.S.O.
5. You talk like *an* M.P.

You have read the above sentences. You must have understood that the Article 'An' is used before that Singular Noun which begins with a consonant but gives the sound of a vowel.

Remember that this rule is applicable to abbreviated forms alone. This rule does not hold validity before the full forms of the words; as:

1. I am *a* Master of Arts.
2. My brother is *a* Member of Legislative Assembly.
3. Your father is *a* Station House Officer.

4. My uncle is *a* Food and Supply Officer.
5. You talk like *a* Member of Parliament.

Examples:

1. Wait for *an* hour.
2. I saw *an* historical building.
3. I am *an* heir to my father's property.
4. I have sent for *an* operator yesterday.
5. Ranjana is *an* honest girl.

Examples:

1. My son is *an* artist.
2. Are you *an* executor?
3. I have sent for *an* operator.

You have read the above sentences. You must have understood that the Article *'An'* is used before that Singular Noun which begins with a Vowel and gives indication to some profession.

Remember that:

(i) The Article *'A'* is used before the Noun which gives the sound of a consonant, irrespective of the fact that it begins either with a vowel or a consonant.

(ii) The Article *'An'* is used before the Noun which gives the sound of a Vowel, irrespective of the fact that it (the said Noun) begins either with a Vowel or a consonant.

(iii) The Article 'An' is used before the Noun which begins with *'h'* but the 'h' is silent in it.

Definite Articles

'The' is called a 'Definite Article because it hints at a definite person, place or thing (definite Noun).

Uses of The

The Article *'The'* is used under the following conditions.

1. *The* earth is round.

3. *The* stars are twinkling.
2. *The* moon shines at night.
4. *The* sun is hot.
5. *The* sky is cloudy.

The Article *'The'* is used here before the names of stars and constellations.

1. My house faces to the North.
2. He has come from *the* South.
3. The sun rises in *the* East.
4. The sun sets in *the* West.

The Article *'The'* is used here before those *directions* which are preceded by a preposition.

1. I read *the* Gita daily.
2. You buy *the* Hindustan Times.
3. I have arranged for *the* India Today.

The Article *'The'* is used here before the names of *religious books, newspapers,* and *magazines.*

1. *The* cow is a milch-animal.
2. *The* Monkey is a beast of burden.
3. *The* dog is a faithful animal.
4. *The* lion is a beast of prey.
5. *The* owl is an ominous bird.

The Article *'The'* is used here before the Singular Nouns which stand for the whole class.

1. Kashmir is *the* Switzerland of Asia.
2. Bangkok is *the* Venice of the East.
3. Dara Singh was *the* Rustam of India.
4. Kalidas is *the* Shakespeare of India.

The Article *'The'* is used here before the Proper Nouns which serve as Common Nouns.

1. *The* rich are proud.

2. *The* poor are honest.
3. *The* brave never fear.
4. *The* shirkers seldom succeed.
5. *The* dishonest suffer in the end.

The Article *'The'* is used here before the adjectives which have been used as Nouns.

1. Bananas are sold by *the* dozen.
2. Ghee is sold by *the* litre.
3. Cloth is sold by *the* metre.

The Article *'The'* is used here before quantitative words showing manner.

1. *The* second boy is my brother.
2. *The* first girl is smart.
3. *The* fourth boy is the loser.
4. *The* third man in the queue is my uncle.

The Article *'The'* is used here before Cardinal Numbers.

1. My sister was born on *the* 8th instant.
2. India got freedom on *the* 15th of August.
3. The School will remain closed on *the* last day of the month.

The Article *'The'* is used here before the date-denoting words.

1. I get up in *the* morning.
2. See me in *the* afternoon evening.
3. I shall return home in *the* afternoon.

The Article *'The'* is used here before the time-denoting words *'evening, morning, afternoon'* (divisions of the day)

1. I returned home last night.
2. I saw him next afternoon.
3. I worship God every evening.

You have read the above sentences. You must have

understood that the Article *'the'* is not used if the words *last, next* or *every* are followed by the words *'evening, morning, afternoon,* etc.

1. Abhay is *the* meanest person on earth.
2. Neelam is *the* prettiest girl in our school.
3. Saurabh is *the* cleverest boy in our street.

The Article *'The'* is used here before Superlative Degrees.

1. Sarla is *the* taller of the two.
2. Manoj is *the* happier of the two.
3. Yash Pal is *the* braver of the two.

The Article *'The'* is used here before such Comparative Degrees as do not have *than* after them.

1. *The* whole colony was irritated.
2. *The* same girl is teasing you.
3. All *the* people are taking tea.
4. Both *the* neighbours are friendly to each other.

You have read the above sentences. It must have become clear to you that the Article *'The'* is used before *'whole* and *same'* (*the whole, the same*) but after *'all* and *both'* (*all the, both the*).

1. *The* Prime Minister of India has a good personality.
2. Shri R. K. Narayanan is *the* ex-President of India.
3. *The* Principal of our school is very strict.

The Article *'The'* is used here before the names of high ranks.

1. Alexander *the* Great believed in speed.
2. Ashoka *the* Great banned the killing of animals.
3. Akbar *the* Great got trees planted on both sides of the roads.

The Article *'The'* is used here before that adjective which succeeds a Noun.

1. *The* Sharmas are very nice people.

2. Beware of *the* Bawariyas.
3. *The* Guptas are usually rich.

The Article *'The'* is used here for the formation of plurals of the Proper Nouns.

1. *The* Mutiny of 1857 shook the Britishers.
2. *The* Battle of Panipat is a memorable event.

The Article *'The'* is used here before the incidents.

1. *The* little Shalini is an outspoken girl.
2. *The* strong Kailash is kind.

The Article *'The'* is used here before Adjectives + Proper Nouns.

1. *The* Congress is a well-knit party.
2. *The* Bhartiya Janata Party is the ruling party in Delhi.
3. *The* Lok Dal is a popular party.

The Article *'The'* is used here before the names of political parties and organisations.

1. *The* workers of the Delhi Cloth Mills are on strike.
2. *The* State Bank of India is a leading bank.
3. *The* Gulati Automobiles remains closed on Monday.
4. Days Nand worked in *the* Alloys and Founderies Works.

The Article *'The'* is used here before the names of Factories, Workshops, Banks, etc.

1. *The* Taj Mahal is located at Agra.
2. *The* Golden Temple is a Gurudwara.
3. The Delhi Public Library is near the Red Fort.
4. Have you ever seen *the* Zoo in Delhi?

The Article *'The'* is used here before the names of Public places and historical buildings.

1. There was a dog. *The* dog was tame.
2. There was a woman. *The* woman was lame.
3. There was a king. *The* king was noble.

The Article *'The'* is used here before those Common Nouns which have been mentioned before and are known already.

1. *The* English ruled in India.
2. *The* French had great respect for Napoleon.
3. *The* Hindus worship Lord Vishnu.

The Article *'The'* is used here before the names of Nations, Communities, etc.

1. *The* U.S.A. is the richest country in the world.
2. Chandigarh is the Capital of *the* Punjab.

The Article *'The'* is used here before the names of certain Countries and Provinces/states.

1. I went to Agra by *the* Taj Express.
2. We travel by *the* D.T.C. bus in Delhi.
3. *The* Himalayas are the highest mountains in India.

The Article *'The'* is used here before the names of *trains, buses, mountains,* etc.

Remember that the Article *'The'* is also used before names of *Canals, islands, lakes, ships, aeroplanes, dams, deserts, oceans, seas, etc.; as:*

The Panama Canal; *the* Andaman and Nicobar Islands; *the* Dal Lake; *the* Vikrant; *the* Bhakra Dam; *the* Sahara Desert, *the* Indian Ocean; *the* Mediterranean Sea.

Miscellaneous Exercise for Recapitulation

Model Sentences

The man you saw here yesterday is an uncle of mine.

The more money one has, the more he wants.

Morning walk is a tonic for the weak.

Who are the men standing there in the street?

Smt. Kamini Sharma is an M.A., B.Ed.

I shall finish this work in an hour and a half.

Milk is a healthy drink for the children.

I visited the village where I was born.

He is neither an honest nor an earnest man.

The sun rises in the east and sets in the west.

I struck him on the head with a hammer.

My father is an engineer and my mother is a teacher.

I bought an H.M.T. watch yesterday.

My father is an N.C.C. officer.

What is the time by your watch?

He is a dishonest boy but his sister is an honest girl.

His father is an Indian but his mother is a European.

He is a one-eyed man.

I bought a pencil and an eraser.

I have lodged an F.I.R. with the police about the theft of my bicycle.

He is a B.A. but his sister is an M.A.

Many a flower is born to fade unseen.

Manorama lost the book that I had presented her.

Madhu is the most intelligent girl in our class.

Diwali is an important festival of the Hindus.

An umbrella is a useful thing.

The tallest man is an engineer.

Leaving the battlefield, the soldier hid himself in a cave.

The Ganges rises from the Himalayas.

I came across a European lady on the way.

Do you not know the girl who had stood first in the examination?

She is an Asian by birth but a European by breed.

The cow is a useful animal.

This is the best film I have seen.

The rich should help the poor.

This is the same person I met.

The more you read, the better marks you will secure.

March is the third month of the year.

Surendra was the Rustam of his time.

He defeated the devil, (situated) within him.

Omission of the Article

The article (A/An/The) is not used under the following conditions and situations.

1. Sheela is the monitor of our class.
2. Perseverance is a virtue.
3. Coal is not found in Delhi.

In the above sentences, no article has been used before Sheela (Proper Noun), Perseverance (Abstract Noun) and Coal (Material Noun) because they have been used in their general sense.

Remember that the Article 'The' is used when the uncountable Nouns (Proper Noun), Material Nouns and Abstract Nouns have been specified; as:

1. Nishant is *the* Dara Singh of our class.
2. *The* Coal of Jharkhand is not inferior to that of Haryana.
3. *The* grace of the girl is praiseworthy.

Examples:

1. Children like sweets.
2. Babies like dolls.
3. Boys like girls.

In the above sentences, children, babies and boys are Common Nouns and Plural Number. No article is used after them.

Remember that the Article 'The' is used before Common Nouns and Plural Numbers in case they are specified by a phrase.

1. *Animals* too are like human beings.
2. *Snakes* should also be protected.
3. *Man* is a social animal.

In the above sentences, *Animals, snakes* and *man* are Common Nouns. They have been used in a broad sense. No article is used after them.

1. Boys, keep quiet.
2. Girls, sit properly.
3. Children, keep to the left.

You have read the above sentences. You must have understood that no article is used before Common Nouns used in Vocative Case.

1. What type of woman is she?
2. What kind of girl are you?
3. What sort of boy is he?

The words *'type of, kind of, sort of'*, have been used in the above sentences. No article is used after these words.

1. Both minors and majors are free.
2. Both husband and wife are stupid.
3. Both son and daughter are equal.

'Common Nouns' have been used in pairs in the above sentences. No article is used after them.

1. We elected him secretary.
2. She was appointed prefect.

The words *'secretary* and *prefect'* are used as complements in the sentences. No article is used after them.

1. Rajiv Gandhi, ex-Prime Minister of India is no more.
2. Zakir Hussain, President of India was the Vice Chancellor of Jamia Millia University.

'A rank' has been used *in apposition to* the Proper Noun in each of the above sentences. No article is used after them.

1. Water of Lake Sambhar is saltish.
2. England is a cultured country.
3. Europe is a continent.
4. Mathura is a city.
5. Monday comes after Sunday.
6. April is fourth month of the year.

No article has been used in the beginning of the above sentences. This makes it clear that no article is used before the names of *lakes, capes, countries, continents, cities, days, months and languages,* etc.

Remember that:

To go to school	—	for studying.
To go to the school	—	for any other purpose.
To go to play	—	for games.
To go to the play	—	for witnessing a drama.
To go to Church	—	for praying to God.
To go to the Church	—	for any other purpose.
To go to sea	—	as a sailor.
To go to the sea	—	on a voyage.
To go to prison	—	as a prisoner.
To go to the prison	—	on a visit.
To leave school	—	to stop being a student.
To leave the school	—	to go away from the premises of the school.

Common Errors in the Use of Articles

Incorrect	*Correct*
1. Ramayana is a sacred book of Hindus.	The Ramayana is a sacred book of the Hindus.
2. The gold is a precious metal.	Gold is a precious metal.

Contd...

	Incorrect	*Correct*
3.	I caught him by neck.	I caught him by the neck.
4.	Cloth is sold by metre.	Cloth is sold by the metre.
5.	Deccan is drier than Delhi.	The Deccan is drier than Delhi.
6.	It is quarter to eight.	It is a quarter to eight.
7.	Sun rises in East.	The sun rises in the East.
8.	This is a news to me.	This is news to me.
9.	Ganges is a sacred river.	The Ganges is a sacred river.
10.	I read *Hindustan Times* daily.	I read the *Hindustan Times* daily.
11.	Why are you making noise?	Why are you making a noise?
12.	She has headache.	She has a headache.
13.	His mother is an European.	His mother is a European.
14.	Lion is a king of beasts.	The lion is the king of the beasts.
15.	This bicycle cost me thousand rupees.	This bicycle cost me a thousand rupees.

11

Determiners

The fixing words which sound a warning that some noun is about to be used are classed (termed) as 'Determiners'. They (the Determiners) modify the succeeding noun in some form or the other.

Read the following sentences:

1. *This* banana is ripe.
2. She wants to be *a* nurse.
3. She has *no* knowledge.
4. Have you got *any* drama of Kalidas?
5. *Some* boys did not get sweets.
6. This is *my* book.

The italicised words *(this, a, no, any, some, my)* in the above sentences are 'Determiners' because they point towards their succeeding nouns in one form or the other or modify it.

Kinds of Determiners

(i) Article Determiners

(ii) Demonstrative Determiners

(iii) Possessive Determiners

(iv) Numeral Determiners

(v) Quantitative Determiners

Article Determiners: They are of the following two types :

Indefinite Articles—A and An

Examples:

1. I have *a* book.
2. *A* cow is grazing.
3. He is *a* B.A.
4. This is *a* useful book.
5. The Taj is *a* unique building.
6. I saw *a* European girl today.
7. Give me *a* one-rupee note.

You have read the above sentences. You must have understood that the Indefinite Article *'A'* is used before the singular noun beginning with a consonant. Those singular nouns are also included in this category which begin with a vowel but give the sound of a consonant.

Examples:

1. I saw *an* ox.
2. He ate *an* apple.
3. Do not touch *an* egg.
4. I shall return in *an* hour.
5. I am *an* S.D.O.
6. He is *an* L.L.B.
7. You are *an* honest man.

You have read the above sentences. You must have understood that the Indefinite Article *'An'* is used before the singular noun beginning with the sound of a vowel. Those singular nouns are also included in this category which begin with a consonant but give the sound of a vowel.

Definite Article—The

Examples:

1. I like *the* guavas of Allahabad.
2. *The* sun is hot.
3. I read *the* Ramayana every day.
4. *The* Hindus go to temples.
5. *The* lion is fearful.
6. There was a crow. *The* crow was cunning.
7. *The* little Dhruvika is a shy girl.

8. *The* Sharmas are gentle people.
9. See me in *the* morning.
10. Who is *the* Prime Minister of India?

You have read the above sentences. You must have understood that the Definite Article *'The'* is used both before the singular and plural nouns.

The Article *'The'* can be used before a noun irrespective of the fact that it begins either with a vowel or a consonant.

Leaving aside the situations where (i) No article is used or (ii) Either of *'A'* or *'An'* is used—*'The'* is used at all places and in all situations.

The Article *'The'* is used before specific and unique nouns.

Demonstrative Determiners

Examples:

1. I like *this* baby.
2. *These* chairs are ours.
3. *That* house is Ramoo's.
4. *These* toys are mine.

The italicised words *(this, these, that, those)* are 'Demonstrative Determiners'. In spite of being used before nouns, they point to the objects specified by them and also modify them.

Remember that:

(1) *This* and *That* are singular.
(2) *These* and *Those* are plural.
(3) *This* and *These* point towards nearby nouns.
(4) *That* and *Those* point towards distant nouns.

Sometimes the above demonstrative adjectives/ determiners are also used without giving an indication of nearness or remoteness; as:

1. *This* is the book which *that* girl presented me.
2. *This* planet is Jupiter.
3. *This* one is Venus.

In the above sentences, the speaker keeps in mind the nearness or remoteness of the object.

Possessive Determiners

Examples:

1. *Your* mother is old.
2. *Our* school is reputed.
3. *My* father is a teacher.
4. *Her* purse is lost.
5. *Its* title page is missing.
6. *Their* books are torn.
7. One should do *one's* duty.

The italicised words (*your, our, my, her, its, their, and one's*) are Possessive Determiners in the above sentences. They are the possessive forms of pronouns. They are used both before singular and plural nouns. They show their relations with their succeeding nouns.

Numeral Determiners

They are of the following three kinds:

1. Definite Numerals.
2. Indefinite Numerals.
3. Distributive Numerals.

Definite Numerals; as:

1. *Fifty* boys are playing.
2. *Ten* girls are running.
3. The *second* boy in the *third* row is my brother.
4. *Both* Rajni and Sushma are present today.

The italicised words (*fifty, ten, second, third, and both*) are definite numerals in the above sentences because they give indication of a definite number.

Indefinite Numerals; as:

1. There are *some* girls in the classroom.
2. *Many* boys have appeared at the test.
3. *Many a* girl has passed.
4. I have bought *few* toys.
5. I have bought a *few* toys.
6. I have lost the *few* toys I had.
7. She gave me *all* the books.
8. She has arrived here after *several* months.

Remember that:

1. Some means 'a certain' amount of something. However, it does not show a specified amount. It is used in affirmative sentences and in questions expecting a positive reply. It is also used with plural Countable Nouns usually referring to three or more (a certain number). It is also used before/with approximate number. It expresses a negative opinion, admiration or approval when used before countable and uncountable nouns.

   It also means a large amount or certain number of something. It means 'a few' when it is used before a Countable Noun.
2. Many means 'a large number of people or things'. A Countable Noun and plural number is used after it.
3. Many a means a large number of people or things. It is used before a singular Countable Noun and a singular verb.
4. Few means 'a too small or negligible number'. It (*few*) is the antonym of many.
5. A Few 'a small number'. It (A few) is the antonym of *none* and synonym of some.
6. The Few means a small but the whole number.

7. All means the whole or entire number.
8. Several means more than three, (some) but fewer than *many*.

Distributive Numerals; as:

1. *Each* boy must bring the book.
2. *Every* girl works hard.
3. *Either* drink (tea/coffee) will do.
4. *Neither* girl (Bimla/Karuna) is smart.

Remember that:

1. Each means 'every individual number out of two or more countable numbers, considered separately'.
2. Every means 'all'. It points to all the nouns collectively out of a large and indefinite number.
3. Either means 'one of the two'. Sometimes it also means 'both of the two'.
4. Neither means 'No one out of the two'.

Quantitative Determiners

Read the following sentences:

1. There wasn't *any* girl in the class. (Negative)
2. Didn't you send her *any* present? (Interrogative)
3. If there is *any* problem, come to me. (Doubt)
4. She has hardly *any* sense. (After...Hardly)

You have read the above sentences. You must have understood that *'Any'* is used both before negative and interrogative sentences. Any means *'several* or *some'*.

5. There is *no* charm on her face.
6. He has *no* friends.

No means *'not at all; not a little; not any; not a; not one iota/ particle; zero in number or quantity'*.

7. Will you give me *more* sweets?
8. I do not need *more* money.

9. I shall buy *more* books.

   More means *'greater or additional number or amount'*.

10. There is *much* tea in the kettle.
11. You need *much* scolding.
12. He does not have *much* wisdom.
13. She has *much* to do yet.

    Much means *'to a great extent or degree'*.

14. You have advised her *many* times.
15. She has *many* frocks.
16. You have made *many* efforts.
17. I have *many* relatives.

    Many means *'a large number'*.

Remember that:

Much shows *'a great extent or degree'* whereas Many shows *'a large number'*.

18. *Some* of you were absent yesterday.
19. *Some* girls are very wise.
20. There is *some* money in my purse.
21. Do you need *some* money?

    Some means *'a certain but small amount'* (*number or quantity*) of something. It is used in the form of adjectives of quality with Uncountable Nouns.

22. Sushma devotes *less* time to her children.
23. As he knew the route, he had *less* trouble.
24. I have *lesser* friends now than I had before.

    Less means *'a smaller number, degree or small quantity'*. It (*less*) is the antonym of *Much* (a larger degree).

25. You have *little* control on your son.

    Little means *'negligible; not much , only slightly, not enough'*. It is used with Uncountable Nouns.

26. *A little* knowledge is a dangerous thing.

    A little means *'not much, a bit less than the required quantity, not adequate, insufficient'*.

27. The *little* experience of swimming saved my life.

28. She has spent the *little* money she had.

    The little means not *much but the whole quantity*.

Common Errors in the Use of Determiners

	Incorrect	*Correct*
1.	English is a language of English.	English is the language of the English.
2.	He gave me any money.	He gave me some money.
3.	Much girls are playing there.	Some/Many girls are playing there.
4.	He does not have some money.	He does not have any money.
5.	She has hardly much money.	She has hardly any money.
6.	Many a men enjoyed the show.	A great many men enjoyed the show. Or Many a man enjoyed the show.
7.	He is a man of much words.	He is a man of few words.
8.	I shall return your money in some days.	I shall return your money in a few days.
9.	I have spent the few money I had.	I have spent the little money I had.
10.	She asked me for any money but I didn't have some.	She asked me for some money but I didn't have any.
11.	How much eggs can you eat at the time?	How many eggs can you eat at a time?
12.	I cannot eat some at dinner.	I cannot eat much at dinner.
13.	Her father has sent her much presents.	Her father has sent her some/many/ a few presents.
14.	Many a little make a mickle.	Many a little makes a mickle.
15.	This book is my.	This book is mine.
16.	How many milk will be needed tomorrow?	How much milk will be needed tomorrow?
17.	Can you give me few money?	Can you give me some money?
18.	Let me thank you in few words.	Let me thank you in a few words.

Contd...

	Incorrect	*Correct*
19.	He did not make some mistakes in his essay.	He did not make any mistakes in his essay.
20.	Do you want any much tea?	Do you want some more tea?
21.	She gave me several advice.	She gave me much advice.
22.	He has usually any money.	He has hardly any money.
23.	Each man is subject to death.	Every man is subject to death.
24.	Every boy of my group sang a song.	Each boy of my group sang a song.
25.	Many a students have failed.	Many a student has failed.
26.	She has fifth sons.	She has five sons.
27.	Both of Ram and Shyam is absent.	Both (of) Ram and Shyam are absent.
28.	I have read few books.	I have read a few books.
29.	The all countries are preparing for war.	All the countries are preparing for war.
30.	There is any truth in what he says.	There is no truth in what he says.
31.	Will you give me much money?	Will you give me more money?
32.	There is the little hope of her success.	There is little hope of her success.
33.	I have warned you much times.	I have warned you many times (many a time).

12

Modals

Basic information about Modals has already been given in the Chapter-Verbs.

The helping verbs which show the mode or attitude of the main verb are called Modals.

Use of Modals

Can

Examples:

1. She *can* teach you if she likes. (*capability* or *strength*)
2. He *can* cheat you. (*nature*)
3. I *can* cross the river. (*ability/skill*)
4. You *can* go home now. (*permission*)
5. Your team *can* use our playground for the match. (*permission*)
6. Accidents *can* happen at any time on G.T. Road. (*probability*)
7. Any one *can't* do these sums. (*incompetence* or *improbability*)
8. You *can't* teach English. (*inefficiency/unability*)

You have read the above sentences. You must have

understood that the Modal *'can'* is used to show *capability, strength, nature, ability, skill, permission, probability, etc.*

The negative of *can* is *cannot* or *can't.*

Cannot (*Can't*) shows *incompetency, improbability, inefficiency* or *unability.* In other words it (*cannot/can't*) *shows lack/absence of capability, strength, nature, ability, skill, permission, probability,* etc.

Note that 'cannot' is written as one word. To write 'can' and 'not' as separate words is wrong according to the traditional grammarians.

Could

Examples:

1. My mother *could* do whatever she wanted to do. (*permission/freedom/determination*)
2. He asked me if I *could* lend him some money. (*capability/strength*)
3. She *could* sing well if she desired. (*ability*)
4. If he had saved enough money he *could* purchase a house. (*capacity and probability*)
5. *Could* you tell me the time? (*polite request*)
6. *Couldn't* he wait for a few minutes more? (*mild annoyance/request*)

You have read the above sentences. You must have understood that the modal *'Could'* is used to show *capacity, probability, polite request, mild annoyance, request,* etc.

The negative of *Could* is *Could not* or *Couldn't.*

Remember that:

Could is the Past form of Can. Therefore, Could shows both the past time and present time situations.

1. I am sorry I *could* not ring you five minutes earlier.

   Here the time, five minutes earlier, can be taken either as past or as present time.

2. *Could* I help you in lifting the load?

   It means 'should I help you in lifting the load'? It shows present time situation.

May

Examples:

1. You *may* use my pen. (*desire/permission*)
2. *May* I have your scooter?

   (*request/desire to seek permission*)
3. She *may* stand first in her class. (*probability*)
4. It *may* rain tonight. (*likelihood/probability*)
5. *May* she have a son! (*keen desire*)
6. I eat so that I *may* remain fit. (*aim/objective*)
7. *May* she get a good partner! (*desire/request*)
8. He *may* not attend my birthday party.

   (*lack of probability*)

You have read the above sentences. You must have understood that the modal *'May'* is used to show *desire, permission, request, probability, likelihood, aim/objective. May not* shows *lack of probability.*

The negative of May is May not or Mayn't.

Might

Examples:

1. She thought that she *might* return home in time.

   (*probability*)
2. *Might* I use your scooter?

   (*excessive modesty/humility*)
3. She *might* have finished her breakfast. (*guess*)
4. He ran fast so that he *might* reach school in time.

   (*purpose*)

5. He has not promised, but he *might* lend me money.

(*doubtful probability in future*)

6. The referee said that we *might* play the match.

(*permission*)

You have read the above sentences. You must have understood that the modal *'Might'* is used to show *probability, excessive modesty/humility, guess, purpose, doubtful probability in future, permission,* etc.

Remember that:

Might is the past form of *May.* Therefore, *Might* shows both the past time and present time situations. *Might* I use your phone?

Here desire is expressed and permission is sought to use the phone. The negative of *Might* is *Might not.*

Shall

Examples:

1. I *shall* take part in the tournament next week.

(*Simple Future*)

2. We *shall* serve our country. (*Simple Future*)
3. *Shall* I visit your house? (to know the *desire of the hearer*)
4. *Shall* we prepare coffee for you?

(to know the *desire of the hearer*)

5. She *shall* get a saree if she stands first. (*Shows promise*)
6. You *shall* be expelled from school for your misbehaviour. (*threat/warning*)
7. I say you *shall* post this letter. (*order*)
8. *Shall* we have some rest now?

(*suggestion/proposal*)

9. We *shall* accept your present. (*desire*)
10. I *shall* buy the blankets. (*intention* or *planning*)

You have read the above sentences. You must have understood that the modal *'Shall'* is used to show *promise, threat/warning, order, suggestion/ proposal, desire, intention* or *planning.*

Shall is also used with first Person Pronouns (I, we) to show future (time) intention, programme or reference.

Will

Examples:

1. We *will* go for a picnic next week. (Simple Future)
2. I *will* help the poor lady with money. (Simple Future)
3. *Will* you take your seat, please? (*humble request*)
4. He *will* often burn midnight oil. (*routine*)
5. If you insult your parents, you *will* be ruined. (*forewarning*)
6. We *will* not yield before any pressure. (*firm determination*)
7. After reaching Madurai, we *will see* the Meenakshi temple. (*speaker's keen desire*)
8. I *will* repay your loan next month. (*promise*)
9. We *will* help Sushma as far as possible. (*proposal/ardent desire*)
10. You *will* be honest in future. (*order/instruction/warning*)
11. This bag *will* hold all the books. (*capacity*)
12. The machine *will* do all types of calculations. (*quality*)
13. I *will* teach her a lesson. (*threat*)

You have read the above sentences. You must have understood that the Modal *'Will'* is used to show *humble request, routine, forewarning, firm determination, speaker's keen desire, promise, proposal / ardent desire, order/ instruction/warning, capacity, quality and threat.* Will is also used with First person Pronouns to show determination.

Would

Examples:

1. She said that she *would* help me in my need. (Past Tense of *Will*)
2. *Would* you please post this letter for me?
3. My mother *would* go to the temple every morning. (*Humble request/Routine*)
4. *Would* you like to stay with me tonight? (to know *hearer's intention*)
5. Our scooter *wouldn't* start, therefore, we reached the office by bus. (*failure of an activity*)
6. *Would* that I were the Prime Minister of the country! (*Improbable situation*)
7. I *would* like to give you some trouble. (*Desire*)
8. I *would* rather quit than submit to undue pressure. (*Preference*)
9. *Would* you mind giving me a lift in your car? (to *know intention*)

You have read the above sentences. You must have understood that the modal *'Would'* is used to show *humble request, routine, intention, failure of an activity, improbable situation, desire, preference*, etc.

'Would' is also used as the past tense of *Will*.

Should

Examples:

1. She said that I *should* not bother her. (*Past form of will/shall*)
2. The teacher *should* show good result. (*Duty*)
3. You *should* keep your word. (*obligation*)
4. She *should* serve her mother-in-law. (*Advice*)
5. You *should* engage a tutor for your son. (*Suggestion*)

6. *Should* you go to the post office, bring me some post cards. (*Imagination*)
7. *Should* I speak to Rajni? (*Desire*)
8. You *should* see a doctor at once. (*Opinion*)
9. *Should* she come here, we shall protect her. (*Probability*)
10. Fatimah *should* be here by now. (*Guess*)

You have read the above sentences. You must have understood that the Modal *'Should'* is used to show *duty, obligation, advice, suggestion, imagination, desire, opinion, probability and guess.*

Should is also used as the Past Tense of *Will/Shall.*

Must

Examples:

1. You *must* return my book at once. (*Obligation*)
2. I *must* buy a wrist-watch because I get late everyday. (*Compulsion*)
3. You *must* teach her a lesson. (*Necessity*)
4. Everyone *must* follow the traffic rules. (*Necessity/compulsion*)
5. The bride *must* serve her aged mother-in-law. (*Sincere advice*)
6. You *must* appear at the test. (*Necessity*)
7. She *must* reach her school in time daily. (*Advice*)
8. The old lady *must* be around seventy. (*Guess*)
9. My uncle *must* have reached home by now. (*Probability*)
10. There is a heavy downpour; you *must* take your umbrella with you. (*logical necessity*)
11. She caught a thief. She *must* have been very brave. (*Guess about past activity*)
12. You must not (*mustn't*) go out in the dark. (*Denial/Restriction/Advice*)

You have read the above sentences. You must have understood that the modal *'Must'* is used to show *obligation, compulsion, necessity, sincere advice, guess, probability, logical necessity, guess about past activity, denial/restriction,* etc.

Ought

Examples:

1. The students *ought* to respect their teacher. (*Duty*)
2. We *ought* to serve our old parents. (*Social bondage*)
3. We *ought* to do our duty. (*Moral duty/obligation*)
4. You *ought* to join some tutorial group. (*Suggestion*)
5. Anuradha *ought* to be here by now. (*Guess*)
6. She has burnt midnight oil. She *ought* to score a high percentage of marks. (*Strong probability*)
7. You *ought* to have obeyed your father. (*Neglectful conduct*)

You have read the above sentences. You must have understood that the *modal 'Ought' is used to show duty, social bondage, moral duty/obligation, suggestion, guess, strong probability, neglectful attitude, etc.*

Remember that:

Ought to = should

Oughtn't is the negative of Ought.

Oughtn't we respect our elders?

Need

Examples:

1. I *need* money. (*Present*)
2. You *needed* my help. (*Past*)
3. You will *need* these books. (*Future*)
4. She does not *need* woollen clothes. (*Negative*)

In the above sentences, *need* has been used as Principal

Verb. Here *need* means to *feel* the *necessity for. Need* can be conjugated as:

Need (Present), Needed (Past), Needed (Past Participle) and Needing (Present Participle).

Use of 'Need' as Modal

Examples:

1. You *need not* wait for him. (*Absence of necessity*)
2. What *need* you go to her house? (*necessity*)
3. She *need* not go to school on Sundays. (*Absence of necessity/Negation*)
4. *Need* she serve you a cup of hot tea? (*Interrogation*)

You have read the above sentences. You must have understood that the modal *'Need'* is used to show *absence of necessity, necessity, negation* and *interrogation.*

Needn't is the negative of Need.

Need does not have a past form when used as Modal Auxiliary.

Need is invariably used in the Present Tense. The infinitive, without 'to' is used as its object.

Needn't + Perfect Infinitive (needn't + have + V^3) is used in expressing the unnecessary activities which have been done by mistake; as:

You *needn't* have given her your shawl because she has many shawls.

This means 'You made a mistake in giving her your shawl'.

Dare

Examples:

1. I *dare* say that Kailash is a mean fellow.
2. The child *dares* to go in the dark.
3. She *dared* to risk her life.

In the above sentences, *dare* has been used as a Principal Verb. It means *'Misadventure/negative courage/undesired courage'*.

Dare can be conjugated as

Dare (Present), Dared (Past), Dared (Past Participle), and Daring (Present Participle)

The infinitive 'to' is normally used with *'Dare'*.

Uses of 'Dare' as Modal

Examples:

1. *Dare* he say so? (*Interrogative misadventure*)
2. *Dare* they speak against you?(*Interrogative Misadventure*)
3. *Dare* you step in her room? (*Interrogative misadventure*)
4. You *daren't* meet me after school hours. (*Negative misadventure*)
5. She *daren't* help you against the police. (*Negative misadventure*)

You have read the above sentences. You must have understood that the modal *'Dare'* is used to show *challenge* or *misadventure*. It (*Dare*) is used in negative as well as interrogative sentences.

'Dare' is also used in prohibitory sentences.

Examples:

You *dare* not abuse your seniors.

As a 'Defective verb—*Dare*' is used only in prohibitory and interrogative sentences.

Dare as a defective verb can be conjugated as Dare (Present), Durst/Dared (Past and Past Participle).

The infinitive 'to' is not used in such sentences, as:

1. You *dare* not say so. (*Present*)
2. How *dare* you call her names? (*Present-Interrogative*)
3. She *dare* not oppose her husband. (*Past*)
4. How *dare* she open my box? (*Past-Interrogative*)

Remember that:

'Dare' is an odd type of Verb. As a matter of principle, the infinitive with 'to' is used with *do/did* in the negative and interrogative forms of *'Dare'* but 'to' is generally elided (dropped) in usage; as:

1. Did he *dare* (to) oppose my proposal?
2. How does he *dare* (to) criticize what I said?
3. He *dared* not (to) speak a word against the decision.

'Used To'

Examples:

1. I *used to* bathe in the river. (*but don't*) (*Past Habit*)
2. He *used to* drink before going to bed daily. (*old/Past Habit*)*-now given up*)
3. She *used not to* disobey her husband. (*negative*)

   In the above sentences, *used to* has been used to show old habit (in or out of practice at the time of speakings).

'Used to' does not have the Present Tense Form. It is invariably used in the Past.

Also read the following sentences:

1. I am not *used to* such treatment.
2. She got *used to* drinking.
3. I am *used to* a life of struggle.
4. Mind it. I am not *used to* this kind of silly behaviour.
5. I am not *used to* going out in the dark.

In the above sentences *'Used to'* means 'accustomed to'. Some form of *be/seem/get/become* is used before *'used to'* in such sentences.

More/Further Information about Modals.

1. *Can, could, may, might, shall, will, would, should, must, ought (to), need, dare* and *used* to are called Modals or Modal Auxiliaries.

2. Specific Qualities of Modals: Modals show *willingness, advice, promise, determination, threat, supposition, inference, duty, obligation, request, possibility, permission, suggestion, instruction, power, capability, ability,* etc.
3. Modals are never used alone. They are always used with such words as are applied (clear) or implied (understood).
4. Modals are not governed by the number, gender and person of the subject. In other words, no change takes place (is effected) in their basic (genuine) form. They always remain unchanged (alike).
5. Only the First/Crude form of Verb (V^1) is used with the Modals. The Infinitive, without 'to' is used with them. The Infinitive 'to' is used only with the Modals—*used* (*used to*) and *ought* (*ought to*).

Miscellaneous Exercise 1 (For Recapitulation)

Uses of 'shall', 'will', 'should', 'ought to' and 'would'.

Model Sentences

I *shall* reach Jaipur on Sunday morning.

We *shall* finish this work tomorrow.

Shall I make a cup of tea for you?

Shall we not go out and sit in the garden?

We *shall* arrange a meeting next month.

She *will* accept (comply with) my request.

You *will* come to see us now and then.

Will she stay here tonight?

This basket *will* hold all the apples.

Will you take your seat, please?

You *will* get ill if you eat stale food.

Kamla *will* be twelve on her next birthday.

We *should* always speak the truth.

Should you not keep your word?

Work hard lest you *should* fail.

You *should/ought* to learn the poem.

He/She *should/ought* to serve his/her country.

Should you go there, convey my message to them.

She *would* swim in the tank for hours.

Would you please lend me your book?

Miscellaneous Exercise 2 (For Recapitulation)

Uses of May', Might', Can', Could'

Model Sentences

We eat that we *may* live.

It *may* rain tonight.

This medicine *may* cure your cough.

She *may* or *may not* come.

May she never fail in life!

She *might* have lost her purse.

The patient *might* recover soon.

Might I use your scooter for a week?

She thought that I *might* buy her a gold ring.

She asked if he *might* help her.

You *cannot* drive a motor car.

You *can* go home now.

Accidents *can* take place at any time on this busy road.

Anyone *can* make mistakes.

Can't you sit properly?

Could you tell me the time?

If I had the money, I *could* buy that car.

She *couldn't* win the first prize.

Sorry. I *couldn't* inform you duly.

We *could* reach there with much difficulty.

Miscellaneous Exercise 3 (For Recapitulation)

Uses of 'Must', 'Need', Dare', 'Used to'

Model Sentences

You *must* obey your parents and teachers.

You *must* not waste your money.

You *must* return immediately.

You *must* leave the room at once.

You *must* apologise for your rude behaviour.

Children *must* not play in this garden.

You *need* not worry about me.

Need I go there and talk to them?

Need I bring all my certificates with me?

You *needn't* repay my loan this month.

You *dare* not challenge your officers.

Dare you climb up that tree?

I wonder how he *dare* come here!

How *dare* he enter my room without my permission.

Why *daren't* you speak to him/her?

She *used to* visit our house every week.

She *usedn't to* speak the truth.

Used he *to* smoke in childhood?

I *used* to study day and night in my student life.

He *used* to wander here and there ten years ago.

Common Errors in the use of Modals

Incorrect	*Correct*
1. Shanti *should* lift the box by herself.	Shanti *can* lift the box by herself.
2. They *may* play football very well.	They *can* play football very well.
3. He *could* swim upstream though he is bulky.	He *can* swim upstream though he is bulky.
4. *Would* you call back tomorrow?	*Can* you call back tomorrow?
5. She is well read. She *might* speak in English fluently.	She is well read. She *can* speak in English fluently.
6. She *would* do as she likes.	She *can* do as she likes.
7. You *may* not keep a gun without a valid licence.	You *cannot* keep a gun without a valid licence.
8. *Should* the news of her failure be true?	*Can* the news of her failure be true?
9. I *can* speak Sanskrit when I was ten years old.	I *could* speak Sanskrit when I was ten years old.
10. She *should* not buy a dictionary for want of money.	She *could* not buy a dictionary for want of money.
11. *Must* I use your phone for a week?	*Could* I use your phone for a week?
12. *Would* you come tomorrow and have breakfast with me?	*Could* you come tomorrow and have breakfast with me?
13. *May* I have four tickets please?	*Could* I have four tickets please?
14. She *can* be successful if she had tried hard.	She *could* be successful if she had tried hard.
15. *Would* you peel these apples for me?	*Could* you peel these apples for me?
16. She told me that she *can* read very fast.	She told me that she *could* read very fast.
17. *Should* I have a smoke here?	*May* I have a smoke here?
18. *Could* I know what she wants?	*May* I know what she wants?
19. *Can* I come in, sir?	*May* I come in, sir?
20. You *would* ask for anything you want?	You *may* ask for anything you want.
21. She *should* see me if she wishes.	She *may* see me if she wishes.

Contd...

Incorrect	Correct
22. *Would* you succeed in life!	*May* you succeed in life!
23. She *would* (perhaps) be able to remember what you said.	She *might* (perhaps) be able to remember what you said.
24. She is gasping for breath. She *could* have come running.	She is gasping for breath. She *might* have come running.
25. *Can* I have a word with you?	*Might* I have a word with you?
26. You *would* like to comment on the latest fashions.	You *might* like to comment on the latest fashions.
27. We *will* leave for Mathura tomorrow.	We *shall* leave for Mathura tomorrow.
28. Let us go, *will* we?	Let us go, *shall* we?
29. *Would* we take a taxi.	*Shall* we take a taxi?
30. *Will* I bring you a cup of milk?	*Shall* I bring you a cup of milk?
31. What do you suppose, I *will* do tomorrow?	What do you suppose, I *shall* do tomorrow?
32. Mind it! you *will* not make a noise.	Mind it! you *shall* not make a noise.
33. If you do not work hard, you *will* fail.	If you do not work hard, you *shall* fail.
34. You *would* not drink and drive.	You *should* not drink and drive.
35. Work *hard,* lest you *might* fail.	Work hard, lest you *should* fail.
36. You *could* buy a new pen: this one leaks.	You *should* buy a new pen; this one leaks.
37. If I *would* meet her now, she will not recognise me.	If I *should* meet her now, she will not recognise me.
38. I *might* like to make a phone call, if possible.	I *should* like to make a phone call, if possible.
39. I *must* say she is over thirty.	I *should* say she is over thirty.
40. *Could* they play well, they will win.	*Should* they play well, they will win.
41. You *might* not be so unfriendly.	You *should* not be so unfriendly.
42. Madhuri *shall* be twelve next month.	Madhuri *will* be twelve next month.
43. *Would* you please come back later?	*Will* you please come back later?
44. I *shall* talk to her on your behalf.	I *will* talk to her on your behalf.

Contd...

Incorrect	Correct
45. We *shall* stop smoking.	We *will* stop smoking.
46. I *shall* give her a sumptuous feast.	I *will* give her sumptuous feast.
47. I *shall* visit your house every week.	I *will* visit your house every week.
48. I *shall* beat you if you abuse me again.	I *will* beat you if you abuse me again.
49. Engines *shall* not run without lubricants.	Engines *will* not run without lubricants.
50. She *shall* never deceive you.	She *will* never deceive you.
51. You *shall* have to pay for the repairs.	You *will* have to pay for the repairs.
52. It *should* be a pity to miss the main film.	It *would* be a pity to miss the main film.
53. *Should* you pay me in cash, please?	*Would* you pay me in cash, please?
54. I *might* like to ask you a question.	I *should* like to ask you a question.
55. *Can* you like to sit down?	*Would* you like to sit down?
56. I *should* prefer tea to coffee.	I *would* prefer tea to coffee.
57. *Could* you like me to get something for you?	*Would* you like me to get something for you?
58. She *shall* often come home tired out.	She *would* often come home tired out.
59. I *must* not like to see him again.	I *would* not like to see him again.
60. She *should* rather stay at home than go for a walk.	She *would* rather stay at home than go for a walk.
61. I wish you *should* not chatter so much.	I wish you *would* not chatter so much.
62. I *might* do my best to help you.	I *would* do my best to help you.
63. You *can* pay your fees in time.	You *must* pay your fees in time.
64. She *would* be back by 6.40 p.m.	She *must* be back by 6.40 p.m.
65. You *should* not worry about me.	You *must* not worry about me.
66. She *may* be tired after working for twelve hours.	She *must* be tired after working for twelve hours.

Contd...

Incorrect	Correct
67. You *can* serve your aged parents.	You *must* serve your aged parents.
68. She *should* not come here again.	She *must* not come here again.
69. A servant *should* carry out his master's orders.	A servant *must* carry out his master's orders.
70. You *must* not see her; just pen a letter.	You *dare* (need) not see her; just pen a letter.
71. She *should* not have gone alone in the jungle at midnight.	She *need* not have gone alone in the jungle at midnight.
72. She *must* not disobey her in-laws.	She *dare* not disobey her in-laws.
73. I *should* not oppose my boss.	I *dare* not oppose my boss.
74. I *would* have helped her.	I *ought* to have helped her.
75. They *would* widen this road.	They *ought* to widen this road.
76. I *would* run a mile every morning in my youth.	I *used* to run a mile every morning in my youth.
77. I *would* go to school on foot.	I *used* to go to school on foot.

13

Sentence

Speech is a gift of God to human beings. We use words in speaking and writing. We generally use a group of words in order to communicate our thoughts to others (during our speech or writing); as:

The Sun rises in the east.

Definition: A group of words (like this) that makes complete sense is called a *sentence.*

Kinds of Sentences

We can classify the sentences into the following two groups: (i) on the basis of their meanings or sense. (ii) on the basis of their form or structure.

(i) Division of the sentences on the basis of meaning/sense:

1. Statements
2. Commands
3. Questions
4. Exclamations.

Statements

We use the statements most of all, in our compositions or speeches. Therefore, the statements have vital importance in the sentences. Read the sentences given below carefully.

Nupur buys a pen.

Dhruvika works hard.

The boys are reading.

Roopangi has a nice frock.

Such type of commonplace sentences are called declarations or statements. They apprise us of some situation.

Kinds of Statements:

(i) Mukul is coming. Sonu is playing.
Madhu is sleeping. Bimla is reading.

All of the above sentences bear positive declarations or assertions. Therefore, they are called *Positive Statements or Declarative Sentences.*

(ii) Mukul is not coming. Sonu is not playing.
Madhu is not sleeping. Bimla is not reading.

The presence of the word *not* in the above sentences has rendered them into *Negative Statements.*

Remember that both of the positive statements and the negative statements are called *Assertive Sentences.*

Conversion of Positive Statements into Negative Statements

Read the following sentences carefully:

(a)	***Positive Statement***		***Negative Statement***
	I *am* a good boy.		I am *not* a good boy.
	Sarla *is* a nice woman.		Sarla is *not* a nice woman.
	They *are* gentle girls.		They are *not* gentle girls.
	Sohan *was* angry.		Sohan was *not* angry
	You *were* ill.	—	You were *not* ill.

Explanation:

(i) We have used the verbs *to be* (*is, am, are, was, were*) as Full Verb in a positive statement.

(ii) We have used the word *not* after the verbs *to be* (*is, am, are, was, were*) in a negative statement.

(b) ***Positive Statement***	***Negative Statement***
She has a doll.	She has no doll(s).
We have books.	We have no books.
You had a brother.	You had no brother(s).

Explanation:

(i) We have used the verbs *to be* (*has, have, had*) as Full Verb in a positive statement.

(ii) We have used the word *no* after the verbs *to be* (*has, have, had*) in a negative statement.

Remember that the insertion of the word *not* or *no* after the Full Verb renders the positive statements into negative sentences.

(c) ***Positive Statement***	***Negative Statement***
I *am* writing.	I am *not* writing.
She *is* reading.	She is *not* reading.
You *are* sleeping.	You are *not* sleeping.
We *were* playing.	We were *not* playing
She *was* eating.	She was *not* eating.
I *have* done this.	I have *not* done this.
He *has* gone.	He has *not* gone.
They *had* fallen.	They had *not* fallen.

Explanation:

(i) We have used the verbs *to be* (*is, am, are, was, were, has, have, had*) as Helping/Auxiliary Verb in the positive statements given above.

(ii) We have used the word *not* after the Helping/Auxiliary Verbs (*is, am, are, was, were, has, have, had*) to convert the positive statements given above into negative sentences.

Positive Statement	***Negative Statement***
She *will* return home.	She *will not* return home.
I *shall* help you.	I *shall not* help you.

You *can* swim.	You *cannot* swim.
He *could* read.	He *could not* read.
They *may* come.	They *may not* come.
He *might* take tea.	He *might not* take tea.
The car *would* start.	The car *would not* start.
You *should* work hard.	You *should not* work hard.
You *must* obey me.	You *must not* obey me.

Explanation:

(i) We have used the first (crude) form after verbs (V^I) after the modal Auxiliaries (*will, shall, can, could, may, might, would, should, must*) in the positive statements given above.

(ii) We have used the word *not* after the Modal Auxiliaries (*will, shall, can, could, may, might, would, should, must*) and before the first (crude) form of the verbs (V^I) to convert the positive statements given above into negative sentences.

Remember that the insertion of the word *not* after the Helping/Auxiliary Verb or Modal Auxiliary and before the first/crude form of the verb (V^I) converts the positive sentences into negative sentences.

Distinction between Helping/Auxiliary verbs and Modal Auxiliary

	Helping/Auxiliary Verb	*Modal Auxiliary*
(i)	Any form of the verb can be used after the Helping/ Auxiliary verb.	Only the first (crude) form of the verb (V^I) is used after the Modal Auxiliary.
(ii)	Helping verb can be used as a Full verb	Modal Auxiliary is never used as a Full verb.
(iii)	Helping verbs are changed according to the number,	Modal Auxiliaries are not changed according to the

gender and person of the subject.	number, gender and person of the subject 'to' is not used after any other Modal Auxiliary except 'used' and 'ought'.

(d)

Positive Statement	*Negative Statement*
I *live* here.	I do *not* live here.
She sings well.	She does *not* sing well.
The boys come here.	The boys do *not* come here.
He reaches home.	He does *not* reach home.
I lived here.	I did *not* live here.
She sang well.	She did *not* sing well.
The boys came here.	The boys did *not* come here.
He reached home.	He did *not* reach home.

Explanation:

Positive Statements	*Negative Statements*
Simple Present Tense.	Subject + do not + V^I
Full verb *Or*	*Or*
Full verb + *S or es*	Subject + does not + V^I
Simple Past Tense. 2nd form of Full verb	Subject + did not + V^I

Short (Contracted/Abbreviated/form of Negative (Auxiliary Verbs/ Modal Auxiliaries + not)

Auxiliary Verb (Modal Auxiliary)	*Negative*	*Short (Contracted/ Abbreviated form)*
do	not	don't
does	not	doesn't
is	not	isn't
am	not	ain't
are	not	aren't

Contd....

Auxiliary Verb (Modal Auxiliary)	*Negative*	*Short (Contracted/ Abbreviated form)*
has	not	hasn't
have	not	haven't
did	not	didn't
was	not	wasn't
were	not	weren't
had	not	hadn't
will	not	won't
shall	not	shan't
can	not	can't
could	not	couldn't
would	not	wouldn't
should	not	shouldn't
must	not	mustn't
may	not	mayn't
ought	not	oughtn't
need	not	needn't
might	not	mightn't
used to	not	usedn't to
dare	not	daren't

Please note that the use of *usedn't to* is considered obsolete and informal now. The use of *didn't use to* in place of *usedn't to* has become acceptable now.

Commands

Read the sentences given below:

Strike a match.

Give up smoking.

Please help this poor man.

Always speak the truth and be honest.

Obey your parents.
Respect your teachers.
Post this letter.
Observe silence.
Stand up on the bench.
Rub the board.
Do your work and go home.
Give me something to eat.
Take care of your health.
Do not strike a match near the petrol.
Beware of pick-pockets.
Trust in God and do the right.
March forward and attack the enemy.
Never tell a lie.
Do not mix with bad boys.
Go to your room and study.
Let us take tea.
Let the boys go to bed.
Let us go out for a walk.

The sentences given above are *Imperative Sentences* because the verbs used in them express *command, humble request, suggestions, instructions, advice,* etc.

The sentences which express *a desire* are called optative sentences, *e.g.*

1. May he live long!
2. May she get a son!
3. May God bless you!
4. May God grant him long life!
5. Good-bye, my friend!
6. Good morning, sir!
7. Farewell, my countrymen!

The bare (crude) form of the verb is used in the imperative sentences. Though the subject 'you' is not given, it (you) is implied.

Questions

A sentence that asks a question is called an *Interrogative* sentence.

Read the sentences given below:

Do you know me?
Had I written a letter?

Does he help you?
Is she present?
Are you tall?
Am I wrong?
Has he failed?
Have you taken rest?
Did you swim?
Were they joking?
Will you eat rice?
Shall we dance?
Can you kill a snake?
Could he sing a song?
Dare she abuse you?
Should I see him?
Need he come here?
Would he go with you?

Interrogative sentences begin with a helping verb. They can be answered in *'Yes'* or *'No'*. Therefore, they are also called as 'Yes — No' questions. You can answer them simply by moving your neck without using your tongue.

Examples of 'Yes — No' Questions:

Q. Is she reading?

Ans. Yes; Yes, she is; Yes, she is reading. No; No, she isn't; No, she is not reading.

Q. Can you solve this sum?

Ans. Yes; Yes, I can; Yes, I can solve this sum. No; No, I can't; No, I can't solve this sum.

Q. Were you sleeping?

Ans. Yes; Yes, I was; Yes, I was sleeping. No; No, I wasn't; No, I wasn't sleeping.

Q. Will you buy a sweater?

Ans. Yes; Yes, I shall; Yes, I shall buy a sweater. No; No, I shan't; No, I shan't buy a sweater.

Look at the sentences given below:

What is her name?
Where do you live?
Which is your frock?
When do you take tea?
Why have you come here?
How do you do?
Who is your best friend?
Whom do you like most?
Whose book is this?

The above interrogative sentences also begin with a helping verb. We cannot answer them without using the tongue.

Conversion of Positive statements into Interrogative statements

(a) ***Positive Statements***	***Interrogative Statements***
Ram is happy.	Is Ram happy?
I am a student.	Am I a student?
You are my uncle.	Are you my uncle?
She was very poor.	Was she very poor?
The girls were absent.	Were the girls absent?

Explanation:

Positive Statements: S + Verb to be (*is, am, are, was, were*)...

Interrogative Statements: Full Verb (*is, am, are, was, were*) + S?

(b) ***Positive Statements***	***Interrogative Statements***
A cow has two horns	Has a cow two horns?
I have four pencils.	Have I four pencils?
She had two brothers.	Had she two brothers?

Explanation:

Positive Statements: S + Full Verb (*has, have, had*)

Interrogative Statements: Full Verb (*has, have, had*)+S?

(c) ***Positive Statements***	***Interrogative Statements***
I walk fast.	Do I walk fast?
She does her work.	Does she do her work?
You played cricket.	Did you play cricket?

Explanation:

Positive Statements	***Interrogative Statements***
Simple Present Tense. Full	Do + S + Full verb...?
Verb or Full Verb + s or es.	Does + S + Full Verb...?
Simple Past Tense.	Did + S + Full Verb?
2nd form of Full Verb.	

(d)

Positive Statements	*Interrogative Statements*
I am writing a letter.	Am I writing a letter?
She is reading a book.	Is she reading a book?
You are singing a song.	Are you singing a song?
He was drinking tea.	Was he drinking tea?
They were singing a song.	Were they singing a song?
I have done my work.	Have I done my work?
He has bought a radio.	Has he bought a radio?
She had gone to market.	Had she gone to market?
I shall sell my scooter.	Shall I sell my scooter?
You will ride a horse.	Will you ride a horse?

Explanation:

Positive Statements: S + helping verb

Interrogative Statements: Helping verb + S?

(e)

Positive Statements	*Interrogative Statements*
She will sing a song.	Will she sing a song?
I shall go to school.	Shall I go to school?
You can run fast.	Can you run fast?
She could lift the table.	Could she lift the table?
You might help me.	Might you help me?
It would rain.	Would it rain?
You should work hard.	Should you work hard?

Explanation:

Positive Statement: S + Auxiliary Modal

Interrogative Statements: Auxiliary Modal + S?

(f)

Positive Statements	*Interrogative Statements*
My name is Sharda.	What is your name?
I live at Lodhi Road.	Where do you live?
Mr. Negi is our teacher.	Who is your teacher?
I came to Delhi in 1991.	When did you come to Delhi?

I went there by bus.	How did you go there?
I took your pen by mistake.	How/Why did you take my pen?
I want to see Shalini.	Whom do you want to see?
I shall buy this doll.	Which doll will you buy?
This is Rajni's house.	Whose house is this? *Or* Which is Rajni's house?

All the above sentences have been converted into interrogative statements according to the nature of the question.

Question Tags — Usage and Answers

Q. I am a tall boy, ain't I?

Ans. Yes, you are; Yes, you are a tall boy. *Or*
No, you aren't; No, you aren't a tall boy.

Q. The earth is round, isn't it?

Ans. Yes, it/she is; Yes, it/she is round.

Q. You are a fool, aren't you?

Ans. No, I ain't; No, I ain't (am not) a fool.

Q. You live at Kanpur, don't you?

Ans. Yes, I do; Yes, I live at Kanpur.

Q. She reads in tenth class, doesn't she?

Ans. Yes, she does; Yes, she reads in tenth class.

Q. You have four brothers; haven't you?

Ans. Yes, I have; Yes, I have four brothers. *Or*
No, I haven't; No, I haven't four brothers.

Q. You returned from school, didn't you?

Ans. Yes, I did; Yes, I returned from school *Or*
No, I didn't; No, I didn't return from school.

Q. You were making a noise, weren't you?

Ans. Yes, I was; Yes, I was making a noise. *Or*
No, I wasn't; No, I wasn't making a noise.

Q. You had broken my slate, hadn't you?

Ans. Yes, I had; Yes, I had broken your slate. *Or*
No, I hadn't; No I hadn't broken your slate.

Q. She will dance on the stage, won't she?

Ans. Yes, she will; Yes, she will dance on the stage .

Q. I shall solve this sum, shan't I?

Ans. Yes, you will; You will solve this sum. *Or*
No, you won't; No, you won't solve this sum.

Q. Sarla can stand first, can't she?

Ans. Yes, she can; Yes, Sarla can stand first. *Or*
No, she can't; No, Sarla can't stand first.

Q. You should work hard, shouldn't you?

Ans. Yes, I should; Yes, I should work hard.

'Question Tag' is such a type of phrase as is used at the tail (end) of a statement. If the statement is positive, the question tag will be negative and vice versa.

Exclamations

Exclamatory sentences are those sentences which express the abrupt (feeling of *wonder, sorrow, pain, joy, admiration,* etc. (sudden) and spontaneous.

Examples:

Oh God!

Oh! What is this?

Hush! keep quiet.

Well done! you have won the race.

What a pity! you did not come to my house.

Bravo! you fought bravely.

Ah! Rohit has joined us.

Alas! you are ruined.

Hello! what do you want?

Hurrah! mother has come.

Bravo! you have stood first.

Fie upon him! he failed for the second time.

Pooh! you cheated that child.

14

Classification of Sentences

Sentences can be classified into the following types:

Simple Sentences

Definition: A sentence which has one subject and one predicate is called a Simple sentence. Examples:

1. Rama killed Ravana with an arrow.
2. Dhruvika plays with her toys and dolls.
3. Nand Ram is a very diligent chap.

Complex Sentences

Definition: A sentence which has one Principal clause and one or more Subordinate (dependent) clauses is called a Complex Sentence.

Examples:

1. Youth is the time when seeds of character are sown.
2. Uneasy lies the head that wears the crown.
3. That he will fail in the examination is certain.
4. When the patient will recover cannot be said.
5. I informed Radha that she was wanted by the Principal.
6. The truth is that Urmilla has deceived all her lovers.
7. Seeing that a barking dog was running towards her, she started shedding tears.

8. The teacher called the roll to see whether all were present.
9. There is no sense in what she says.
10. The news that Babita has won a prize in lottery does not seem to be true.
11. Do not board the bus until it comes to a dead stop.
12. The puppy followed wherever Pushpa went.
13. Madhuri fell asleep on the ground because she was weary.
14. Were I to go unarmed, I should surely come to grief.
15. You may enjoy yourself as you please.
16. Though Rehman tried his level utmost, he could not defeat his adversary.
17. Step forward that I may bless you.
18. The bride spoke in such a low voice that the bridegroom could hardly hear her.
19. The son is as arrogant as the father is.
20. Lucy's parents searched for Lucy as far as they could reach.

Look at the sentences printed above.

Sentences 1 and 2 are of Adjective Clauses.

Sentences 3 to 10 are of Noun Clauses.

Sentences 11 to 20 are of Adverb Clauses.

The sentences pertaining to Noun clauses, Adjective Clauses and Adverb clauses are called complex sentences :

Complex Sentence

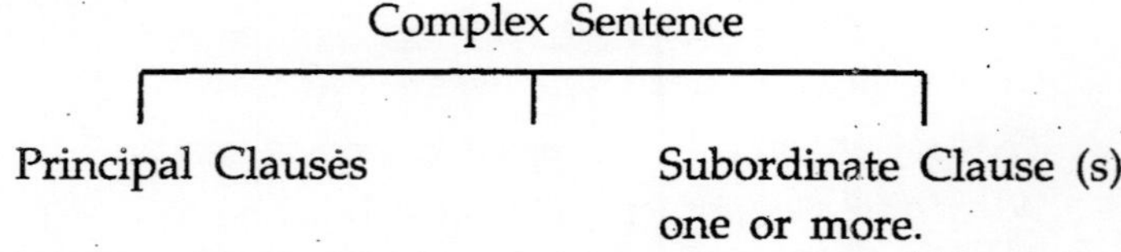

Principal Clauses

Subordinate Clause (s) one or more.

The Principal or Subordinate clause can exist anywhere in the sentence.

Compound Sentences

Definition: A chain of Simple Sentences joined by Co-ordinate Conjunctions is called a Compound Sentence.

There is no division of a Compound Sentence into Principal or Subordinate Clauses. Rather all the clauses are of equal importance and are called co-ordinate clauses.

Examples:

1. She is slow but (she is) steady.
2. The way was long and the time was short.
3. She was guilty, therefore, she was expelled from college.
4. Work hard or you will suffer.
5. Run hard or you will lose the race.
6. The sun was setting and we were still far away from our destination.
7. She cannot run, for she has pain in her leg.
8. The Chinaman took Mikali home and (he) gave him food.
9. He is more intelligent than his brother (is).
10. Can Chanchal read (English) and write English.
11. Mahatma Gandhi was not only a good statesman, he was also a great patriot.
12. Babita tried her level best, nevertheless, she failed.
13. Run fast, else you will not reach school in time.

The sentences which contain Co-ordinate clauses are called Compound Sentences.

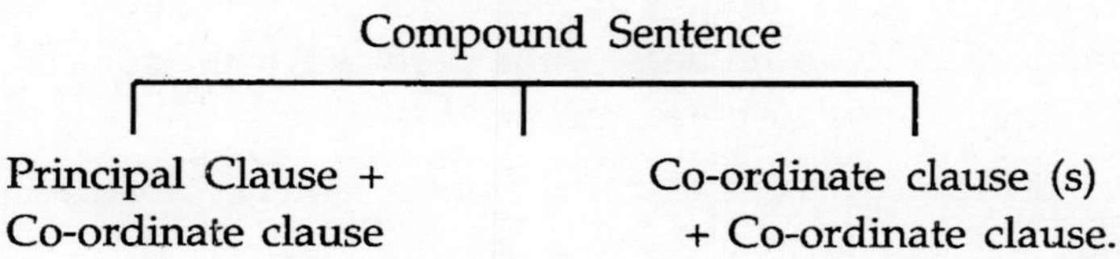

Parts of a Sentence

Every sentence has two parts:

Subject: The word about which something is said is called the subject, e.g.

(i) I like milk. (ii) You are a man.

In sentence (i) Who likes milk? The answer is — I. In sentence (ii) Who is a man? The answer is — You. Therefore, 'I' and 'You' are subjects in sentences (i) and (ii) above respectively.

Predicate: That word is called the predicate which tells something about the subject, *e.g.*

(i) Mohan falls (ii) Sita dances

In sentence (i) What does Mohan do? Answer — falls.

In sentence (ii) What does Sita do? Answer — dances.

Therefore, 'falls' and 'dances' are predicates in sentences (i) and (ii) above respectively.

Read the following sentences carefully:

(i) I love little Pussy. (ii) They are four sisters.

In sentence (i) What do I do? Answer — I love little Pussy.

In sentence (ii) What are they? Answer — They are four sisters.

Therefore, the words 'I' and 'they' are subjects in sentences (i) and (ii) above respectively.

The remaining parts of sentences (i) ....love little Pussy and sentence (ii) ....are four sisters — are predicates.

Remember that 'The sentence — the subject = the predicate'. 'The sentences — the predicate = the subject' Even a single word can be a *predicate.*

If the Subject is extricated from a sentence, the remaining part will be called the *predicate.*

15

Sentence Formation

We do not use only Simple Sentence in our day-to-day lives. We usually combine Simple Sentences to form Complex and Compound Sentences. Forms of Synthesis:

1. To Combine Simple Sentences to make Simple Sentences.
2. To Combine Simple Sentences to form Compound Sentences.
3. To Combine Simple Sentences to form Complex Sentences.

Combining Simple Sentences into Simple Sentences

	Simple Sentences	*Combined Simple Sentences*
1.	I do not like that child. He ever-weeps.	I do not like that ever-weeping child.
2.	She took bath. She used Lux soap.	She took bath using Lux soap.
3.	She made remarks. Her remarks pinched me.	She made pinching remarks on me.
4.	The young lady cried for help. She pointed to a tree.	Pointing to a tree, the young lady cried for help.

Here, the Simple Sentences have been Combined into Simple Sentences by using Participles (V. + ing form)

5.	He has come here. He will see you.	He has come here to see you.

Contd...

	Simple Sentences	*Combined Simple Sentences*
6.	I am going to market. I shall buy some paper.	I am going to market to buy some paper.
7.	I shall meet you. I shall discuss this matter with you.	I shall meet you to discuss this matter with you.
8.	She is too weak. She cannot walk.	She is too weak to walk.
9.	My mother was much delighted. She had heard of my brilliant success.	My mother was much delighted to hear of my brilliant success.

Here, the Simple Sentences have been combined into Simple Sentences by using Infinitive (to + V^1).

10.	I brushed my teeth. I took my breakfast.	Having brushed my teeth, I took my breakfast.
11.	The film was over. The spectators returned to their houses.	The film having been over, the spectators returned to their houses.
12.	She finished her work. She rang to her husband.	Having finished her work she rang to her husband.
13.	The mob was uncontrollable, the police let off tear-gas.	The mob having been uncontrollable, the police let off tear-gas.

Here, the Simple Sentences have been combined into Simple Sentences by using Participle (Participial) Phrases.

14.	Rama was a benign rule. He treated his subjects as his brothers.	Rama, the benign ruler treated his subjects as his brothers.
15.	Gandhi was a typical leader. He believed in the principle of Ahimsa.	Gandhi, a typical leader believed in the principle of Ahimsa.
16.	Anuradha is my cousin. She is a famous dancer.	Anuradha, my cousin is a famous dancer.
17.	Shambhu is my next-door neighbour. He is a pilot.	Shambhu, my next-door neighbour is a pilot.

Here, the Simple Sentences have been combined into Simple Sentences by using 'Noun Phrases in Apposition'.

18.	She reached Madras safe and sound. She is lucky.	Luckily, she reached Madras safe and sound.
19.	He secured distinction marks. He secured it through his diligence.	He secured distinction marks by dint of his diligence.
20.	She was happy. She blessed me a great deal.	Happily she blessed me a great deal.

Contd...

	Simple Sentences	*Combined Simple Sentences*
	Here, the Simple Sentences have been combined into Simple Sentences by using 'Adverbs' or 'Phrases'.	
21.	I advised him. He did not serve his aged parents.	He did not serve his aged parents even on my advice.
22.	This car must be purchased. There is no question of cost.	This car must be purchased at any cost.
23.	Let him succeed. You may demand a party from him then.	You may demand a party from him after his success.
	Here, the Simple Sentences have been combined into Simple Sentences by using 'Propositions with Nouns'.	

Combining Simple Sentences into Compound Sentences

Read the following sentences:

	Simple Sentences	*Compound Sentences*
1.	I can read. I can sing. I can draw a sketch.	I can read, sing and draw a sketch.
2.	She is a writer. She is an orator.	She is a writer as well as an orator.
3.	Mohan is taller than Sohan. Mohan is taller than Sham. Mohan is taller than Harnam.	Mohan is taller than Sohan, Sham and Harnam.
4.	Mohan is smart. Mohan is equally intelligent.	Mohan is both smart and equally intelligent.
5.	Mohan is healthy. Mohan is wealthy.	Mohan is not only healthy but wealthy also.
	Here, the Simple Sentences have been combined into Compound Sentences by using 'Cumulative Conjunctions'.	
6.	Run fast. You will miss the first period.	Run fast or you will miss the first period.
7.	Work hard. You will be a laggard in studies.	Work hard otherwise you will be a laggard in studies.
8.	Revise your courses. You will get a poor percentage of marks.	Revise your courses or (or else/ else) you will get a poor percentage of marks.
	Here, the Simple Sentences have been combined into Compound Sentences by using 'Alternative Conjunctions.'	

Contd...

	Simple Sentences	Compound Sentences
9.	She burnt midnight oil. She got a low percentage of marks.	She burnt midnight oil but she got a low percentage of marks.
10.	Do what you like. Do not argue with me.	Do what you like, only do not argue with me.
11.	She had to face bitter criticism. She persevered.	She had to face bitter criticism nevertheless she persevered.
12.	My uncle is rich. My father is poor.	My uncle is rich, while (whereas my father is poor.

Here, the Simple Sentences have been combined into Compound Sentences by using 'Adversative Conjunctions.'

13.	She was a woman of loose morals. She was divorced.	She was a woman of loose morals therefore she was divorced.
14.	You must be put behind the bars. You have stolen my scooter.	You must be put behind the bars because you have stolen my scooter.
15.	The days are short. It is November.	The days are short for it is November.

Here, the Simple Sentences have been combined into compound Sentences by using 'Illative Conjunctions.'

16.	She is not tall. She is not dwarfish.	She is not tall and not dwarfish either.
17.	She is not a dancer. She is not an orator.	She is not a dancer and not an orator either.

Here, the Simple Sentences have been combined into Compound Sentences by using 'Appropriate Words.'

Combining Simple Sentences into Complex Sentences

Read the following sentences:

	Simple Sentences	Complex Sentences
1.	He will fail in the examination. It is certain.	It is certain that he will fail in the examination.
2.	His daughter was doing well at school. He was pleased to learn this.	He was pleased to learn that his daughter was doing well at school.
3.	You must exercise daily. It is essential.	That you must exercise daily is essential.
4.	She should be promoted. This is a decision. It is a good one.	That she should be promoted is a good decision.
5.	We should do something to help the refugees. I felt strongly that way.	I felt strongly that we should do something to help the refugees.

Contd...

	Simple Sentences	*Complex Sentences*

Here, the Simple Sentences have been combined into Complex Sentences by using 'that' as connective. It combines the sentences pertaining to—'Noun Clauses'.

6.	We saw the heroine. She had played a nice part in a film.	We saw the heroine who had played a nice part in a film.
7.	I know a lady. She has come to inspect the school.	I know the lady who has come to inspect the school.
8.	I know the boy. He has topped the merit list.	I know the boy who has topped the merit list.
9.	Two men were fighting. They were arrested by a policeman.	The two men who were fighting were arrested by a policeman.
10.	He said something. No one understood it.	He said something which no one understood .

Here, the Simple Sentences have been combined into Complex Sentences by using 'Who/Which' as connective. Who/Which are called 'Relative Pronouns'. They combine the sentences pertaining to 'Adjective Clauses.'

11.	This is the only field. Roses grow here.	The is the only field where roses grow.
12.	I know the time. The train leaves for Delhi then.	I know the time when the train leaves for Delhi.

Here, the Simple Sentences have been combined into Complex Sentences by using 'Where/When' as connectives. Where/when are called 'Relative Adverbs'. However, the above sentences combined by them (Where/When) are of Adjective Clauses because where is qualifying field and When is qualifying time.

13.	You go out in rain. You will get wet.	If you go out in rain you will get wet.
14.	She is very clever. She can solve this sum.	She can solve this sum because she is very clever.
15.	She shifted there. Living was safe there.	She shifted where the living was safe.
16.	My sister has gone to Meerut. It is now a dull place.	It is now a dull place since my sister has gone to Meerut.
17.	The prince was enthroned. The king had died.	After the king had died, the prince was enthroned. *Or* The prince was enthroned after the king had died.
18.	She is very pretty. She is a humble girl.	She is very pretty, yet she is a humble girl.

Contd...

	Simple Sentences	*Complex Sentences*
19.	Sharda will definitely stand first. She had revised the course thoroughly.	Sharda will definitely stand first because she had revised the course thoroughly.
20.	The police chased the thief. The thief ran faster.	When the police chased the thief, he ran faster.

Here, the Simple Sentences have been combined into Complex Sentences by using 'If / because / where / since / after / yet / when' as connectives. The sentences combined by the above connectives are of 'Adverb Clauses'.

Remember that, like the *adverb*, the *adverb clause* too shows *'Time, place, Reason, Condition, Manner, Contrast Concession, Result/Effect, Extent, Purpose and comparison,'* etc.

Compound sentences make 'Co-ordinate Clauses'.

Complex sentences make 'Noun Clauses, Adjective Clauses and Adverbial Clauses'.

16

Syntax

Syntax means the (rules for the) arrangement of words into phrases and phrases into sentences. There are syntactic differences between English and several other languages.

The very meaning of the sentence will change a great deal if the words are not properly arranged in the sentence. Therefore, it is quite essential for a student to have thorough knowledge about grammatical rules to write and speak correct English 'Syntax' includes parts of speech and articles.

We have already discussed Parts of speech and Articles in full details. You are required to memorise the rules pertaining to them so that you may not hesitate in using them.

Position of Subject, Verb and Object—Some languages differ widely from English in the manner of writing a sentence. The position of words in English is:

Subject (S)	*Verb (V)*	*Object (O)*
Sheela	is	a girl
Kamal	is	a naughty boy
This boy	has	four books
I	had	three brothers

Read the following sentences:

Sheela a girl is	This four books has.
Kamal a naughty boy was	I three brothers had.

These sentences are incorrect according to the syntax of English language but they are correct according to the rules of Hindi Grammar. Most of the students in India speak wrong English because they lack the syntactical knowledge, rich vocabulary and knowledge of correct uses of words, phrases and idioms. They also try to translate their ideas from their vernacular to English. Literal translation of phrases most often becomes incorrect, odd, humorous and harsh.

Look at the following sentences.

My head is eating circle.

My heart became garden-garden.

First weigh the words then open the mouth.

The above sentences are the literal translation of sentences of Hindi language. They are quite acceptable in Hindi. But their translation into English is incorrect odd, humorous and harsh.

Look at the following sentences:

(1) I am feeling giddy

(2) I was overjoyed.

(3) Think twice before you speak.

The above sentences are correct English.

LESSON 1

Verb 'To Be'—(Is)

Model Sentences

I. Affirmative	*II. Interrogative*
1. He is a man.	Is he a man?
2. Sohan is a soldier.	Is Sohan a soldier?
3. The crow is thirsty.	Is the crow thirsty?

4. She is my sister.	Is she my sister?
5. It is a toy.	Is it a toy?
6. It is a costly turban.	Is it a costly turban?
7. That pole is tall.	Is that pole tall?
8. She is a dancer and painter.	Is she a dancer and painter?
9. Nikunj is a skilled swimmer.	Is Nikunj a skilled swimmer?
10. He is noble and honest.	Is he noble and honest?

III. Negative	*IV. Interrogative-Negative*
1. He is not a man.	Is he not a man?
2. Sohan is not a soldier.	Is Sohan not a soldier?
3. The crow is not thirsty.	Is the crow not thirsty?
4. She is not my sister.	Is she not my sister?
5. It is not a toy.	Is it not a toy?
6. It is not a costly turban.	Is it not a costly turban?
7. That pole is not tall.	Is that pole not tall?
8. She is not a dancer and painter.	Is she not a dancer and painter?
9. Nikunj is not a skilled swimmer.	Is Nikunj not a skilled swimmer?
10. He is not noble and honest.	Is he not noble and honest?

LESSON 2

Verb 'To Be'-(Am)

Model Sentences

I. Affirmative	*II. Interrogative*
1. I am a boy.	Am I a boy?
2. I am a student.	Am I a student?
3. I am a poor student.	Am I a poor student?
4. I am your fast friend.	Am I your fast friend?

5. I am very honest.	Am I very honest?
6. I am the monitor of my class.	Am I the monitor of my class?
7. I am a good player of hockey.	Am I a good player of hockey?
8. I am thin and tall.	Am I thin and tall?
9. I am quite good at studies.	Am I quite good at studies?
10. I am jolly and playful.	Am I jolly and playful?

III. Negative	*IV. Interrogative-Negative*
1. I am not a boy.	Am I not a boy?
2. I am not a student.	Am I not a student?
3. I am not a poor student.	Am I not a poor student?
4. I am not your fast friend.	Am I not your fast friend?
5. I am not very honest.	Am I not very honest?
6. I am not the monitor of my class.	Am I not the monitor of my class?
7. I am not a good player of hockey.	Am I not a good player of hockey?
8. I am not thin and tall.	Am I not thin and tall?
9. I am not quite good at studies.	Am I not quite good at studies?
10. I am not jolly and playful.	Am I not jolly and playful?

LESSON 3

Verb 'To Be'—(Are)

Model Sentence

I. Affirmative	*II. Interrogative*
1. You are a woman.	Are you a woman?
2. We are good swimmers.	Are we good swimmers?
3. They are our aunts.	Are they our aunts?

4. Ram and Krishna are neighbours.	Are Ram and Krishna neighbours?
5. You are children (a child).	Are you children (a child)?
6. You are a naughty girl.	Are you a naughty girl?
7. They are healthy and wealthy.	Are they healthy and wealthy?
8. You are my nephews and nieces.	Are you my nephews and nieces?
9. Motu and Chhotu are loafers and scoundrels.	Are Motu and Chhotu loafers and scoundrels?
10. My friends are selfish.	Are my friends selfish?

III. Negative	***IV. Interrogative-Negative***
1. You are not a woman.	Are you not a woman?
2. We are not good swimmers.	Are we not good swimmers?
3. They are not our aunts.	Are they not our aunts?
4. Ram and Krishna are not neighbours.	Are Ram and Krishna not neighbours?
5. You are not children (a child).	Are you not children (a child)?
6. You are not a naughty girl.	Are you not a naughty girl?
7. They are not healthy and wealthy.	Are they not healthy and wealthy?
8. You are not my nephews and nieces.	Are you not my nephews and nieces?
9. Motu and Chhotu are not loafers and scoundrels.	Are Motu and Chhotu not loafers and scoundrels?
10. My friends are not selfish.	Are my friends not selfish?

A few Rules about the verb 'To Be' (Is, Am, Are)

Affirmative sentences: Is—It is used with third person singular pronouns (*He, She, It* and any singular name)

Am: It is used with first person singular pronoun (I)

Are: It is used with first person plural pronoun (we); second person, both singular and plural pronoun (you); and third person plural pronoun (They and more than one noun).

Negative Sentences— is not = isn't ....
am not = ain't —.
are not = aren't —.

Interrogative Sentences—Is / Subject / Predicate?
Am / Subject / Predicate?
Are/ Subject / Predicate?

Interrogative-Negative Sentences— Is / Subject + not + predicate?
Am / Subject + not + predicate?
Are / Subject + not + predicate?

Some uses of simple 'Be'

	Affirmative Sentences	*Negative Sentences*
1.	Be useful and clever.	Do not (Don't) be useless and dullard.
2.	Be diligent and fast.	Do not (Don't) be indolent and slow.
3.	Be fearless and bold.	Do not (Don't) be fearful and timid.
4.	Be social and tolerant.	Do not (Don't) be unsocial and intolerant.
5.	Be noble and honest.	Do not (Don't) be ignoble and dishonest.
6.	Be faithful and obedient.	Do not (Don't) be faithless and disobedient.
7.	Be kind and reliable.	Do not (Don't) be unkind and unreliable.
8.	Be civilized and cultured.	Do not (Don't) be uncivilized and uncultured.
9.	Be pure and true.	Do not (Don't) be impure and untrue.

LESSON 4

Verb 'To Be'—(was)

Model Sentences

I. Affirmative	*II. Interrogative*
1. Hari was very poor.	Was Hari very poor?
2. I was very naughty.	Was I very naughty?
3. He was my uncle.	Was he my uncle?
4. She was my teacher.	Was she my teacher?
5. It was a fine day.	Was it a fine day?
6. She was an examiner and invigilator.	Was she an examiner and invigilator?
7. He was a goldsmith and jeweller.	Was he a goldsmith and jeweller?
8. The toy was cheap and pretty.	Was the toy cheap and pretty?
9. The coat was costly and loose.	Was the coat costly and loose?
10. It was a cloudy and stuffy day.	Was it a cloudy and stuffy day?

III. Negative	*IV. Interrogative-Negative*
1. Hari was not very poor.	Was Hari not very poor?
2. I was not very naughty.	Was I not very naughty?
3. He was not my uncle.	Was he not my uncle?
4. She was not my teacher.	Was she not my teacher?
5. It was not a fine day.	Was it not a fine day?
6. She was not an examiner and invigilator.	Was she not an examiner and invigilator?
7. He was not a goldsmith and jeweller.	Was he not a goldsmith and jeweller?

8.	The toy was not cheap and pretty.	Was the toy not cheap and pretty?
9.	The coat was not costly and loose.	Was the coat not costly and loose?
10.	It was not a cloudy and stuffy day.	Was it not a cloudy and stuffy day?

Remember that 'was' is used with 'I' and 'he, she, it and single nouns', to denote past events / situations, etc. The Negative of 'Was' is 'Was not' = Wasn't'

LESSON 5

Verb 'To Be'-(Were)

Model Sentences

	I. Affirmative	*II. Interrogative*
1.	We were players.	Were we players?
2.	You were my friend.	Were you my friend?
3.	You were angry.	Were you angry?
4.	They were very cunning.	Were they very cunning?
5.	Ramu and Shamu were thieves.	Were Ramu and Shamu thieves?
6.	The slum dwellers were poor and helpless.	Were the slum dwellers poor and helpless?
7.	We were smart and clever.	Were we smart and clever?
8.	You were indolent and indocile.	Were you indolent and indocile?
9.	Both the sisters were cultured and courteous.	Were both the sisters cultured and courteous?
10.	They were frugal and miserly.	Were they frugal and miserly?

	III. Negative	*IV. Interrogative-Negative*
1.	We are not players.	Were we not players?
2.	You were not my friend.	Were you not my friend?

3. You were not angry.	Were you not angry?
4. They were not very cunning.	Were they not very cunning?
5. Ramu and Shamu were not thieves.	Were Ramu and Shamu not thieves?
6. The slum-dwellers were not poor and helpless.	Were the slum dwellers not poor and helpless?
7. We were not smart and clever.	Were we not smart and clever?
8. You were not indolent and indocile.	Were you not indolent and indocile?
9. Both the sisters were not cultured and courteous.	Were both the sisters not cultured and courteous?
10. They were not frugal and miserly.	Were they not frugal and miserly?

Remember that *'Were'* is used with 'We, You, They and plural nouns/pronouns' to denote part relations, activities, etc. The negative of *'Were'* is 'Were not = Weren't'

LESSON 6

Verb 'To Be'—(Has)

Model Sentences

I. Affirmative	*II. Interrogative*
1. Mohan has a (one) sister.	Has Mohan a (one) sister?
2. He has two brothers.	Has he two brothers?
3. She has a pen.	Has she a pen?
4. It has a tail.	Has it a tail?
5. Shama has ten sarees.	Has Shama ten sarees?
6. The farmer has a large family.	Has the farmer a large family?
7. Manorama has charming eyes.	Has Manorama charming eyes?

8.	The hunter has two guns.	Has the hunter two guns?
9.	This house has only one door.	Has this house only one door?
10.	The elephant has a trunk.	Has the elephant a trunk?

	III. Negative	*IV. Interrogative-Negative*
1.	Mohan has no sister. *Or* Mohan has not a sister.	Has Mohan not a (one) sister?
2.	He has not two brothers.	Has she not two brothers?
3.	She has not a pen.	Has she not a (no) pen?
4.	It has not a tail.	Has it no (not a) tail?
5.	Shama has not ten sarees.	Has Shama not ten sarees?
6.	The farmer has not a large family.	Has the farmer not a large family?
7.	Manorama has not (does not have) charming eyes.	Has Manorama not (Doesn't Manorama have) charming eyes?
8.	The hunter has not (doesn't have) two guns.	Has the hunter not (Doesn't the hunter have) two guns?
9.	This house has not (doesn't have) only one door.	Has this house not (Doesn't this house have) only one door?
10.	The elephant has not (doesn't have) a tusk.	Has the elephant not (Doesn't the elephant have) a tusk?

Remember that Has is used with 'He, She, It and other third person singular nouns', to denote ownership or possession.

The negative of 'Has' is 'Has not' = Hasn't or 'Does not-(Doesn't) have'.

LESSON 7

Verb 'To Be'-(Have)

Model sentences

	I. Affirmative	*II. Interrogative*
1.	They have books.	Have they books?
2.	I have toffees.	Have I toffees?
3.	Sushma and Radha have a scooter.	Have Sushma and Radha a scooter?
4.	We have shops.	Have we shops?
5.	You have a knife.	Have you a knife?
6.	The children have interest in games.	Have the children interest in games?
7.	They have many shops in the city.	Have they many shops in the city?
8.	The passengers have heavy luggage.	Have the passengers heavy luggage?
9.	The farmers have many animals.	Have the farmers many animals?
10.	You have thousands of books.	Have you thousands of books?

	III. Negative	*IV. Interrogative-Negative*
1.	They have no (not) books.	Have they no (not) books?
2.	I have no (not) toffees.	Have I no (not toffees)?
3.	Sushma and Radha have no (not a) scooter.	Have Sushma and Radha no (not) a scooter?
4.	We have no shops.	Have we no shops?
5.	You have no (not a) knife.	Have you no (not a) knife?
6.	The children have no (do not have any) interest in games.	Have the children no (Don't the children have any) interest in games?
7.	They have not many shops in the city.	Have they not (Do they have not) many shops in the city?

8. The passengers have no (do not have any) heavy luggage.	Have the passengers (Don't the passengers have) heavy luggage?
9. The farmers have not many animals.	Have the farmers not (Don't the farmers have) many animals?
10. You have not thousands of books.	Have you not thousands of books?

Remember that 'Have' is used with 'I, we, you, they and plural nouns' to denote ownership or possession.

The negative of *Have* is *Have not* = *Haven't*, or *'Do not (Don't) have'*.

LESSON 8

Verb 'To Be'—(Had)

Model Sentences

I. Affirmative	*II. Interrogative*
1. She had curly hair.	Had she curly hair?
2. We had a holiday on Saturday.	Had we a holiday on Saturday?
3. You had a house to live in.	Had you a house to live in?
4. He had two brothers.	Had he two brothers?
5. I had four buffaloes.	Had I four buffaloes?
6. Ram had a great personality.	Had Ram a great personality?
7. The sky had stars in the night.	Had the sky stars in the night?
8. The farmer had cows and goats.	Had the farmer cows and goats?
9. Their house had many windows.	Had their house many windows?
10. They had vast knowledge.	Had they vast knowledge?

I. Negative	*II. Interrogative—Negative*
1. She had no curly hair.	Had she no curly hair?
2. We had no (not a) holiday on Saturday.	Had we no (not a) holiday on Saturday?
3. You had no (not a) a house to in.	Had you no (not a) house to live in?
4. He had not two brothers.	Had he not two brothers?
5. I had not four buffaloes.	Had I not four buffaloes?
6. Ram had not (did not have) a great personality.	Had Ram not (Did not) (Didn't Ram have) a great personality?
7. The sky had no stars in the night.	Had the sky no stars in the night?
8. The farmer had not cows and goats.	Had the farmer no (not) cows and goats?
9. Their house had not many windows.	Had their house not many windows?
10. They had not (did't have) vast knowledge.	Had they not (Didn't they have) vast knowledge?

Remember that 'Had' is used with all the nouns/pronouns. The negative of *'Had'* is *'Hadn't,* or *'Did not (Didn't)'* have Remember that these forms of 'Be' (*Is/Am/Are/Was/Were/Has/Have/Had*) have been used in this chapter as main verbs. No other verb has been used with them here.

As auxiliary (helping) Verbs *they* (*Is/Am/Are/Was/Were/Has/Have/Had*) have been discussed in the separate chapter of tenses.

EXERCISE I

Use of There

Model Sentences

1. Once there was a prince.
2. Was there no well in your village?

3. Is there no tea in the cup?
4. There was a white lion in the zoo.
5. Was there no water in the pot?
6. There are thirty boys in our class.
7. There was only one note in my pocket.
8. How many doors are there in this room?
9. Is there no sense in you at all?
10. How many bananas are there in the basket?

'There' has the following meaning and uses:

(i) In /At / To That place.

(ii) That place or thing (used after a preposition)

(iii) At/ With reference to that point (in a story, a series of actions, an argument, etc.)

(iv) Used for emphasis before some verbs which show the location of semebody/ something (go, stand, lie, etc.)

(v) Used to call attention to something.

'There is used both for singular and plural nouns in both the simple present and simple past.

EXERCISE 2

Uses of 'It'

Model Sentences

1. It is close today.
2. It is very hot today.
3. It is ten minutes to ten.
4. It is noon.
5. It was cloudy yesterday.
6. Was it she?
7. Is it her frock?
8. It is no time to go to bed.
9. It is very cold in (inside) the room.
10. It is time to take tea.

'It' has the following meanings and uses.

(i) Subject/object of a verb or after a preposition.

(ii) Animal/thing mentioned earlier or being observed now.

(iii) Baby especially whose sex is not known or is unimportant.

(iv) Fact/situation already known/implied.

(v) Identification of a person.

(vi) Subject position to make a statement about *time, distance,* or *weather.*

(vii) Things/circumstances/conditions in general.

(viii) Emphasis on any part of a sentence.

'It' is used for singular number in both the present and past tenses.

EXERCISE 3

Uses of 'Has to', 'Have to', 'Had to', 'Shall have to' and 'Will Have to'

Model Sentences

I *have to* take my bath just now.

We *have to* go to school daily.

You *have to* wash your clothes your self/yourselves.

They *have to* do their home-work yet.

She *has to* go to the picnic.

He *has to* help me in Mathematics.

It (The dog) *has to* guard our house.

I *had to* go there all of a sudden.

He *had to* join the wedding party.

They *had to* go to the market every day.

You *will have to* lend me Rs. 500.

She *will have to* make tea for the guests.

They *will have to* repay my loan.

I *shall have to* write several letters.

We *shall have to* arrange a feast.

Have you *not to* go there? *Or*

Haven't you to go there?

Has she *not to* solve the sums? *Or*

Hasn't she *to* solve the sums?

Had she *not to* wait for you? *Or*

Hadn't she *to* wait for you?

Shall I *not have to* cook my own food? *Or*

Shalln't I *have to* cook my own food?

Will she not *have to* take part in the debate? *Or*

Won't she *have to* take part in the debate?

Rules: The infinitive *'To'* is added after (attached to) *has, have, had, shall have and will have,* to show the necessity/ compulsion.

'Have to' is used in Present Tense with' *I, we, you* and *they'*.

'Has to' is used in Present Tense with *'He, She, It* and other Third person singular subjects/nouns.'

'Had to' is used in Past Tense with subjects of all persons (*I/we/you/he/she/it/they*) without any discrimination.

'Shall have to' is used in Future Tense with subjects of First Person (*I, We*).

'Will have to' is used in Future Tense with subjects of second and Third Person (*You, He, She, It, They*).

'Had to' is used ın Past Tense with subjects of all persons (*I/We/You/He/She/It/They*) without any discrimination.

17

Tenses

Definition: Any of the forms of a verb that may be used to indicate the time of the action or state expressed by the verb is known as 'Tense' in English Grammar.

The word 'Tense' is derived from the Latin word *'tempus'* meaning 'time'.

Kinds: Tenses are of the following three kinds:

1. Present Tense
2. Past Tense
3. Future Tense

Division according to degree of completeness:

Tenses

Present Tense   Past Tense   Future Tense

Division of the Tenses

1. Present Indefinite Tense	Past Indefinite Tense	Future Indefinite Tense
2. Present Continuous Tense	Past Continuous Tense	Future Continuous Tense
3. Present Perfect Tense	Past Perfect Tense	Future Perfect Tense
4. Present Perfect Continuous Tense	Past Perfect Continuous Tense	Future Perfect Continuous Tense

Read the following sentences:

1. I *play* football every day.
2. He *played* football yesterday.
3. We *shall play* football tomorrow.

In sentence 1, the verb ***play*** refers to *Present time.*

In sentence 2, the verb ***played*** refers to *Past time.*

In sentence 3, the verb ***shall play*** refers to *Future time.*

In this way, the verb may refer to (i) *Present* time (ii) *Past* time (iii) *Future* time.

The verb that refers to present tense is said to be in the *Present Tense;* as:

I sing. I jump.

The verb that refers to *past* time is said to be in the *Past Tense;* as:

I sang. I jumped.

The verb that refers to *Future* time is said to be in the *Future Tense;* as:

I shall sing. I shall jump.

The tense of a verb shows the *time* of an action or event.

Remember that sometimes a Present tense may express future time; as:

Let us play till the teacher *comes.*

Here *comes* (Present tense, conveys the sense of *will come* (Future tense).

Similarly, sometimes the Past tense may express present time, as:

I wish I knew the man. This sentence means 'I am sorry, I don't know the man.

Here *knew* (Past tense) conveys the sense I *do not know'.* (Present tense)

Below we give the main tenses (Active voice, Indicative mood) of the verb to *sing*.

Name of the Tense	*Rules to be Followed*	*Use in Sentence*
1. Present Indefinite	Verb—1st form s/es with Third Person singular	I/we/you/they sing. He/she/it sings.
2. Present Continuous Progressive	Verb 1st form + ing I-am You/we/they-are He/she/it-is	I am singing. you/we/they are singing. He/She/It is singing.
3. Present Perfect	Verb 3rd form I/We you/they-have He/She/It-has	I/We/You/They/ have sung. He/She/It has sung.
4. Present Perfect Continuous	I/You/We/They- have been He/She/It has been Verb-Ist form+ing (since/for)	I/We/You/They have been singing. ...... since for He/She/It has been singing ...... since/for
5. Past Indefinite	Verb—2nd form She/It/they	I/We/ You /He sang.
6. Past Continuous/ Progressive	Verb—Ist form+ing I/ He /She/It-was You /We/ They-were	I /He/ She /It was singing. You/ We/ They were singing.
7. Past Perfect	Verb-3rd form-had	I/We/You/He/ She/It/They-had sung.
8. Past Perfect Continuous	-had been- Verb-Ist form +ing (since/for)	I/We /You/He/She/It/ they-had been singing. ...... since/for
9. Future Indefinite	I/we-shall You/He/She/It/They- *will* verb- Ist form	I/ We/ shall sing. You/He/ She/ It/ They will sing.
10. Future Continuous/ Progressive	Verb Ist form+ ing I, we, shall be You/ He/ She/It/ They will be	I/ We/ shall be singing. You /He /She It/ They-will be singing.

11	Future Perfect	Verb-3rd form I/ We- shall have You/ He/ She/ It/ They-will have	I/ We shall have sung. He/ She/ It/ You/They will have sung.
12.	Future Perfect Continuous	I/We-shall have been He/She/It/You/They - will have been. Verb-1st form+ing (since/for)	I/We shall have been singing. since/for He/She/It/You They will have been singing (since/for)

Exercises

LESSON 1

Present Indefinite Tense

Model Sentences

I. Affirmative	*II. Interrogative*
I *buy* a toy.	Do I buy a toy?
We *go* to school.	Do we go to school?
He *takes* tea.	Does he take tea?
She *does* her home work.	Does she do her home work?
It *rains.*	Does it rain?
You *run* very fast.	Do you run very fast?
They *read* daily.	Do they read daily?
Mohan *plays* in the morning.	Does Mohan play in the morning?
Sita and Sushma *sing* a song.	Do Sita and Sushma sing a song?
Rani *learns* her lesson.	Does Rani learn her lesson?

III. Negative	*IV. Interrogative-Negative*
1. I do not buy a toy.	Do I not buy a toy?
2. We do not go to school.	Do we not go to school?
3. He does not take tea.	Does he not take tea?
4. She does not do her home-work.	Does she not do her home-work?

5. It does not rain.	Does it not rain?
6. You do not run very fast.	Do you not run very fast?
7. They do not read daily.	Do they not read daily?
8. Mohan does not play in the morning.	Does Mohan not play in the morning?
9. Sita and Sushma do not sing a song.	Do Sita and Sushma not sing a song?
10. Rani does not learn her lesson.	Does Rani not learn her lesson?

* *Indefinite* means *'Vague; not clearly defined or stated; lasting* an unspecified time.

Affirmative Sentences: Those sentences are called *affirmative sentences* that express *'agreement'*; indicating 'yes'.

Interrogative Sentences: Those sentences are called interrogative sentences which *ask or seem to ask a question or make an enquiry.* The interrogative sentences beginning with a helping verb can be answered without opening the mouth.

Negative Sentences: Those sentences are called *negative sentences* which express *denial* or *refusal;* indicating 'no' or 'not'.

Interrogative-Negative Sentences: Those sentences are called *interrogative-negative sentences* which ask or *seem to ask* a *question* and express *denial or refusal.*

Informative Recapitulation

Name of the Tense	***Affirmative***	***Interrogative***	***Negative***	***Interrogative Negative***
Present	V^1	Do.?	....do not	Do...not V3
Indefinite	V^1+s/es	Does..V...?	does not V^1	Does.. not V^1?

Put a full stop (•) at the end of Affirmative and Negative sentences. Put the mark of interrogation (?) at the end of interrogative and interrogative-negative sentences.

Always use the First /Crude form of the verb (V^1) after Do or Does. (Drop s/es attached with V^1)

Other types of Interrogative Sentences:

Where do I go?	Who does not know this?
What do you eat?	Which book do you like?
When do we get up?	Whom does she want to see?
Why do they weep?	Whose book do you buy?
How does she work?	

If one is required to open the mouth to answer a certain question, the relevant word of 'wh' family or 'How' will be used to begin the Sentence.

Present Indefinite Tense

Examples:

1. She does smoke but does not confess.

   This is an *emphatic* sentence. Here emphasis has been laid on the two facts. (i) She smokes, (ii) She does not confess.

2. I always reach the school in time.

   A habitual action or (a regular routine (habit) is expressed here).

3. The rose smells sweet. (Normal/General truth is shown here).

4. Our school closes at 6 p.m. these days. (The activity which is true at the time of speaking is shown here.)

5. My house faces to the East. (Here permanent position/ location/situation or fact is shown)

6. The ship sails for Nicobar next week. (Here a planned activity is shown which is scheduled to take place in future)

7. If you work hard, you will pass.

   The condition (beginning with 'if') is shown here. Present Indefinite Tense has been used here in the subordinate clause of condition beginning with 'If' *'If you work hard'* here means *'if you will work hard'*.

8. Always speak the truth. (This is an Imperative sentence).
9. Sharat carries the ball. He hits it hard and scores a goal. (We use Present Indefinite Tense to broadcast commentaries on sporting events).

   This sentence shows different actions taking place simultaneously.
10. Laxmi Bai draws her sword and attacks the enemy.

    This sentence is a vivid narrative and serves as substitute for the simple past.
11. There goes the stupid girl. (This is an exclamatory sentence beginning with 'There' to express the actual happening in the present.
12. Kalidas says, "Beauty needs no ornamentation" (Present Indefinite Tense has been used here to introduce a quotation).
13. (i) I smell a flower.

    (ii) He seems mischievous.

    (iii) I want a cup of hot tea.

    (iv) I think she is right.

    (v) She owns a bungalow.

(Here Present Indefinite Tense has been used to show verbs of perception, appearing, emotion, thinking and possession to convey the sense of Present Continuous Tense. Such verbs are normally not used in Present Continuous Tense).

LESSON 2

Present Continuous Tense

Model Sentences

I. Affirmative	*II. Interrogative*
1. I am learning my lesson.	Am I learning my lesson?
2. You are flying kites now.	Are you flying kites now?

3. We are revising our lesson now.	Are we revising our lesson now?
4. Munna is telling a lie.	Is Munna telling a lie?
5. She is speaking the truth.	Is she speaking the truth?
6. They are cheating you.	Are they cheating you?
7. It is raining outside.	Is it raining outside?
8. Smoke is coming out of the window.	Is smoke coming out of the window?
9. The boys are swimming in the tank.	Are the boys swimming in the tank?
10. The postman is delivering letters in the street.	Is the postman delivering letters in the street?

III. Negative	*IV. Interrogative-Negative*
1. I am not learning my lesson.	Am I not learning my lesson?
2. You are not flying kites now.	Are you not flying kites now?
3. We are not revising our lesson now.	Are we not revising our lesson now?
4. Munna is not telling a lie.	Is Munna not telling a lie?
5. She is not speaking the truth.	Is she not speaking the truth?
6. They are not cheating you.	Are they not cheating you?
7. It is not raining outside.	Is it not raining outside?
8. Smoke is not coming out of the window.	Is smoke not coming out of the window?
9. The boys are not swimming in the tank.	Are the boys not swimming in the tank?
10. The postman is not delivering the letters in the street.	Is the postman not delivering the letters in the street?

Continuous means 'that which goes or moves further (beyond a certain point) without stopping for a period of time. It means the work is incomplete/imperfect.

Informative Recapitulation

Name of the Tense	*Affirmative*	*Interrogative*	*Negative*	*Interrogative*
Present Continuous	......is/am/are V^1+ing	is/am/are/ V^1+ing?	is/am/are/ not V^1+ing	is/am/are/ not V^1+ ing?

Remember that Present Continuous is also known as Present Progressive or Present Imperfect.

(Other instructions—same as given in Present Indefinite Tense).

Indefinite Tense

Other Types of Interrogative Sentences:

What are you doing?

How are you progressing at your studies?

Why is she laughing?

Who is disturbing you?

Which book are you reading?

Whom are you abusing?

When are you returning home?

Whose scooter are you driving?

Where is Rani working?

Present Continuous Tense

Examples:

1. What are you writing these days? (It shows that an activity is going on around the time though it is not being done at the time of speaking).
2. I am not leaving for Mathura tomorrow. (To show the action which has been planned for future though the response is positive or negative).
3. She is always showing you down. (It shows the repeated action which has become a habit).
4. She is weeping now. (Shows an action going on at the time of speaking.)
5. I am reading 'Hamlet'. (However, I am not reading it at

this moment. Shows an action which is temporary and may or may not be actually happening at the time of speaking.)

6. Sushma is arriving tomorrow. (Shows an action that has been arranged to take place in the near future).
7. Our neighbouring girl is very silly. She is always throwing rubbish in the street. (Shows an obstinate habit). *Present Continuous Tense* is used here with the Adverb- 'Always'.

The following verbs are not normally used in the Continuous forms.

(a) Verbs of *appearance:* look; seem; appear.

(b) Verbs of *emotion:* desire, feel, like, hate, love, hope, prefer, refuse, wish, want.

(c) Verbs of *Perception:* notice, recognise, see, smell, hear.

(d) Verbs *of possession:* belong to, own, possess, consist of, contain.

(e) Verbs of *thought:* believe, suppose, agree, think, trust, consider, know, forget, imagine, mind, understand, mean.

Examples:

Wrong	***Right***
She is *thinking* you are wrong.	She *thinks* you are wrong.
The old man *is looking* gay.	The old man *looks* gay.
Nikunj is *having* a car.	Nikunj *has* a car.
These peaches are *tasting* sour.	These peaches taste sour.

However, the above *verbs—think, look, have, taste* can be used in the Continuous tenses but with a changed meaning.

Examples: I am thinking of helping the widow with money.

She is looking there.

Mother is having breakfast.

LESSON 3

Present Perfect Tense

Model Sentences

	I. Affirmative	*II. Interrogative*
1.	I have taken a bath.	Have I taken a bath?
2.	We have finished our breakfast.	Have we finished our breakfast?
3.	You have revised your lesson.	Have you revised your lesson?
4.	They have made a noise.	Have they made a noise?
5.	The shopkeeper has sold the books.	Has the shopkeeper sold the books?
6.	She has gone to school.	Has she gone to school?
7.	It has rained.	Has it rained?
8.	He has stood first in his class.	Has he stood first in his class?
9.	She has reached home safe and sound.	Has she reached home safe and sound?
10.	The police have arrested the robbers.	Have the police arrested the robbers?
11.	Tripta has eaten all the apples.	Has Tripta eaten all the apples?

	III. Negative	*IV. Interrogative-Negative*
1.	I have not taken a bath.	Have I not taken a bath?
2.	We have not finished our breakfast.	Have we not finished our breakfast?
3.	You have not revised your lesson.	Have you not revised your lesson?
4.	They have not made a noise.	Have they not made a noise?
5.	The shopkeeper has not sold the books.	Has the shopkeeper not sold the books?
6.	She has not gone to school.	Has she not gone to school?
7.	It has not rained.	Has it not rained?
8.	He has not stood first in his class.	Has he not stood first in his class?

9. She has not reached home safe and sound.	Has she not reached home safe and sound?
10. The police have not arrested the robbers.	Have the police not arrested the robbers?
11. Tripta has not eaten all the grapes.	Has Tripta not eaten all the grapes?

Perfect means 'excellently and fully completed'.

Informative Recapitulation

Name of the Tense	*Affirmative*	*Interrogative*	*Negative*	*Interrogative Negative*
Present Perfect	...has/have/	Has/Have/.. V^3....?	...has/have not V^3	Has/Have... not V^3....?

(Other instructions—same as given in Present Indefinite Tense).

Never means 'at no time'—Never is the antonym of always. 'Not' is not used after 'Never'.

Interrogative Sentences

Whose book have you stolen?

Where has she gone?

Whom have you cheated?

When have you returned home?

How have they solved this sum?

Which fruit have you plucked?

Who has broken this slate?

What has she snatched from you?

Present Perfect Tense

Examples:

1. I have just received her message. (Shows the action which was completed a shortwhile ago using 'just').
2. I have seen a lion in the zoo. (Shows some proper action

the time of which has neither been mentioned nor is definite).

3. I have seen the Republic Day Parade several times. (To show past experience).
4. I have not met Murli since March Last. (To show the action which began in the past and is dormant, not in a state of progress)
5. She has cut her finger and it is still bleeding. (To describe past events which show their effect in the present).
6. Sarla has known me since 1997.

   Sushma has been ill since last Monday.

   They have stayed here for two days.

   I haven't seen Urmilla for several weeks.

   The above sentences denote an action which began at some time in the past and is continuing upto the present moment (often with *since* and *for phrases*).

   Remember that Present Perfect Tense is never used with adverbs of past time. In such cases, simple past should be used; as:

   Rajni *went* to Allahabad yesterday. (Correct)

   Rajni has gone to Allahabad yesterday. (wrong)

   We can also use the following adverbs or adverb phrases with the Present Perfect Tense.

   Never, ever, in question only, *yet* (in negatives and questions) *so far, till now, today, this week, already, this* month, etc.

LESSON 4

Present Perfect Continuous Tense

Model Sentences

I. Affirmative	*II. Interrogative*
1. I have been standing first for four years.	Have I been standing first for four years?

2. We have been swimming in the river since morning.	Have we been swimming in the river since morning?
3. You have been reading since 4 o' clock.	Have you been reading since 4 o' clock?
4. They have been viewing TV for many days.	Have they been viewing TV for many days?
5. He has been solving the sums for two hours.	Has he been solving the sums for two hours?
6. She has been sleeping since 8 o' clock.	Has she been sleeping since 8 o' clock?
7. It has been blowing hard since morning.	Has it been blowing hard since morning?
8. It has been raining heavily here for the last two days.	Has it been raining heavily here for the last two days?
9. She has been working since noon.	Has she been working since noon?
10. We have been knocking at the door for over ten minutes.	Have we been knocking at the door for over ten minutes?

III. Negative	*IV. Interrogative-Negative*
1. I have not been standing first for four years.	Have I not been standing first for four years?
2. We have not been swimming in the river since morning.	Have we not been swimming in the river since morning?
3. You have not been reading since 4 o'clock.	Have you not been reading since 4 o' clock?
4. They have not been viewing TV for many days.	Have they not been viewing TV for many days?
5. He has not been solving the sums for two hours.	Has he not been solving the sums for two hours?
6. She has not been sleeping since 8 o'clock.	Has she not been sleeping since 8 o'clock?
7. It has not been blowing hard since morning.	Has it not been blowing hard since morning?
8. It has not been raining heavily here for the last two days.	Has it not been raining heavily here for the last two days?

9. She has not been working since noon.	Has she not been working since noon?
10. We have not been knocking at the door for over ten minutes.	Have we not been knocking at the door for over ten minutes?

Perfect Continuous means 'that which began at some time in the past and is still continuing, as:

1. She has been reading for four hours (and is still reading).
2. The masons have been repairing the house for many months (and are still repairing it).

Present Perfect Continuous Tense is also sometimes used for an action already finished. The continuity of such activity is emphasised as an explanation of something; as:

1. 'Why are you perspiring profusely?'— I have been playing for an hour.

Informative Recapitulation

Name of the Tense	*Affirmative*	*Interrogative*	*Negative*	*Interrogative Negative*
Present Prefect Continuous	...... has been/ have been/ V^1 + ing/ since/for	Has/Have....been/ V^1+ since/for ....?	..... has/have/ +not been/ V^1 + ing since/for	has/have...... not been V^1 + ing/ since/for-?

'Since' is used for *'Point of time'* 'For ' is used for *'Period of time'*

In negative sentences *not* is inserted after *has/have* but before *been* (*has not been /have not been*).

Other Forms of Interrogative Sentences

1. What have you been reading for two hours?
2. Why has she been weeping since morning?
3. Why has he been laughing for many minutes?
4. How has he been staying in Delhi for four years?
5. Where has she been reading since 1990?
6. Which lesson has he been revising since morning?

7. Whose scooter have you been driving for a week?
8. Whom have you been teasing for an hour?
9. Who has been teaching you for two periods?

LESSON 5

Past Indefinite Tense

Model Sentences

	I. Affirmative	*II. Interrogative*
1.	I went to Madras last week.	Did I go to Madras last week?
2.	We ate many apples.	Did we eat many apples?
3.	You flew kites the whole day. day?	Did you fly kites the whole
4.	The postman delivered letters in the colony.	Did the postman deliver letters in the colony?
5.	Mridula sang a sweet song.	Did Mridula sing a sweet song?
6.	The leaf fell from the tree.	Did the leaf fall from the tree?
7.	They played cards the whole night.	Did they play cards the whole night?
8.	I took great interest in her talks.	Did I take great interest in her talks?
9.	An accident took place here yesterday.	Did an accident take place here yesterday?
10.	I taught in this school for ten years.	Did I teach in this school for ten years?
	III. Negative	*IV. Interrogative-Negative*
1.	I did not go to Madras last week.	Did I not go to Madras last week?
2.	We did not eat many apples.	Did we not eat many apples?
3.	You did not fly kites the whole day.	Did you not fly kites the whole day?
4.	This postman did not deliver letters in the colony	Did the postman not deliver letters in the colony?
5.	Mridula did not sing a sweet song.	Did Mridula not sing a sweet song?
6.	The leaf did not fall from the tree.	Did the leaf not fall from the tree?

7. They did not play at cards the whole night.	Did they not play at cards the whole night?
8. I did not take great interest in her talks.	Did I not take great interest in her talks?
9. An accident did not take place here yesterday.	Did an accident not take place here yesterday?
10. I did not teach in this school for for ten years.	Did I not teach in this school ten years?

Informative Recapitulation

Name of the Tense	*Affirmative*	*Interrogative Negative*	*Negative*	*Interrogative*
Past Indefinite	V^2	Did-V^1....? V^1	...did not	Did/...not V^1?

Past Indefinite Tense is used when a single activity is given.

Other Types of Interrogative Sentences

1. When did you come here?
2. Where did they go yesterday?
3. What did he/she eat this morning?
4. How much (what) did it cost you?
5. Who made tea for us?
6. Why did she not return?
7. Which toy did he/she like?
8. Whose house did you buy?
9. Whom did you hand over my book?

Past Indefinite Tense

Examples:

1. She did sing but not with a tune.

   Here *did* is used before first form of the verb to lay emphasis on an action.
2. A murder took place in front of my house.

   Here, such action has been shown as was finished in the past but is related with the time of speaking.

3. Your father scolded you every day.

   Here, a past habit or routine action has been shown.

4. The bride walked gracefully round the fire.

   Here, some particular event of the past is shown.

5. We studied in this school for seven years. (Do not study now).

   Here, such action has been shown which was done for many years in the past but got finished before the time of speaking.

6. I received Bimla's parcel a fortnight ago.

   Here such an action is shown as was completed in the past. An adverb or adverb phrase of past time is often used in such sentences.

7. I learnt Sanskrit at Rohtak.

   The sentence doesn't contain an adverb of time. The time, here is implied.

8. He worked in the field many hours every day .

   Here, the *past habit* is shown.

LESSON 6

Past Continuous Tense

Model Sentences

I. Affirmative	II. Interrogative
1. I was looking at the bridge.	Was I looking at the bridge?
2. We were speaking on the stage.	Were we speaking on the stage?
3. You were shaking hands with him.	Were you shaking hands with him?
4. He was riding a horse.	Was he riding a horse?
5. She was receiving the prize.	Was she receiving the prize?
6. The train was moving.	Was the train moving?
7. They were helping us in Hindi.	Were they helping us in Hindi?
8. He was lying in bed due to sickness.	Was he lying in bed due to sickness?

9.	It was snowing and we were shivering with cold.	Was it snowing and were we shivering with cold?
10.	I was waiting for you, when the bell rang.	Was I waiting for you, when the bell rang?

	III. Negative	*IV. Interrogative-Negative*
1.	I was not looking at the bridge.	Was I not looking at the bridge?
2.	We were not speaking on the stage.	Were we not speaking on the stage?
3.	You were not shaking hands with him.	Were you not shaking hands with him?
4.	He was not riding a horse.	Was he not riding a horse?
5.	She was not receiving the prize.	Was she not receiving the prize?
6.	The train was not moving.	Was the train not moving?
7.	They were not helping us in Hindi.	Were they not helping us in Hindi?
8.	He was not lying in bed due to sickness.	Was he not lying in bed due to sickness?
9.	It was not snowing and we were not shivering with cold.	Was it not snowing and were we not shivering with cold?
10.	I was not waiting for you, when the bell rang.	Was I not waiting for you, when the bell rang?

Informative Recapitulation

Name of the Tense	*Affirmative*	*Interrogative*	*Negative*	*Interrogative Negative*
Past Continuous	....was/were/ V^1+ing/....	Was/were.... V^1+ing?	was/were/ not V^1+ing	Was/were/ - Not V^1+ing...?

Other types of Interrogative Sentences

1. What were you doing then?
2. Why was she making a noise?
3. Where were we playing?
4. When was she writing a letter?
5. How were they driving the scooter?
6. Whose clothes were they ironing?

7. Which book were you reading?
8. Whom was she scolding?
9. Who was teasing you?

Remember that Past Continuous Tense is used to show such action as was being done before the time of speaking.

Examples:

1. The milkmen were milking the cows.
2. He was laughing heartily.

Past Continuous Tense

1. His parents were viewing TV all evening.
2. The light went out while we were taking our meal.

(Here, the actions going on at some time in the past are shown. The time of the action may or may not be indicated).

In sentence 2 above, the Simple Past and the Past Continuous have been used together when a new action took place in the middle of a longer action. The Simple past is used for the new action.

3. Kalawati was always quarrelling.
4. She was continually churning milk.

(Here Past Continuous Tense is used with *always, continually,* etc., to show persistent habits in the past.

LESSON 7

Past Perfect Tense

Model Sentences

	I. Affirmative	*II. Interrogative*
1.	I had finished my homework.	Had I finished my homework?
2.	We had revised our lesson.	Had we revised our lesson?
3.	You had stood first in the class.	Had you stood first in the class?
4.	She had quarrelled with me.	Had she quarrelled with me?
5.	He had deceived me.	Had he deceived me?

6. The train had left the station.	Had the train left the station?
7. They had failed in the examination.	Had they failed in the examination?
8. Tilak Raj had joined the army at the age of eighteen.	Had Tilak Raj joined the army at the age of eighteen?
9. I had received his letter after a week.	Had I received his letter after a week?
10. You had made such a mistake before also.	Had you made such a mistake before also?

III. Negative	***IV. Interrogative-Negative.***
1. I had not finished my home-work.	Had I not finished my home-work?
2. We had not revised our lesson.	Had we not revised our lesson?
3. You had not stood first in the class.	Had you not stood first in the class?
4. She had not quarrelled with me.	Had she not quarrelled with me?
5. He had not deceived me.	Had he not deceived me?
6. The train had not left the station.	Had the train not left the station ?
7. They had not failed in the examination.	Had they not failed in the examination?
8. Tilak Raj had not joined the army at the age of eighteen.	Had Tilak Raj not joined the army at the age of eighteen?
9. I had not received his letter after a week.	Had I not received his letter after a week?
10. You had not made such a mistake before also.	Had you not made such a mistake before also?

Informative Recapitulation

Name of the Tense	*Affirmative*	*Interrogative*	*Negative*	*Interrogative-Negative*
Past Perfect	....had V^3	had....V^3...?	....had not V^3	had not V^3...?

Other Forms of Interrogative Sentences

1. Who had teased you?
2. What had we done?

3. Where had you gone at that time?
4. When had he left Delhi?
5. Which state had the storm hit?
6. Whose roof had fallen yesterday?
7. How had you reached Bombay?
8. Who had beaten Hari?
9. Whom had Sushma robbed the other days?

Remember that normally there are two actions in Past Perfect Tense. The action taking place earlier is shown by Past Perfect Tense and the action taking place later is shown by simple Past Tense; as

1. Sushma had left her house before Lata rang.
2. The patient had died before the doctor came.

It shows the Simple Past is used in one clause and Past Perfect is used in the other clause.

Past Perfect Tense

1. I defeated him in the cycle race in 1998. I had done so last few years before.

(Here, the past Perfect describes an action completed before a certain moment in the past).

LESSON 8

Past Perfect Continuous Tense

Model Sentences

	I. Affirmative	*II. Interrogative*
1.	I had been reading the book since morning.	Had I been reading the book since morning?
2.	We had been swimming in the river since 4 o'clock.	Had we been swimming in the river since 4 o'clock?
3.	You had been wasting your time for two days.	Had you been wasting your time for two days?

4.	She had been making tea for five minutes.	Had she been making tea for five minutes?
5.	He had been going to the club for many years.	Had he been going to the club for many years?
6.	It had been drizzling since this afternoon.	Had it been drizzling since this afternoon?
7.	They had been smiling for ten minutes.	Had they been smiling for ten minutes?
8.	I had been teaching my brother for half an hour.	Had I been teaching my brother for half an hour?
9.	Kamla had been coming late for the last ten days.	Had Kamla been coming late for the last ten days?
10.	Rajeshwari had been cheating her lover for several years.	Had Rajeshwari been cheating her lover for several years?

	III. Negative	***IV. Interrogative-Negative***
1.	I had not been reading the book since morning.	Had I not been reading the book since morning?
2.	We had not been swimming in the river since 4 o'clock.	Had we not been swimming in the river since 4 o'clock?
3.	You had not been wasting your time for two days.	Had you not been wasting your time for two days?
4.	She had not been making tea for five minutes.	Had she not been making tea for five minutes?
5.	He had not been going to the club for many years.	Had he not been going to the club for many years?
6.	It had not been drizzling since this afternoon .	Had it not been drizzling since this afternoon?
7.	They had not been smiling for ten minutes.	Had they not been smiling for ten minutes?
8.	I had not been teaching my brother for half an hour.	Had I not been teaching my brother for half an hour?
9.	Kamla had not been coming late for the last ten days.	Had Kamla not been coming late for the last ten days?
10.	Rajeshwari had not been cheating her lover for several years.	Had Rajeshwari not been cheating her lover for several years?

Informative Recapitulation

Name of the Tense	*Affirmative*	*Interrogative*	*Negative*	*Interrogative Negative*
Past Perfect Continuous	....had been/ V^1+ing/since/ for	had...been/ V^1+ing/since/ for......?	....had not been/V^1+ing	had....not been/ V^1+ing/since/ for......?

'Since' is used for *'Point of Time'* *'For* is used for *'Period of Time'*.

(For other information look at the rules gives in the lesson—Present Perfect Continuous Tense).

Other Forms of Interrogative Sentences

1. Where had you been playing for two hours?
2. Why had she been weeping since morning?
3. What had she been doing for two hours?
4. When had she been preparing breakfast for ten minutes?
5. How had he been opposing you for twenty years?
6. Who had been felling trees since morning?
7. Which poem had you been learning by heart for half an hour?
8. Whose money had you been spending for several days?
9. Whom had you been beating for five minutes?

Past Perfect Continuous Tense:

Before her marriage, Rekha had been writing a book for two years.

(Here Past Perfect Continuous Tense has been used for the action that began before a certain point in the past and continued upto that time).

LESSON 9

Future Indefinite Tense

Model Sentences

I. Affirmative	*II. Interrogative*
1. I shall buy some books.	Shall I buy some books?
2. We shall go to picnic tomorrow.	Shall we go to picnic tomorrow?

3. You will revise your lesson tomorrow.	Will you revise your lesson tomorrow?
4. The teacher (s) will punish him.	Will the teacher (s) punish him?
5. Mohini will recite a poem.	Will Mohini recite a poem?
6. It will rain today.	Will it rain today?
7. They will return to Delhi tonight.	Will they return to Delhi tonight?
8. My mother will milk the cow.	Will my mother milk the cow?
9. The teacher will give us a test.	Will the teacher give us a test?
10. She will adopt a different career.	Will she adopt a different career?

III. Negative	*IV. Interrogative-Negative*
1. I shall not buy some (any) books.	Shall I not buy some (any) books?
2. We shall not go to picnic tomorrow.	Shall we not go to picnic tomorrow?
3. You will not revise your lesson tomorrow.	Will you not revise your lesson tomorrow?
4. The teacher(s) will not punish him.	Will the teacher(s) not punish him?
5. Mohini will not recite a poem.	Will Mohini not recite a poem?
6. It will not rain today.	Will it not rain today?
7. They will not return to Delhi tonight.	Will they not return to Delhi tonight?
8. My mother will not milk the cow.	Will my mother not milk the cow?
9. The teacher will not give us a test.	Will the teacher not give us a test?
10. She will not adopt a different career.	Will she not adopt a different career?

Informative Recapitulation

Name of the Tense	*Affirmative*	*Interrogative*	*Negative*	*Interrogative Negative*
Future Indefinite	....shall/will V^1	shall/will/ V^1......?	....shall/will not V^1......?	shall/will not V^1......?

Use *'Shall'* with First Person Pronouns (I, We)

Use *'Will'* with Second and Third Person Pronouns (You, He, She, It, They)

Use the Crude/ First Form of Verb (V^1)

Remember that *'Shall not'* = *'Shan't'* and *'Will not'* = *'Won't'*.

Other Forms of Interrogative Sentences

1. Where will she go tomorrow?
2. Which book will you borrow from the library?
3. Who will help you in English?
4. Whom will you present this gift?
5. Why will you not repay my loan?
6. When shall I see you again?
7. How will you evade your responsibility?
8. What will you buy if you win a lottery?
9. Whose book will you steal?

Some Other Uses of Future Indefinite Tense

Examples:

1. Our team leaves for Nehru Stadium tomorrow morning.

   (The future Tense (*will leave*) is indicated by the use of present Indefinite Tense (*leaves*).
2. I am leaving for Kanpur next month.

   (Here Future (*shall leave*) Tense is shown by the use of Present Continuous Tense (*am leaving*). It talks about future planning.
3. (i) I *am going* to buy a new scooter. (It means I shall buy a new scooter in near future).

   (ii) She *is going to have* a baby. (It means she will have a baby in near future).

   Here, some definite event likely to take place in near future is shown by the use of 'going to'. We use the *'going to'* form when preparation for an action has already been made.

4. I *am to finish* my work by next month.

   Here Future Tense (*shall finish*) is shown by the use of *be + to +* V^1

5. It *will be* Holi in a week.

   Nupur *will be* fourteen next month.

   Here, Simple Future Tense is used to talk about things scheduled to take place naturally.

6. I'm sure India *will win* the trophy.

   Here, Simple Future is used to talk about something most likely to happen.

7. It's very cold. I *shall bring* you tea.

   Here, Simple Future is used when something is decided to be done just at the time of speaking instant decision.

8. Dark clouds are hovering in the sky. It is going to rain. Here, it is going to rain means 'It shall probably rain. The 'going to' form is used here in talking about what seems likely.' It gives the sense of Simple Future.

9. Let us get into the compartment. The train is *going to* leave. The train *is going to* leave is an indication /signal that the train *will leave* soon (after a short time).

   Here it shows that the action of the leaving of the train is on the point of happening.

10. Let us get into the shed. It's about to rain.

    'It's about to rain' means it will definitely start raining soon'. Here, *about to* is used to express the immediate future.

11. The school *opens* on 1st July.

    (It means the school *will open* on 1st July.)

    Here, the Simple Present Tense is used to show official programmes.

12. The film starts at 1.30 and finishes at 4.25.

    It means 'the film will start at 1.30 and will finish at 4.25. Here, the Simple Present Tense is used to show the scheduled time table.

13. (i) Let us chat till (until) he *arrives*.

    (ii) Please inform me as soon as the typist *comes*.

    (iii) Can I have tea before I *board* the school bus?

    (iv) I won't attend the meeting if it *rains*.

    (v) I won't attended his party unless he *invites* me.

    (vi) I shall help her, when she *asks* me.

    (vii) Don't make a noise, while I *work*.

    (viii) Don't talk loudly as mother *sleeps* inside.

    (ix) I shall leave the house after my father *sleeps*.

    (x) Wait here, by the time I *return*.

In the above sentences the clauses with *till; until; soon as; before; if; unless; when; while; as; after, by the time* are used in Simple Present but they convey the sense of Simple Future Tense.

LESSON 10

Future Continuous Tense

Model Sentences

I. Affirmative	*II. Interrogative*
1. I shall be taking the test tomorrow.	Shall I be taking the test tomorrow?
2. We shall be swimming in the river tomorrow.	Shall we be swimming in the river tomorrow?
3. You will be reaching Jaipur tomorrow.	Will you be reaching Jaipur tomorrow?
4. She will be singing songs tonight.	Will she be singing songs tonight?
5. He will be travelling by train.	Will he be travelling by train?
6. They will be cooking food.	Will they be cooking food?
7. The bus will be running very fast.	Will the bus be running very fast?

8. The gardener will be watering the plants tomorrow morning.	Will the gardener be watering the plants tomorrow morning?
9. She will be inviting all her relatives.	Will she be inviting all her relatives?
10. We shall be staying in Kanpur for a week.	Shall we be staying in Kanpur for a week?

III. Negative	*IV. Interrogative-Negative*
1. I shall not be taking the test tomorrow.	Shall I be not taking the test tomorrow?
2. We shall not be swimming in the river tomorrow.	Shall we not be swimming in the river tomorrow?
3. You will not be reaching Jaipur tomorrow.	Will you not be reaching Jaipur tomorrow?
4. She will not be singing songs tonight.	Will she not be singing songs tonight?
5. He will not be travelling by train.	Will he not be travelling by train?
6. They will not be cooking food.	Will they not be cooking food?
7. The bus will no the running very fast.	Will the bus not be running very fast?
8. The gardener will not be watering the plants tomorrow morning.	Will the gardener not be watering the plants tomorrow morning?
9. She will not be inviting all her relatives.	Will she not be inviting all her relatives?
10. We shall not be staying in Kanpur for a week.	Shall we not be staying in Kanpur for a week?

Informative Recapitulation

Name of the Tense	*Affirmative*	*Interrogative*	*Negative*	*Interrogative-Negative*
Future Continuous	....shall/will be V^1+ing	shall/will... be V^1+ing.....?	....shall/will not be V^1+ing	shall/will not be V^1 +ing......?

Other Types of Interrogative Sentences

1. What shall I be buying from the bazaar?
2. Where shall we be sleeping tomorrow?
3. When will you be reaching Delhi?
4. Who will be teaching you English?
5. Why will the farmers not be ploughing their fields tomorrow?

6. Whose scooter will he be driving?
7. How will she be managing her household?
8. Which class will you be teaching?
9. Whom will you be deceiving life-long?

Future Continuous Tense

1. (i) I suppose it will be drizzling after an hour.

   (ii) *This time, next Sunday, I shall be enjoying myself at* Dehradun.

   (Here, Future Continuous Tense is used to express the actions which will be in progress at a time in future.)

2. We shall be holding the next meeting the next week.

   (Here, Future Continuous Tense is used to express the action which has already been planned for future and is normally expected to happen.)

3. The Chief Minister is to take around of the flood affected area.

   (Here, the form of *be* + *to* + crude (base) form of the verb is used in place of Future Continuous Tense to talk about official arrangements and plans.)

   This sentence can also be written as The Chief Minister will take a round of the flood-affected area.

   (*Be to* + V^1 is often used in news reports. *Be* is usually dropped in headlines, as...... Chief Minister to visit flood affected area)

LESSON 11

Future Perfect Tense

Model Sentences

I. Affirmative	*II. Interrogative*
1. I shall have bathed in the river.	Shall I have bathed in the river?
2. We shall have started our journey.	Shall we have started our journey?

3. You will have bought a scooter.	Will you have bought a scooter?
4. He will have crossed the boundary.	Will he have crossed the boundary?
5. She will have earnt enough money.	Will she have earnt enough money?
6. The police will have caught the thief.	Will the police have caught the thief?
7. They will have returned to their houses.	Will they have returned to their houses?
8. We shall have won the match by a big margin.	Shall we have won the match by a big margin?
9. He will have left his place by now.	Will he have left his place by now?
10. We shall have sold our scooter by Monday.	Shall we have sold our scooter by Monday?

III. Negative	***IV. Interrogative-Negative***
1. I shall not have bathed in the river.	Shall I not have bathed in the river?
2. We shall not have started our journey.	Shall we not have started our journey?
3. You will not have bought a scooter.	Will you not have bought a scooter?
4. He will not have crossed the boundary.	Will he not have crossed the boundary?
5. She will not have earnt enough money.	Will she not have earnt enough money?
6. The police will not have caught the thief.	Will the police not have caught the thief?
7. They will not have returned to their houses.	Will they not have returned to their houses?
8. We shall not have won the match by a big margin.	Shall we not have won the match by a big margin?
9. He will not have left this place by now.	Will he not have left this place by now?

Future Perfect Tense shows that the desired or proposed activity is scheduled (expected) to be excellently and fully completed in future.

Informative Recapitulation

Name of the Tense	*Affirmative*	*Interrogative*	*Negative*	*Interrogative-Negative*
Future Perfect	....shall/will/ have V^3	shall/will/ have V^3......?	....shall/will not have V^3	shall/will not have V^3....?

Other Types of Interrogative Sentences

1. Where will she have reached?
2. What will you have bought?
3. When shall we have arrived here?
4. How will they have entered there?
5. Why will you have sold your house?
6. Who will have quarrelled with you?
7. Which bus will you have boarded?
8. Whose field will you have tilled?
9. Whom will you have slained?

Some Other Uses of Future Perfect Tense

1. I shall have written this book by the end of this month.
2. She will have left before you visit her house.
3. By the end of 2000, I shall have worked in this organisation for fifteen years.

   (In the above sentences, Future Perfect Tense is used to talk about such actions as will be completed by the stipulated time in future)
4. (i) The spectators will have occupied their seats before the film starts.

   (ii) He will have reached home before the rain starts.

   (iii) We shall not have taken milk before you sleep.

   (iv) Will Rajni have taken her bath before she takes her breakfast?

(In the above sentences two activities have been shown in each sentence. The Future Perfect Tense is used for the action to be completed earlier. Similarly, the Present Indefinite Tense is used for the latter action to be completed next.)

LESSON 12

Future Perfect Continuous Tense

Model Sentences

I. Affirmative	*II. Interrogative*
1. I shall have been playing for one (an) hour in the evening.	Shall I have been playing for one (an) hour in the evening?
2. We shall have been sleeping since 10 o'clock.	Shall we have been sleeping since 10 o'clock?
3. You will have been watering the field since morning.	Will you have been watering the field since morning?
4. He will have been preparing for the test since 2001.	Will he have been preparing for the test since 2001?
5. They will have been swimming in the river since morning.	Will they have been swimming in the river since morning?
6. The police will have been chasing him since next June.	Will the police have been chasing him since next June?
7. We shall have been residing in Delhi for ten years.	Shall we have been residing in Delhi for ten years?
8. Reeta will have been sewing clothes for two hours.	Will Reeta have been sewing clothes for two hours?
9. We shall have been revising our course since December.	Shall we have been revising our course since December?
10. The team will have been practising for an hour.	Will the team have been practising for an hour?

III. Negative	*IV. Interrogative-Negative*
1. I shall not have been playing for one (an) hour in the evening.	Shall I not have been playing for one (an) hour in the evening?
2. We shall not have been sleeping since 10 o'clock.	Shall we not have been sleeping since 10 o'clock?
3. You will not have been watering the field since morning.	Will you not have been watering the field since morning?

4. He will not have been preparing for the test since 2001.	Will he not have been preparing for the test since 2001?
5. They will not have been swimming in the river since morning.	Will they not have been swimming in the river since morning?
6. The police will not have been chasing him since next June.	Will the police not have been chasing him since next June?
7. We shall not have been residing in Delhi for two years.	Shall we not have been residing in Delhi for two years?
8. Reeta will not have been sewing clothes for two hours.	Will Reeta not have been sewing clothes for two hours?
9. We shall not have been revising our course since December.	Shall we not have been revising our course since December?
10. The team will not have been practising for an hour.	Will the team not have been practising for an hour?

Informative Recapitulation

Name of the Tense	*Affirmative*	*Interrogative*	*Negative*	*Interrogative-Negative*
Future Perfect Contin-uous	....shall have been/will have been/ V^1+ ing/since/ for	shall/will have been/ V^1+ ing/since for......?	shall not have been /will not have been/ V^1+ ing/since/ for	shall/will not have been/ V^1/since/for......?

Interrogative Sentences

1. Why will she not have been coming to the library since next year?
2. When will he have been serving in this factory for ten years?
3. How will she have been feeling since next month?
4. Who will have been cleaning our utensils since tomorrow?
5. Whose trees will you have been cutting for several months?
6. What will you have been reading for two hours?

7. Where will they have been staying for a week?
8. Which book will you have been revising since the coming Monday?
9. Whom will she have been cursing for two days?

Remember that the Future Perfect Continuous Tense is used for such actions as will be in progress over a period of time that will end in the future; as

1. By next year, we shall have been reading in this school for seven years.
2. Sushma will have been teaching in this school for four years by next December.

18

Voice

Kinds of Voice

(i) Active Voice

(ii) Passive Voice

Read the following sentences:

1. Sushma sings a song.
2. A song is sung by Sushma.

In Sentence 1 above the verb (sings) is in active voice because Sushma is the doer of the action (sing).

In Sentence 2, song is sung by another person 'Sushma'. Hence its verb (*is sung*) is in the passive voice.

Remember that

Only that sentence of Active Voice can be converted/ transformed into Passive Voice which has a subject, a verb and an object. (In other words, only transitive verbs can be changed into passive voice).

Rules for Conversion of sentences (From Active Voice to Passive Voice)

1. Replace the subject by the object (of the active voice)
2. Use the relevant helping verb + Third form of the verb after the object:

3. Put 'By' after the third form of the verb.
4. Put the subject of the active voice after *'By'*

Change the subject of the Active Voice as follows if it is a Pronoun.

Active Voice	*Passive Voice*
I	me
We	us
You	you
He	him
She	her
It	it
They	them
Whom	By whom

Remember that the sentences pertaining to Future Continuous and Perfect Continuous Tenses (Present/Past/Future) cannot be changed into Passive Voice.

Present Indefinite Tense

Active Voice	*Passive Voice*
1. I eat a mango	A mango is eaten by me.
2. We sing songs.	Songs are sung by us.
3. You help me.	I am helped by you.
4. He writes a letter.	A letter is written by him.
5. Do you not buy a pen?	Is a pen not bought by you?
6. Does she beat you?	Are you beaten by her?
7. Who abuses you?	By whom are you abused?
8. The farmers grow wheat in the fields.	Wheat is grown by the farmers in the fields.
9. The rich hate the poor.	The poor are hated by the rich.
10. The mother manages the house.	The house is managed by the mother.

Use Is/am/are + V^3 while transforming this tense into Passive Voice.

Past Indefinite Tense

	Active Voice	Passive Voice
1.	I rang the bell.	The bell was rung by me.
2.	The farmers reaped the crops.	The crops were reaped by the farmers.
3.	Did you play hockey?	Was hockey played by you?
4.	Did she pluck the flowers?	Were the flowers plucked by her?
5.	Who broke the window pane?	By whom was the window pane broken?
6.	He wrote a letter.	A letter was written by him.
7.	Chauhan kicked the ball.	The ball was kicked by Chauhan.
8.	I did not commit the mistake.	The mistake was not committed by me.
9.	The hen did not lay an egg.	An egg was not laid by the hen.
10.	Did we admire Sarita's beauty?	Was Sarita's beauty admired by us?

Use 'was/were + V^3' while transforming this tense into Passive Voice.

Future Indefinite Tense

	Active Voice	Passive Voice
1.	I shall help you.	You will be helped by me.
2.	They will support us.	We shall be supported by them.
3.	Shall we buy fruits?	Will the fruits be bought by us?
4.	Will she teach us?	Shall we be taught by her?
5.	Who will worship him?	By whom will he be worshipped?
6.	Shall I not learn English?	Will English not be learnt by me?
7.	Will Prem not fly a kite?	Will a kite not be flown by Prem?
8.	She will not do these sums.	These sums will not be done by her.
9.	Arun will not pay the bill.	The bill will not be paid by Arun.
10.	I shall take tea.	Tea will be taken by me.

Use 'shall/will + be + V^3' while transforming this tense into Passive Voice.

Present Continuous Tense

	Active Voice	*Passive Voice*
1.	I am carrying my bag.	My bag is being carried by me.
2.	You are beating me.	I am being beaten by you.
3.	He is cheating us.	We are being cheated by him.
4.	Am I writing a letter?	Is a letter being written by me?
5.	Are they singing songs?	Are the songs being sung by them?
6.	Who is disturbing you?	By whom are you being disturbed?
7.	You are teasing me.	I am being teased by you.
8.	Shamu is telling a lie.	A lie is being told by Shamu.
9.	Ram is not running a race.	A race is not being run by Ram.
10.	Am I not revising my lesson?	Is my lesson not being revised by me?

Use 'Is/Am/Are + being + V^3' while transforming this tense into Passive Voice.

Past Continuous Tense

	Active Voice	*Passive Voice*
1.	I was driving my car.	My car was being driven by me.
2.	You were biting your nails.	Your nails were being bitten by you.
3.	Was he growing the plants?	Were the plants being grown by him?
4.	Were they stealing your books?	Were your books being stolen by them?
5.	Who was scolding her?	By whom was she being scolded?
6.	You were not wasting your time.	Your time was not being wasted by you.
7.	The shopkeepers were not. selling goods.	Goods were not being sold by the shopkeepers.

8. Sohan was doing nothing.	Nothing was being done by Sohan.
9. Were the farmers ploughing the fields?	Were the fields being ploughed by the farmers?
10. Was she cleaning the room?	Was the room being cleaned by her?

Use 'was/were + being + V^3' while transforming this tense into Passive Voice.

Present Perfect Tense

Active Voice	*Passive Voice*
1. I have solved the sums.	The sums have been solved by me.
2. We have bought a car.	A car has been bought by us.
3. Have you won the race?	Has the race been won by you?
4. Has she returned your toys?	Have your toys been returned by her?
5. Who has torn your shirt?	By whom has your shirt been torn?
6. They have not insulted us.	We have not been insulted by them.
7. The police have traced the thief.	The thief has been traced by the police.
8. Have our countrymen honoured Mahatma Gandhi?	Has Mahatma Gandhi been honoured by our countrymen?
9. Have you not solved the sums?	Have the sums not been solved by you?
10. Have I done my duty?	Has my duty been done by me?

Use 'Has/Have + been + V^3' while transforming this tense into Passive Voice.

Active Voice	*Passive Voice*
1. I had run a race.	A race had been run by me.
2. She had boiled rice.	Rice had been boiled by her.
3. They had thrown the ball.	The ball had been thrown by them.

4. Had he ironed his clothes?	Had his clothes been ironed by him?
5. Had you not disobeyed your teacher?	Had your teacher not been disobeyed by you?
6. Who had used my scooter?	By whom had my scooter been used?
7. Had our team not won the match?	Had the match not been won by our team?
8. We had not crossed the river.	The river had not been crossed by us.
9. Had Veena bought a saree?	Had a saree been bought by Veena?
10. Had I never seen such a horrible sight?	Had such a horrible sight never been seen by me?

Use 'Had+ been+ V^3' while transforming this tense into Passive Voice.

Future Perfect Tense

Active Voice	*Passive Voice*
1. I shall have caught the train.	The train will have been caught by me.
2. You will have annoyed me.	I shall have been annoyed by you.
3. Shall we have recited a poem?	Will a poem have been recited by us?
4. Will she have repaid your loan?	Will your loan have been repaid by her?
5. Who will have tortured her?	By whom will she have been tortured?
6. The labourers will have repaired the road.	The road will have been repaired by the labourers.
7. Will you not have taught me?	Shall I not have been taught by you?
8. Will Ram have bought the book?	Will the book have been bought by Ram?

9. The grandmother will have told a tale.	A tale will have been told by the grandmother.
10. They will not have informed the police.	The police will not have been informed by them.

Use 'Shall/Will + have been+ V^3' while transforming this tense into Passive Voice.

Verb with Two Objects

Active Voice	***Passive Voice***
1. He sent me a gift.	A gift was sent to me by him. *Or* I was sent a gift by him.
2. I am telling you a tale.	A tale is being told to you by me. *Or* You are being told a tale by me.
3. She will write me a letter.	A letter will be written to me by her. *Or* I shall be written a letter by her.
4. We offered her tea.	She was offered tea by us. *Or* Tea was offered to her by us.
5. I was giving you good advice.	Good advice was being given to you by me. *Or* You were being given good advice by me.
6. She presents me a gift.	A gift is presented to me by her. *Or* I am presented a gift by her.
7. He has lent me some money.	Some money has been lent to me by him. *Or* I have been lent some money by him.
8. Will you ask her some questions?	Will some questions be asked of her by you? *Or* Will she be asked some questions by you?

Verb with Modal Auxiliaries

	Active Voice	*Passive Voice*
1.	I can do this sum.	This sum can be done by me.
2.	He could not stop the car.	The car could not be stopped by him.
3.	She would knit her sweater.	Her sweater would be knitted by her.
4.	You may take tea.	Tea may be taken by you.
5.	He might recite a poem.	A poem might be recited by him.
6.	We should serve our country.	Our country should be served by us.
7.	You need not welcome him.	He need not be welcomed by you.
8.	You must show your homework.	Your homework must be shown by you.
9.	We ought to love our country.	Our country ought to be loved by us.
10.	I used to play hockey everyday.	Hockey used to be played by me everyday.

Use the given 'Modal Auxiliary + be + V^{3}' while transforming the sentences with Modals into Passive Voice.

Question—Word Questions

	Active Voice	*Passive Voice*
1.	What is she sewing?	What is being sewn by her?
2.	Why are you robbing her?	Why is she being robbed by you?
3.	Whom did you call?	Who was called by you?
4.	Where did you hide your purse?	Where was your purse hidden by you?
5.	Which present did you buy?	Which present was bought by you?

6. How much milk can you carry?	How much milk can be carried by you?
7. How many apples have you eaten?	How many apples have been eaten by you?
8. How have you solved this sum?	How has this sum been solved by you?
9. Whose pen had you stolen?	Whose pen had been stolen by you?

The sentences with the question-word *'Who'* have already been solved in each tense.

Use the given 'question-Word + the relevant form of *'be* + V^{3}' while transforming these tenses into Passive Voice.

Imperative Sentences

Active Voice	*Passive Voice*
1. Speak the truth.	Let the truth be spoken. *Or* The truth should be spoken.
2. Obey your seniors.	Let your seniors be obeyed. *Or* Your seniors should be obeyed.
3. Post this letter.	Let this letter be posted. *Or* This letter should be posted.
4. Close the door.	Let the door be closed. *Or* The door should be closed.
5. Open the shutters.	Let the shutters be opened. *Or* The shutters should be opened.
6. Switch on the light.	Let the light be switched on. *Or* The light should be switched on.
7. Do not insult the poor.	Let the poor be not insulted. *Or* The poor should not be insulted.
8. Never tell a lie.	Let a lie be never told. *Or* A lie should never be told.

9. Do not keep bad company.	Bad company should not be kept. *Or* Let bad company be not kept.
10. Please lend me some money.	Let some money be lent to me. *Or* Some money should be lent to me.

Use 'Let + the object of the active voice + be+ V^3' Or 'The object of the active voice + should be + V^3'

Some Typical Sentences

Active Voice	*Passive Voice*
1. Do not mix with bad boys.	You are advised not to mix with bad boys. *Or* You are forbidden to mix with bad boys.
2. Please lend me your book.	You are requested to lend me your book.
3. Leave the class at once.	You are ordered to leave the class at once.
4. Engage a tutor for your son.	You are suggested to engage a tutor for your son.
5. Attack the enemy posts.	You are commanded to attack the enemy posts.
6. God helps those who help themselves.	Those who help themselves are helped by God.

In such sentences 'you' is taken as subject and the words like *advised, ordered, requested, suggested, commanded,* etc. are used according to the sense of the sentence. Infinitive (with/without to) is also used.

Change of Voice in the Infinitive

Active Voice	*Passive Voice*
1. You will have to take tea.	Tea will have to be taken by you.
2. The pen is to write with.	The pen is to be written with.

3. It is time to revise your lesson.	It is time for your lesson to be revised.
4. Women like men to praise them.	Women like to be praised by men.
5. Rani wants to please Mohit.	Rani wants Mohit to be pleased.
6. It is time to sow the seeds.	It is time for the seeds to be sown.
7. Do this work.	This work has (is) to be done.
8. Ashoka wanted to annex Kalinga.	Ashoka wanted Kalinga to be annexed.
9. There is no shop to let.	There is no shop to be let.
10. She worked hard to win the game.	She worked hard for the game to be won.
11. He is to do this job.	This job is to be done by him.

In the above sentences the 'to' infinitive has been changed to 'to *be* + V^3'.

Where 'by' is not used

Active Voice	*Passive Voice*
1. My remark offended him.	He was offended at my remark.
2. Your honesty pleases me.	I am pleased with your honesty.
3. Her behaviour vexes me.	I am vexed at her behaviour.
4. Social service interests her.	She is interested in social service.
5. This glass contains milk.	Milk is contained in this glass.
6. My performance amazed her.	She was amazed at my performance.
7. Quinine is bitter in taste.	Quinine is bitter when (it is) tasted.
8. Sweep this house.	This house needs to be swept.
9. They have defeated the enemy.	The enemy has been defeated.
10. They have declared the result.	The result has been declared.

11. The police arrested the thief.	The thief was arrested.
12. They are punishing the children.	The children are being punished.

There in no need of using the agent 'by' in the above sentences.

Sentences Involving Prepositions

Active Voice	*Passive Voice*
1. Your behaviour surprised us all.	We were all surprised *at* your behaviour.
2. I looked at her face.	Her face was looked at by me.
3. My mother has interest in gardening.	My mother is interested in gardening.
4. Your good fortune rejoices me.	I am rejoiced at your good fortune.
5. Her behaviour has astonished me.	I have been astonished at her behaviour.
6. Does she know you?	Are you known to her?

There in no need of using the agent 'by' in the above sentences. Use the Fixed/Appropriate Preposition in place of the agent *'by'*.

19

Clauses and Analysis

Observe the following sentences:

1. She knows *where you live.* (Knows what?)
2. She knows the place *where you live.* (Which place?)
3. She will reach *where you live.* (Shall reach where?)

The clause, *where you live* in sentence 1 is object of the verb *knows.* Therefore it is a Noun clause. The clause, *where you live* in sentence 2 qualifies the noun *place.* Therefore it is an Adjective clause. The clause, *where you live* in sentence 3 modifies the verb *will reach.* Therefore, it is an Adverb Clause.

Please note that the same clause (where you live) may be a Noun Clause, and Adjective Clause and an Adverb Clause in different sentences according to its function.

Therefore, we cannot state the kind of a clause without finding its function.

Definition: Those parts of a sentence which have subjects and predicates are called Clauses. There are as many clauses in a sentence as there are Finite Verbs.

Kinds of Clauses

(a) Co-ordinate Clauses
(b) Subordinate Clauses
(c) Principal Clauses

Co-ordinate Clauses

Observe the following sentences:

1. The bus arrived *and* I boarded it.
2. Run fast *or* you will lose the race.
3. He ran fast *but* (he) lost the race.

The above sentences are joined by co-ordinate conjunctions *e.g. 'and , or* and *but'*. They are the examples of Co-ordinate clauses.

Some more Co-ordinate Conjunctions are: *not only....... but also; either....... or, neither....... nor, or else; otherwise, as well as, for, therefore, both....... and, etc.* They also join Co-ordinate Clauses.

Kinds of connection between two Co-ordinate Clauses

Copulative:

Examples:

1. Gandhi was *not only* a good leader, he was *also* a reformer.
2. She cannot sing *nor* can she dance.
3. She *as well as* her parents is stupid.
4. I took my lunch packet *and* boarded the bus.

In the above sentences, the italicised words (Co-ordinate Conjunctions) simply couple together two sentences.

Alternative:

Examples:

1. *Either* you *or* your sister is haughty.
2. *Neither* a borrower *nor* a lender be.
3. Obey your teachers *or* you will repent.
4. Walk fast, *else* you will not catch the bus.

In the above sentences, the italicised words (Co-ordinate Conjunctions) simply offer a choice between the clauses disjointed in meaning.

Adversative:

Examples:

1. She is intelligent *but* slow-working.
2. She ran fast, *yet* she missed the train.
3. I am weak, *however,* I shall carry your box.
4. Everybody cursed her, *nevertheless,* she did not come round.

In the above sentences, the italicised words (Co-ordinate Conjunctions) show contrast and are opposite in meaning.

Illative:

Examples:

1. She didn't show her homework, *therefore,* she was expelled from school.
2. Her father is poor, *so* he cannot give a fat dowry.
3. He missed the bus, *for* he did not run fast.

In the above sentences, the italicised words (Co-ordinate Conjunctions) join two clauses wherein the second clause draws inference from the first clause. Also observe the following sentences:

1. He cursed his parents, *which* (and this) was wrong.
2. She went to Agra, *where* (and there) she saw the Taj.
3. Then he called on the Principal, *who* (and he) promised him to help.

In the above sentences the Co-ordinate clauses begin with Relative Pronouns (He/She) or Adverbs (Then). Here the Subordinate Conjunctions (which / where / who) are used in a continuative sense. Therefore, they introduce Co-ordinate Clauses and form a compound sentence.

Analysis of Compound Sentences

Definition: Analysis is the process of breaking up a sentence into its component parts.

Points to Remember. Analysis of a Compound Sentence

(i) Pick out all the finite verbs to ascertain the number of clauses.

(ii) Break up the sentence into clauses.

(iii) Write the clauses in full (by supplying the missing verb or subject).

(iv) Separate the connective.

(v) Show the function of each clause.

Model Solutions

Example: 1. He is strong but he is dull.

Analysis: (i) He is strong (*Principal Clause*)
(ii) He is dull (*Co-ordinate Clause*)
Co-ordiante to (ii). Connective 'but'

Example: 2. He was stupid; therefore, he was punished.

Analysis: (i) He was stupid (*Principal Clause*)
(ii) He was punished (*Co-ordinate Clause*)
Co-ordinate to (i) Connective 'therefore'

Example: 3. I have bought a bicycle, which has proved a white elephant to me.

Analysis: (i) I have bought a bicycle (*Principal Clause*)
(ii) (It) has proved a white elephant to me (*Co-ordinate Clause*)
Co-ordinate to (i) Connective 'which'

Example: 4. You can fool some of the people all of the times and all of the people some of the times; but you cannot fool all the people all the time.

Analysis: (i) You can fool some of the people all of the times. (*Principal Clause*)
(ii) You can fool all of the people some of the times (*Co-ordinate Clause*)
Co-ordintate to (i) and (ii) Connective 'and'

(iii) You cannot fool all the people all the time.
(*Co-ordinate Clause*)
Co-ordinate to (ii) and (iii)
Connective 'but'

***Subordinate Clauses* (Complex Sentences)**

The Noun Clause: A Noun Clause may be (a) Subject to a Transitive verb.

Observe the following sentences:

1. *That God exists everywhere* is true.
2. *Why the old lady cursed him* is known to me.
3. *When my father will return* is uncertain.
4. *How she has got this job* is an open secret.

In the above sentences the italicised words are the Noun Clauses. A Noun Clause always performs the function of a noun and answers the question. "What"?

The above sentences can be broken (disjoined) into clauses as follows:

1. It is true — (*Principal Clause*)
   God exists everywhere. — (*Subordinate / Noun Clause*)
   That — *Conjunction*
2. It is known to me — (*Principal Clause*)
   the old lady cursed him. — (*Subordinate / Noun Clause*)
   Why — *Conjunction*
3. It is uncertain — (*Principal Clause*)
   My father will return — (*Subordinate/Noun Clause*)
   When — *Conjunction*
4. It is an open secret — (*Principal Clause*)
   She has got this job — (*Subordinate / Noun Clause*)
   How — *Conjunction*

To find the Noun clause, we should ask questions like—

1. What is true
2. What is known to me?
3. What is uncertain?
4. What is an open secret?

The answers to the above questions will locate the Subordinate Noun Clause. They stand as subject to the Finite Verbs *'is, is known, is* and *is'* respectively.

Object to a Transitive Verb

Observe the following sentences:

1. The beggar asked me *if I could help him.*
2. Everybody knows *why* you are *late.*
3. The teacher said *that hard work is the key to success.*
4. She asked me *if I would lend her a hundred rupees.*

The italicised words in the above sentences are Noun Clauses because they answer the question "What"? They are joined by the connectives (*if/why/that/if*) and they are object to the verbs—asked, knows, said and asked respectively.

Complement to an Incomplete Verb

Observe the following sentences:

1. It seems *that she is very selfish.*
2. My opinion *is that we should quit this place.*
3. He found *that his cash was missing.*
4. Everybody felt *that the old man would not recover.*

The italicised words in the above sentences are Noun Clauses because they answer the question. "What?" They are joined by the connectives (*'that'*). They serve as complement to the verbs (*seems, is, found* and *felt*) preceding them.

Object to a Preposition

Observe the following sentences:

1. There is no truth in *what she says.*
2. I am surprised at *what step she has taken.*
3. Don't crave for *what you cannot achieve.*
4. You must stick to *what you have promised.*

The italicised words in the above sentences are Noun Clauses. They serve as objects to the prepositions (*'in/at/ for/ to'*) preceding them.

Object to a Participle

Observe the following sentences:

1. Hoping *that I will see her,* I visited her house.
2. Hearing *that he was ill,* I rang up to him.
3. Fearing *that the wolf would kill the sheep,* the shepherd boy began to cry.
4. Seeing *that the bear had gone away,* the boy climbed down the tree.

The italicised words in the above sentences are Noun Clauses. They serve as objects to the participles (*'Hoping/ Hearing/Fearing/Seeing'*) preceding them.

Object to an Infinitive

Observe the following sentences:

1. I want to know *what help you expect from me.*
2. The girl was made to tell *where she had stayed for the night.*
3. He was shocked to learn *that his father had met with a serious accident.*
4. I want to ascertain *whether you would accompany me.*

The italicised words in the above sentences are Noun Clauses. They serve as objects to the infinitives (*'to know/to tell/to learn/to ascertain'*) preceding them.

Apposition to a Noun or a Pronoun

Observe the following sentences:

1. The saying *that pride hath a fall* is true.
2. Then came the news *that Mahatma Gandhi was shot dead.*
3. It is quite certain *that she is not at home.*

4. The idea *that man is a humble tool in the hands of destiny* seems to be true.

The italicised words in the above sentences are Noun Clauses. They stand in Apposition to a Noun (*saying/news/idea*) or Pronoun (*'it'*) preceding them.

The following Connective Words begin the Noun Clauses: The Conjunction *'that'*; as:

1. He thought *that* he was right.
2. I am sure *that* she would write a letter to me.

Sometimes the conjunction *'that'* is omitted but its meaning is implied; as:

1. She thought she was mistaken.
2. I am sure you would stand first.

The Interrogative or Relative words; as:

1. That is *what he means.*
2. Tell me *why you disobeyed your teachers.*
3. I know *where you go every night.*
4. *How she manages her household,* is very astonishing.

The Interrogative or Relative Pronoun; as:

1. I can't say *whose house it is.*
2. Can you guess *who is wandering in the street?*

The Conjunction 'if/whether'; as:

1. I asked him *if* (*whether*) he had packed his luggage.
2. She asked me *if* (*whether*) I would teach her Mathematics.

Adjective Clause

Definition: The Adjective Clause performs the function of an adjective to qualify a noun or pronoun of the main clause. Observe the following sentences:

1. This is the old man *who stumbled against a stone.*
2. The elephant is an animal *which has tusks.*

3. She is the girl *whose husband divorced her*.
4. This is the place *where my friend lives*.

Analysis of Adjectival Clauses

Clause	*Kind*	*Function*
1. (a) This is the old man	Main Clause	
(b) Who stumbled against a stone	Adjectival Clause	Qualifying— 'Old man'
2. (a) The elephant is an animal	Main Clause	
(b) Which has tusks	Adjectival Clause	Qualifying —'elephant'
3. (a) She is the girl	Main Clause	
(b) Whose husband divorced her	Adjectival Clause	Qualifying—'girl'
4. (a) This is the place	Main Clause	
(b) Where my friend lives	Adjectival Clause	Qualifying —'place'

Relative Pronouns (*'who, which* and *whose*) join the Adjective Clause to the Principal Clause in sentences 1, 2 and 3 above.

Relative Adverb (*'where'*) also joins the Adjective Clause to the Principal Clause in sentence 4 above.

Sometimes an Adjectival Clause is introduced by *'but'* which is equivalent to a Relative Pronoun followed by 'not' as:

1. There was not a woman *but* shed tears at the bride's departure. *Or*

   There was not a woman *who did not* shed tears at the bride's departure.
2. There are few of us *but* love their motherland. *Or*

   There are few of us *who do not* love their motherland.
3. There is none in the neighbourhood *but* was prepared to help her. *Or*

   There was none in the neighbourhood *who was not* prepared to help her.

Adverb Clause

Definition: The Adverb Clause performs the function of an adverb. It can modify a verb, an adjective or another adverb.

Time-denoting Adverbial Clauses

Observe the following sentences:

1. All stood up *when the* President came.
2. Wait here *till I do not come back.*
3. She sang *while I danced.*
4. The doctor had reached there *before the patient died.*
5. *As the hot* air cools, the balloon comes down.

The italicised words in the above sentences are Adverb Clauses. Their introducing words (*'when, till, while, before* and *as'*) are time denoting adverbs.

Some other time-denoting adverbs are: after, since, as soon as, whenever, as long as, so long as, etc.

Place-denoting Adverbial Clauses: Observe the following sentences:

1. She studies *where I study.*
2. Live *wherever you desire.*
3. She returned *whence (from where) she had arrived.*
4. The soul has reached *where from it might not return.*
5. The ship sailed *whither the wind took her.*

The clauses printed in italics in the above sentences point to the place where the action of the main clause takes place. They are Adverbial Clauses and serve as adverbs of places.

Manner-denoting Adverbial Clauses

Observe the following sentences:

1. Try to finish it *as she has shown you.*
2. He ran *as if he were frightened.*

3. She behaved *as though she were annoyed.*
4. I did *according as I was directed.*

The clauses printed in italics in the above sentences point to the manner in which the action of the Main Clause is done. They are Adverbial Clauses and serve as adverbs of manners.

Reason or Cause-denoting Adverbial Clauses

Observe the following sentences:

1. As *she has been laid up with fever,* she cannot take our class.
2. She cannot solve this sum, *because she is dull in Mathematics.*
3. Since *you recommend him,* I am appointing him.
4. I regret *that I could not see you on the appointed day.*
5. *Now that the sun has set,* we should return home.

The clauses printed in italics in the above sentences point to the reason behind the action expressed in the Main Clauses. They are Adverbial Clauses and serve as adverbs of reason/cause.

Condition-denoting Adverbial Clauses

Observe the following sentences:

1. We cannot get first division, *unless we burn midnight oil.*
2. I will lend you the required money *provided that you promise me to return it in time.*
3. I cannot let you in *if you do not show me your identity card.*
4. *In case you do not return the library books in time,* you will be fined.

The clauses printed in italics in the above sentences point to the condition behind the action in/of the Main Clause. They are Adverbial Clauses and serve as adverbs of condition.

Please note that the condition denoting adverb (which introduces the adverbial clause of condition) is sometimes omitted; as:

1. Should she come to me, I shall bring her round. Or
   If she comes to me, I shall bring her round.
2. Supposing he fails, he can't execute his studies. *Or*
   If he fails, he can't execute his studies.
3. Had you worked hard, you would have got first division.
   Or

   If you had worked hard, you would have got first division.

Extent-denoting Adverbial Clauses

Observe the following sentences:

1. *So far as I know,* she is a dullard.
2. I cannot say *how far I am correct.*
3. There was water and water *as far as I could see.*
4. Can you tell me *how long* you will accompany me?

The clauses printed in italics in the above sentences point to the extent of the action (fact) mentioned in the Main Clause. They are Adverbial Clauses and serve as adverbs of extent.

Comparison-showing Adverbial Clauses

Observe the following sentences:

1. She is as pretty *as she is wise.*
2. I like him *no less than you (do).*
3. Sharda is cleverer *than Kaushalya is.*
4. The aeroplane flies faster *than a railway train can run.*

The clauses printed in italics in the above sentences point to the comparison of the degrees of a quality in the Main Clause. They are Adverbial Clauses and serve as adverbs of comparison.

Result or Effect-denoting Adverbial Clauses

Observe the following sentences:

1. Run fast *so that you may not be late.*
2. She ate so much *that she fell asleep.*

3. He ran so fast *that he got tired.*
4. So bravely did they fight *that the enemies retreated.*

The clauses printed in italics in the above sentences point to the result of the action expressed in the Main Clause. They are Adverbial Clauses and serve as adverbs of result/effect.

Contrast or Concession-denoting Adverbial Clauses

Observe the following sentences:

1. He is miserly *though he is rich.*
2. We must go *although it is raining.*
3. *Whatever you may say,* I don't believe a word of it.
4. *Even if she apologises,* I shall not visit her house.

The clauses printed in italics in the above sentences point to a contrast to the action expressed in the Main Clause. They are Adverbial Clauses and serve as adverbs of contrast/concession.

Purpose-denoting Adverbial Clauses

Observe the following sentences:

1. She works hard, *so that she may get a* scholarship.
2. Keep awake *lest somebody should get down with your luggage.*
3. You eat *that you may live.*
4. I went to the post office *in order that* I might post the letter.

The clauses printed in italics in the above sentences point to the purpose behind the action expressed in the Main Clause. They are Adverbial Clauses and serve as adverbs of purpose.

Important Point about Adverbial Clauses: Some Grammarians treat the Extent-denoting Adverbial Clause at par with the Manner-denoting Adverbial Clause and Proportion-denoting Adverbial Clause.

Subordinate Conjunctions	*Introduce Adverbial Clause of*
When, whenever, after, before, while, as long as, as soon as, till, since, etc.	Time
Where, wherever, whence, whither, wherefrom, etc.	Place
that, in order that, lest, so that, etc.	Purpose
For, because, since, as, that, etc.	Cause/reason
In case, if, unless, on the condition, provided that, etc.	Condition
So........ that, so, such, such that, etc.	Result/Effect
as ... as, so ... as, than, such as, no less than, etc.	Comparison
Even if, however, whatever, though, although, etc.	Concession/ Contrast
as, as if, as though	Manner
the........ the, etc.	Extent

Analysis of Simple Sentences

Definition: A Simple Sentence has only two parts (i) subject, (ii) predicate.

It has only one subject and one finite verb.

The terms *'Subject'*, *'Predicate'* and *'Finite Verb'* have already been elaborated in the relevant chapters. I. Observe the following sentences:

1. A cool breeze is blowing.
2. Barking dogs seldom bite.
3. Laxmi Bai, the brave was honour-loving.
4. Manorama, my cousin is a pretty girl.

The words, *'a cool'*, *'barking'*, *'the brave'* and *'my cousin'* used in the above sentences have been attached to the subjects *'breeze'*, *'dogs'*, *'Laxmi Bai'* and *'Manorama'* respectively. They are called the *enlargement of the subjects* because they qualify or explain them.

Observe the following sentences:

1. The old lady cried bitterly.
2. She went holidaying yesterday.
3. She wishes me to leave.

The word *'bitterly, holidaying yesterday* and *me to leave'* used in the above sentences have been attached to the finite verbs *'cried, went* and *wishes.'* They are called the *enlargement of the predicates.*

Observe the following sentences:

1. This is a romantic novel.
2. I met Sushma, Sheela's mother.
3. This a two-rupee coin.

The words *'romantic, Sheela's mother* and *two-rupee'* used in the above sentences have been attached to the objects proper, *'novel, Sushma* and *coin'* respectively. They are called the enlargement of the object because they qualify or explain them.

Observe the following sentences:

1. The volley ball is round.
2. He looks gloomy.
3. The students elected Nikunj their monitor.
4. The Principal found Rajni guilty.

The words *'round, gloomy, their monitor* and *guilty'* complete the predicate of a verb of incomplete predication in the above sentences. They are therefore, called their complements.

Analysis

A Simple Sentence may have all or some of the following parts:

1. Subject (Proper).
2. Enlargement of the subject.
3. Object (Proper).

4. Enlargement of the object.
5. Finite Verb.
6. Complement.
7. Extension of the Predicate.

Analysis in Tabular Form

1. The company has employed a skilled typist today.
2. The young fisherman brought home a half-dead fish.
3. The judges found her at fault.
4. Sensible girls follow their parents' counsel readily.
5. The students of our college are well-behaved.
6. The injured horse was neighing painfully.
7. Rama, the noble is called Benign Ruler in history.

Analysis of Simple Sentences

Subject		*Predicate*				
Subject proper	*Enlargement of the Subject*	*Finite Verb*	*Object Proper*	*Enlargement of the Object*	*Comple-ment*	*Extension of the Predicate*
1. Company	The	has employed	typist	a skilled	....	today
2. fisherman	The, young	brought	fish	a, half-dead		home
3. judges	The	found	her	....	at fault	....
4. girls	The, sensible	follow	counsel	their parents'	....	readily
5. students	The, of our, college	are	....	....	....	well-behaved
6. horse	The, injured	was neighing	....	....	....	painfully
7. Rama	the noble	is called	Ruler	the Benign	....	in history

Transformation of Sentences

Definition: Transformation means the ways to change various sentences from one grammatical form (pattern) to another without any change in their meanings. It is an excellent form of exercise in composition.

The expression of the same idea in varied forms of language lends it beauty and colour.

Removal of Too

Observe the following sentences:

1. She is too clever to be taken in.
   She is *so* clever *that* she *cannot* be taken in.
2. This information is too good to be true.
   This information is *so* good *that* it *cannot* be true.
3. The old man is too wise not to follow your advice.
   The old man is *so* wise *that* he *can* follow your advice easily.
4. Her morals are too lofty for description.
   Her morals are *so* lofty *that* they *cannot* be described.
5. Sharda is too eager for praise.
   Sharda is *over* eager for praise. *Or*
   She is *more than* enough eager for praise.
6. Her manners were too vulgar.
   Her manners were vulgar beyond the proper limit.
7. He is too honest to accept bribery.
   He is *so* honest *that* he *will not* accept bribery.

Points to Remember:

1. Change the sentence into two clauses (*so that, can / cannot*) if the Adverb 'too' is followed by an infinitive.
   (See sentence 1 and 2)
2. While removing the adverb 'too' change the subordinate clause in the affirmative form. (*so* that, *can*) if the sentence containing the Adverb 'too' is in the negative form.
   (See sentence 3)
3. Use the words *'over'*, *'beyond the proper limit'*, *'more than enough'* etc; if the Adverb 'too' is not followed by an infinitive. (See sentence 4 to 6)

If the Adverb 'too' shows some natural habit 'too' is changed to *so* and is followed by *will/would not* (not by *can/could/not*) (See sentence 7)

ng Too

Observe the following sentences:

1. He is *so* weak *that* he *cannot* walk.
   He is *too* weak *to* walk.
2. She is *so* intelligent that she *will not* win a scholarship.
   She is *too* intelligent not *to* win a scholarship.
3. Sushma is *over* eager *for* dancing.
   Sushma is *too* eager for dancing.
4. He is *so* brave *that* he is afraid of none.
   He is *too* brave *to* be afraid of anyone.
5. The box is *so* heavy that you cannot lift it.
   The box is *too* heavy *for* you to lift (it).

Interchange of Degrees of Comparison

(From Positive Degree to Comparative Degree)

1. Positive : Mohan is not so tall as Sohan.
   Comparative : Sohan is taller than Mohan.
2. Positive : That rope is not so large as this.
   Comparative : This rope is larger than that.
3. Positive : She was as lovely as a lily.
   Comparative : A lily was not lovelier than she.
4. Positive : He is as stupid as a donkey.
   Comparative : A donkey is not more stupid than he.
5. Positive : North India is not so hot as South India.
   Comparative : South India is hotter than North India.

We use *as/so + positive degree + as* in positive sentences and *than* + comparative degree while transforming it into comparative degree.

(From Comparative Degree to Positive Degree)

1. Comparative : Akbar was not greater than Ashok.
   Positive : Ashok was (at least) as/so great Akbar.
2. Comparative : Asha is better than any other painte
   Positive : No other painter is as good as Asha.
3. Comparative : Pushpa is better than most of t. swimmers.
   Positive : Few swimmers are as good as Pushpa
4. Comparative : A crow is not more cunning than a fo:
   Positive : A fox is as cunning as a crow.
5. Comparative : Copper is more precious than brass.
   Positive : Brass is not as/so precious as copper.

(From Comparative Degree to Superlative Degree)

1. Comparative : Sham is stronger than any other athlete.
   Superlative : Sham is the strongest of all the athletes.
2. Comparative : Milk is not more wholesome than some other foods.
   Superlative : Milk is not the most wholesome food.

(From Positive Degree to Superlative Degree)

1. Positive : Some fruits are as cheap as banana.
   Superlative : Banana is not the cheapest fruit
2. Positive : Millet is not so healthful as some other cereals.
   Superlative : Millet is not one of the most healthful cereals.

(From Superlative Degree to Comparative Degree)

1. Superlative : The rose is the loveliest flower.
   Comparative : The rose is lovelier than any other flower.
2. Superlative : Maize is not the most nutritious of all the grains.

Comparative : Maize is not more nutritious than some other grains.

(From Superlative Degree to Comparative Degree and Positive Degree)

1. Superlative : Usha is the fastest runner.
   Comparative : Usha is faster than any other runner.
   Positive : No other runner is as fast as Usha.
2. Superlative : J. C. Bose was one of the greatest scientists of his age.
   Comparative : J. C. Bose was greater than many other scientists of his age.
   Positive : Very few scientists of his age were as great as J. C. Bose.
3. Superlative : Barley is not the most nutritious of all the grains.
   Comparative : Barley is not more nutritious than some other grains.
   Positive : Some grains are at least as nutritious as barley

Interchange of Assertive and Interrogative Sentences

Observe the following sentences:

Assertive Sentences	*Interrogative Sentences*
1. Virtue is its own reward.	Is not virtue its own reward?
2. It does not matter if you fail.	Does it matter if you fail?
3. Man is mortal.	Is man not mortal?
4. Their glory can never fade.	Can their glory ever fade?
5. He returned home after many years.	Did he not return home after many years?
6. Everyone worships the rising sun.	Does not everyone worship the rising sun?
7. This book in of no use to you.	Of what use is this book to you?

8. Nothing succeeds like success.	Does anything succeed like success?
9. No one would like to mix with her.	Would anyone like to mix with her?
10. Blood is thicker than water.	Is not blood thicker than water?
11. She talks nonsense.	Does she not talk nonsense? *Or* Does she talk sense?
12. She did not mean to scold you.	Did she mean to scold you?
13. She backbites others.	Does she not backbite others?

Please remember that the interrogative sentence will have no negative, if the assertive sentence is negative.

14. She can never repay my kindness.	How can she repay my kindness?
15. He will never learn to be humble.	When will he learn to be humble?
16. It is useless to quarrel over trifles.	Why quarrel over trifles?
17. Everyone loves his child.	Who does not love his child?

General Rules for transforming Assertive sentences into Interrogative sentences and vice versa.

(a) Place the verb (or its auxiliary) before the subjects.

(b) Remove the negative if it is there or insert it if it is not there.

(c) Put the Mark of Interrogation at the end of interrogative sentences.

Interchange of Exclamatory and Assertive sentences

Observe the following sentences

Exclamatory Sentences	*Assertive Sentences*
1. O for a cup of tea!	I wish I had a cup of tea.
2. Alas that he failed thrice!	It is extremely sad that he failed thrice.
3. What a jolly time we had today!	We had a very jolly time today.
4. What a charming scene!	This scene is very charming.
5. How well Asha sings!	Asha sings very well.
6. What an intelligent girl Aishna is!	Aishna is a very intelligent girl.
7. What an interesting book it is!	It is a very interesting book.

8. A fireman and afraid of sparks!	It is surprising that a fireman should be afraid of sparks.
9. What a fall!	It is a great fall.
10. How cleverly she tells the story!	She tells the story very cleverly.

General Rules: Remove the words 'what', 'why', 'how', etc. of the exclamatory sentences and insert 'very' in their places to change them into Assertive sentences. Replace the Mark of Exclamation (!) by a Full Stop (•).

Interchange of Positive and Negative Sentences

Removal of 'too' and 'interchange of Degrees of comparison (by making negative sentences) has already been done.

Observe the following Sentences

by the use of the Antonym.

Positive Sentences	***Negative Sentences***
1. Her clothes are *clean.*	Her clothes are not dirty.
2. Mother Teresa was an *old* woman.	Mother Teresa was not a *young* woman.
3. Be mannerly and polite.	Don't be unmannerly and impolite.

by the use of 'No sooner—than'

4. As soon as I reached home, my mother started scolding me.	No sooner did I reach home than my mother started scolding me.
5. As soon as he sees a constable he starts shivering.	No sooner does he see a constable than he starts shivering.

by the use of 'none' in place of 'only'.

6. Only Manorama can oblige me.	None but Manorama can oblige me.
7. Only the school boy came forward to help the old lady.	None but the school boy came forward to help the old lady.

by using 'double Negatives'.

8. Urmilla saw the Taj.	Urmilla did not fail to see the Taj.
9. She loves her neighbour.	She does not hate her neighbour.

10. Everyone present cheered.	There was no one present who did not cheer.
11. She is sometimes foolish.	She is not always wise.
12. Bahadur is a timid soldier.	Bahadur is not a brave soldier.
by using 'preposition'	
13. She has sense.	She is not without sense.
14. The P.M. is within my reach.	The P.M. is not beyond my reach.
15. He loves his cousin.	He is not without love for his cousin.
miscellaneous sentences	
16. The old woman is very tired.	The old woman is not little tired.
17. Every rose has thorn.	There is no rose but has a thorn.
18. Your niece is a girl of marked insight.	Your niece is a girl of no mean insight.
19. It always pours when it rains.	It never rains but it pours.
20. I am willing to walk to the hospital.	I don't mind walking to the hospital.

Interchange of Interrogative and Negative Sentences

Observe the following sentences:

Interrogative Sentences	*Negative Sentences*
1. When can their friendship break?	Their friendship can never break.
2. Does not truth win at last?	Truth does not lose at last.
3. Who says that the soul is mortal?	No one says that the soul is mortal.
4. Who cares for the weak and helpless?	Nobody cares for the weak and helpless.
5. Do you deserve this honour?	You do not deserve this honour.
6. Who has heard about a social poor man?	No one has heard about a social poor man.
7. Does anything succeed like success?	Nothing succeeds like success.
8. Can they ever die that die in a noble cause?	They can never die that die in a noble cause.
9. Does beauty need any ornaments?	Beauty doesn't need any ornaments.
10. Can riches buy happiness?	Riches cannot buy happiness.

* Remember that—An affirmative question always suggests a negative answer.

An assertive sentence may be either affirmative or negative.

Interchange of Simple and Complex sentences

Observe the following sentences:

Simple Sentences	*Complex Sentences*
By changing into a Noun clause	
1. She did not confess her guilt.	She did not confess that she was guilty.
2. Do you consider him reliable?	Do you consider that he is reliable?
3. Your son seems to-be half-minded.	It seems that your son is half-minded.
By changing into an Adjective clause	
1. My mother is a woman of God fearing nature.	My mother is a woman who possesses a God-fearing nature.
2. Sushma stole my purse.	Sushma stole the purse which belonged to me.
3. A closed fist is more powerful.	A fist that is closed is more powerful.
By changing into an Adverbial clause	
1. In spite of honesty, he suffered.	Though he is honest, yet he suffered.
2. He talked like a politician.	He talked as if he were a politician.
3. She cannot read without spectacles.	She cannot read unless she wears spectacles.
4. We eat to live.	We eat so that we may live.

Interchange of Complex into Simple Sentences

Observe the following sentences:

Complex Sentences	*Simple Sentences*
by using a 'Noun Phrase'	
1. I do not know where Kusum is living.	I do not know the place of Kusum's residence.

2. She described that the margosa is a tall tree.	According to her description, the margosa is a tall tree.
by using an 'Adverbial Phrase'	
3. Shama is more cunning than Kamla is.	Shama is more cunning than Kamla.
4. If God wills, she will visit my house next week.	God willing, she will visit my house next week.
5. As she is not rich, she cannot help you financially.	On account of her poverty, she cannot help you financially.
by using an 'Adjectival Phrase'	
6. Purushottam, who is the General Secretary of our P.T.A. is a shrewd politician.	Purushottam, the General Secretary of our P.T.A. is a shrewd politician.
7. The girls who are smart enjoy life heroically.	The smart girls enjoy life heroically.
8. I detected the thief who has stolen my purse.	I detected the purse-thief.
9. The people who are dishonest are punished by God.	The dishonest people are punished by God.

Interchange of Simple and Compound Sentences

Observe the following sentences:

Simple Sentences	*Compound Sentences*
1. She must try to behave herself.	She must try and behave herself.
2. Cursing her maid servant, she stepped out of the house.	She cursed her maid servant and stepped out of the house.
3. You can touch the naked wire at the risk of your life.	Do not touch the naked wire at the risk of your life.
4. In spite of hard work, she got a poor third division.	She worked hard but she got a poor third division.
5. Besides being a fine painter, she is a good dancer.	She is not only a fine painter but also (is) a good dancer.

* Expand a word or a phrase into a Co-ordinate clause while converting Simple Sentences into Compound Sentences.

Interchange of Simple and Compound Sentences

Observe the following sentences:

Compound Sentences	*Simple Sentences*
by using a Participle	
1. The pickpocket saw the policeman and ran away.	Seeing the policeman, the pick-pocket ran away.
2. Sushma, was late, therefore, we were worried.	Sushma being late, we were worried.
by a 'Gerund' or 'Infinitive' as	
3. She must make up her deficiency in English or she will not pass the exam.	She must make up her deficiency in English to pass the exam.
4. You must seek some job or you will starve.	You must seek some job to escape starvation.
5. You should learn how to swim before you jump into deep water.	Learn swimming before you jump into deep water.
by a 'Prepositional Phrase'	
6. He was expelled from service, for he was arrogant.	Due to his arrogance, he was expelled from service.
7. Do not dupe others or you will come to grief.	You will come to grief in the event of duping others.

* Replace a Co-ordinate Clause with a Participle, a Gerund, an Infinitive or a Prepositional Phrase while transforming Compound Sentences into Simple Sentences.

Interchange of Compound and Complex Sentences

Observe the following sentences:

Compound Sentences	*Complex Sentences*

By making the second Co-ordinate clause of the Compound Sentence, the Principal Clause of the Complex Sentence optionally.

1. Look sharp or you will repent forever.	You will repent for ever if you do not look sharp.
2. She burnt midnight oil but did not get first division marks.	Although she burnt midnight oil, yet she did not get first division marks.

3. Speak another word and I will give you a lathi-blow.	If you speak another word, I will give you a lathi-blow.
4. Sushma is talented, but she is not a genius.	Though Sushma is talented, yet she is not a genius.
5. Take care of your health and good fortune will kiss your feet.	If you take care of your health, good fortune will kiss your feet.
6. Spare the rod and spoil the child.	If you spare the rod, the child will be spoiled.
7. She was fully exhausted; therefore, she fell sound asleep.	She fell sound asleep because she was fully exhausted.
8. She is already very late; therefore, there is no fun in standing in the queue.	As she is already late, there is no fun in standing in the queue.
9. She is a flirt and I can prove it.	I can prove that she is a flirt.
10. I bought the pen yesterday but I have lost it.	I have lost the pen which I bought yesterday.

The above rule is optional and is true only in the case of Compound or Complex Sentences having only two clauses.

Interchanging Parts of Speech

Observe the following sentences:

1. Shalini examines the scripts *with care*. *(Noun)*
   Shalini examines the scripts *carefully*. *(Adverb)*
2. Pay *attention* to what I say. *(Noun)*
   Listen *attentively* to what I say. *(Adverb)*
3. She gave me a *rude* reply. *(Adjective)*
   She replied to me *rudely*. *(Adverb)*
4. She has no *sympathy* for her husband. *(Noun)*
   She does not *sympathise* with her husband. *(Verb)*
5. Mala achieved *success* in her attempts. *(Noun)*
   Mala succeeded in her attempts. *(Verb)*
6. Pay *attention* to what I say. *(Noun)*
   Attend to what I say. *(Verb)*

7.	She has sent *invitation* to me.	*(Noun)*
	She has *invited* me.	*(Verb)*
8.	I have no *intention* of harming her.	*(Noun)*
	I do not *intend* to harm her.	*(Verb)*
9.	What she uttered was beyond my *tolerance.*	*(Noun)*
	I could not *tolerate* what she uttered.	*(Verb)*
10.	She reposes her *confidence* in her husband.	*(Noun)*
	She *confides* in her husband	*(Verb)*
11.	She gave her guests a *cold* reception.	*(Adjective)*
	She received her guests *coldly.*	*(Adverb)*

20

Punctuation

Punctuation is the art of putting in proper stops and marks in writing. The wrong use of Punctuation Marks totally changes the meaning of a sentence. Punctuation makes the meaning clear.

Examples:

1. The cow said the master is a faithful animal.
   (*Unpunctuated*)
2. The cow said, "The master is a faithful animal."
   (*Punctuated*)
3. "The cow," said the master, "is a faithful animal."

In the above sentences, sentences gives entirely different meaning than the meaning conveyed by sentence 3.

Sentence 3 is a meaningful sentence because it is properly punctuated.

The Principal Marks of Punctuation: 1. Capital Letters: A.

Observe the following sentences:

(a) *The* farmers are watering their fields.
(b) *Kalidas* said, "*Beauty* needs no ornamentation".
(c) *You* will play football and *I* shall watch you.
(d) Twinkle, twinkle little star.

How I wonder what you are!

Every sentence begins with a capital letter.

Every word that begins a quotation is written with a capital letter. The personal pronoun 'I' is always capitalised, wherever it may occur in a sentence.

Every line of poetry begins with a capital letter.

Observe the following sentences:

(a) Kamal is *Indian* but his friend *Swift* is European.

(b) You have made a *Himalayan* blunder.

Always capitalise the first letter of proper noun or a proper adjective.

(c) The Hindu College, Minto Road , Subhash Street, Chhajju Ram Hospital, Kamal High School.

Always capitalise the first letters of words, forming parts of names of road, street, school, hospital, etc.

(d) I have full faith in *God* and *His* mercy.

The word 'God' and the pronouns standing for him are always capitalised, wherever they may occur in the sentence.

(e) Diwali, Holi, Dussehra, Christmas Day, Id-ul-Fitr and Guru Nanak Birthday are the Chief festivals in India.

The first letter of the names of festivals are always capitalised.

(f) I spoke to Father, Mother, Uncle, Aunt and Cousin about my programme and they all agreed.

Whenever blood relations are used as titles, without determiners, the first letter of each word (denoting relation) is capitalised.

(g) M.B.B.S. M.D, M.L.A., S.D.O., U.N.D., U.S.S.R. All the letters used as abbreviations are capitalised.

Exception: When an abbreviation of a word contains more than one letter, only the first letter is capitalised, *e.g.* B.Sc, M.Sc.

(h) NATO (North Atlantic Treaty Organization).

UNESCO (United Nations Educational Scientific and Cultural Organization)

All the letters of an abbreviation denoting the name of an organization or institution are capitalised when they are put together as one word and no full stop is put after each letter.

Capital letters are also used with: (a) Interjection "O". (b) Names of the days of the week and months of the year. (c) Names of Languages, (d) Names of subjects, (e) Names of religions and sects, (f) Names of newspapers, magazines, etc. (g) Important historical events. (h) Rivers, mountains, lakes and oceans. (i) Personified things or concepts. (j) Words of titles. (k) Important words in the headings of essays and stories.

Full Stop

Observe the following sentences:

(a) The boys are making a noise. (Full stop (.) marks the end of the sentence here)

(b) He asked me when I returned home. (Full stop marks the end of the sentence here because the question 'when *I returned* (*did I return*) home' has been changed into indirect narration. All the sentences of indirect narration end with a full stop.

(c) My brother is *Lieut.* in army.

Full stop marks the end of the abbreviations.

Please note that a full stop denotes the longest pause.

Mark of Interrogation/Question Mark (?)

Observe the following sentences:

(a) When are you leaving for Guwahati?

(b) Where have you been all the while?

Mark of Interrogation is used after every direct question (interrogative sentence) (in direct narration). The mark (note) of interrogation (?) is not used in the indirect form (narration). It is replaced by a full stop there.

Note of Exclamation (!)

Observe the following sentences:

(a) Alas! What a great loss!

(b) Hello! how goes the world with you!

(c) How shameful!

(d) Marvellous!

Mark of Exclamation (!) is used after all interjections, e.g. Hurrah!, alas!, oh, Lo, aha, O, Ha or words, phrases or sentences impressing sudden emotions.

(a) Boys! Look front.

(b) Mother! Mother! where are you?

(c) Have mercy on me, O God!

The Mark of Exclamation (!) is used after an Emphatic Nomination of Address.

(a) May you be crowned with success!

(b) May you be prosperous!

The Mark of Exclamation is used at the end of optative sentences. (Desiderative sentences showing desire/wish).

Comma (,)

The shortest pause, used in punctuation. Observe the following sentences:

(a) Kalidasa, the dramatist surpassed Shakespeare.

Here, the comma separates words/phrases in apposition.

(b) (i) Pt. Deepchand was a wise, learned and upright, old man.

Here, the comma separates the same part of speech

(adjectives) in a sentence. A conjunction is used before the last word in the series in place of the comma.

(ii) Manorama glanced, smiled and bowed before the guests.

Here, the comma separates the same part of speech (verbs) in a sentence.

(c) I presented the bouquet to Madhuri, who handed it over to her mother.

Here, the comma separates a clause used in a continuative sense.

(d) "Yes," said the Principal, "it is a practical suggestion".

Here, the comma separates direct quotation.

(e) She did not, however, achieve her objective.

(i) The words 'yes and no' are also separated by comma in a running sentence.

(ii) Sharda had no hopes of passing the examination, nevertheless, she desired to appear.

(iii) An island is a piece of land surrounded by water, for example/ for instance, Andaman and Nicobar is an island.

(iv) Hitler was a dictator, that is, a ruler who had total power over his country.

Here, commas have been used to mark off words and phrases, *e.g. however, nevertheless, for example* (*for instance,* and *that is.*)

(f) (i) Bimla can't swim, can she?

(ii) I shall help you, shan't I?

Here, the commas mark off question tags.

(g) (i) We said to our guests, "Please come again whenever you like."

(ii) "Hold your tongue," the principal said, "to me."

Here, the commas have been put immediately after the quotation in direct speech when it comes at the beginning of the sentence. Comma is also used to separate the interrupting part of the sentence in direct speech.

(h) (i) Friday, 8th November, 2000 was a holiday.

(ii) I live at 610, Dichaon Kalan, New Delhi-110043.

(iii) Dear Meera, write to me soon.

(iv) Yours sincerely, the residents of Uggarsain Park.

(Here, the commas have been customarily used to separate items in dates and addresses or after the salutations or endings in a letter.)

(Please note that the use of Commas is not given any importance in computerised printing.)

Exception:

(i) I live at 610 Dichaon Kalan in New Delhi-110043.

(No comma is used here because the items are separated by the prepositions (at and *in*). (i) Rajni, fetch me a glass of juice.

(Here, the comma is used to mark off words of nominative of address)

(j) Looking out of the window, Mohini saw a scooterist coming towards her house.

(Here, the comma is used to mark off participial phrase.)

(k) (i) Hari is, at least in my opinion, a mean and selfish person.

(ii) "The decision the Principal has taken, as you may already know, is to expel you from school.

(Here, the commas have been used to mark off parenthetical words, phrases and clauses, etc. which are not the necessary parts of a sentence.)

(l) Since you are so adamant. I won't try to persuade you. If you don't want to accompany me, I am not going to stay here, any longer.

Here, the commas have been used to mark off adverbial clauses used at the beginning of the sentence.

(m) (i) They are, very good friends.

Here, the comma emphasises the friendship.

(ii) "They are very good, friends."

Here, the comma marks off the persons addressed.

(n) (i) Sohan doesn't drink, nor does he gamble.

(ii) Subhash reached the stage, and was cheered by the audience.

Here, the commas have been used before the conjunctions that join two principal clauses having different types of constructions or expressing new or contrasted idea.

(o) Rich and poor, high and low, strong and weak—all must fall a prey to death one day.

Here, the commas have been used to separate pairs of words.

(p) Mr. S.B. Sharma has passed M.A. (English, Sanskrit and Philosophy); B.Ed.

Here, commas have been used to separate degrees.

(q) (i) The dog rose, barked and sprang on the goat.

(ii) The team assembled, they played and they left the playground.

Here, the commas separate short co-ordinate clauses.

(r) Well, come ahead if you dare.

Here, the comma has been used as an interjection.

(s) Kalawanti is too, too shameless.

Here, the comma has been used to mark off an adjective repeated for emphasis.

(t) God willing, India will progress by leaps and bounds.

Here, the comma separates a Nominative Absolute.

(u) Then, at length, the treaty was signed.

Here, the comma has been used to separate two or more Adverbs or Adverbial Phrases coming together.

(v) (i) This scooter is mine, that, hers.

(ii) I am a writer, she, a painter.

Here, the comma has been used to show the omission of a word, especially a verb.

(w) He ran fast, but lost the race.

Here, the comma has been used before a co-ordinate conjunction.

(x) That Pushpa will visit my house today, is uncertain.

Here, the comma has been used to separate a Noun clause which precedes the verb of the Principal clause.

Semicolon (;)

A shorter pause than full stop but a longer pause than the comma.

Observe the following sentences:

(a) (i) To err is human; to forgive is divine.

(ii) The rich are often ungrateful; the poor are usually sympathetic.

(Here, the semicolons have been used to separate long co-ordinate clauses).

(b) (i) The old man is poor; therefore he cannot help you financially.

(ii) He must run fast; else he will miss the train.

(Here, the semicolons have been used to separate co-ordinate clauses joined by *therefore* and *else.*)

(c) (i) There are five chief qualities of a scout; *viz* sincerity, courage (courtesy), obedience, usefulness and truthfulness.

(ii) Some birds cannot fly but they have wings; e.g. kiwi, ostrich, penguin.

(Here, the semicolon has been used before *viz* and *e.g.*).

(d) Distinguish between—male, mail, hale, hail; pail, pale; and cattle, kettle;

Here, the semicolon has been used to separate pairs of words, already separated by commas.

(e) Her conduct was very satisfactory; she was quickly promoted.

Here, the semicolon has been put between two independent clauses not joined by a conjunction.

(f) The two rival groups signed a contract; that is they accepted each other's terms.

Semicolons are used between independent clauses joined by such words or phrases as *that is, besides, moreover, for example,* etc.

(g) The meeting was attended by the following persons. Mr. Mathur, President of the Association; Mrs. Malhotra, the Vice-President; Mr. Sachdeva, the secretary; and Mr. Govind Ram, who is an ex-Treasurer.

Here, the semicolons have been used between items in a series containing commas.

Colon (:)

Observe the following sentences:

(a) (i) Shelley said: If winter has come, can summer be far behind.

(ii) It is said: Pride hath a fall.

Here, the colon has been used to introduce maxims.

(b) Four chief houses in our school are: the Gandhi House, the Patel House, the Subhash House and the Nehru House.

(Here, the colon has been used to enumerate facts.)

(c) (i) Here is a happy news for you: Your father has found a suitable match for your sister.

(ii) I can't eat this apple: It is rotten.

(Here, the colon has been used to introduce a sentence/clause that explains or elaborates what has been said earlier or supports the previous statement directly.

(d) Man proposes: God disposes.

(Here, the colon has been used to separate two contrasted statements).

(e) The main tenses in English Grammar are: the present, the past and the future.

(Here, the colon has been used before examples and explanations).

Dash (—)

Observe the following sentences:

(a) If I were rich—but why grieve over the ill-fortune.

(Here, the dash has been used to mark a sudden or abrupt change in/of thought.)

(b) 1. Bribery, adulteration, adultery—all these have caused the degradation of moral values in India.

(Here, the dash has been used to sum up a series of criminal activities.)

2. Friends, companions, relatives—all deserted him in the hour of adversity.

(Here, the dash has been used to sum up a series of names.

3. Health, wealth, fame—everything she had.

   (Here, the dash has been used to resume a scattered subject)

4. She will not—of this I am very sure—repay your loan.

   (Here, the dash has been used to mark a parenthesis.)

5. She herself, her family, her property—all were ruined.

   (Here, the dash has been used to sum up several things or facts.)

Hyphen (-)

(A hyphen is a short straight line, much shorter than the dash).

Observe the following sentences:

1. His sister-in-law went to the garden and touched the touch-me-not.
2. The teacher ordered the boys to go to their class-room.

   (Here, the hyphens have been used to join words in order to make compound words.)

Some more words joined by hyphens.

Father-in-law, mother-in-law, sister-in-law, foot-ball, land-lord, Commader-in-chief, looking-glass, hiding-place, passer-by, man-of-war, un-finished, etc.

Inverted Commas ("............")

Observe the following sentences:

(a) (i) The teacher said, "I am indisposed today."

(ii) Shakespeare says, "Woman! frailty is thy name."

(Here, the inverted commas have been used to enclose quotations).

(b) (i) 'The Ramayana" is a classical epic.

(ii) The ship "Titanic" met with its watery grave.

(Here, the inverted commas have been used to single out some special name).

(c) She said to her husband, "Buddha says: 'To fast once a week' means to purify oneself."

(Here, the inverted commas are used to express the view of some great men but single inverted (raised) commas are used to introduce a quotation within a quotation.)

Apostrophe (')

Observe the following sentences:

(a) (i) I *won't* help you because I *don't* want to help you.

(Here, the apostrophe has been used to indicate the omission of a letter or letters to show contraction.)

(ii) *Rohit's* toy is costlier than *Mukul's* toy.

(Here, the apostrophe has been used to form the possessive case of animate objects.)

(iii) Your t's and 5's are incorrect.

(Here, the apostrophe has been used to form the plurals of letters and figures.)

Brackets ( )

Observe the following sentences:

1. The old lady has lost all she had (wealth, hut, honour).
2. Pt. Prabhu Dayal (may his soul rest in peace!) was a learned scholar of Sanskrit.
3. The moon is............. everybody knows............. the jewel of the sky.

(The brackets, parenthesis and double dashes have been used in the above sentences to separate a phrase or clause from the main parts of a sentence which are grammatically unrelated.)